ONES I'VE SURFED
WAINUI BEACH
BACK BEACH
OAKURA - S

Wavetrack

New Zealand Surfing Guide

CONTENTS

Introduction   5
User Guide   6
Weather   8
About New Zealand   12
Gallery   213
Index   545

NORTH ISLAND

NE	**Northland East Coast**, Cape Reinga south to Tawharanui	14
NW	**Northland West Coast**, Cape Maria Van Demen south to Pouto	48
AE	**Auckland East Coast**, Waiwera south to Takapuna	72
AW	**Auckland West Coast**, Muriwai south to Port Waikato	84
GB	**Great Barrier Island**, Little Barrier and Great Barrier Islands	104
WK	**Waikato**, Te Akau south to Kiritehere	112
TN	**Taranaki**, Awakino south to Wanganui	134
CO	**Coromandel**, Waikawau to Whiritoa	184
BP	**Bay of Plenty**, Waihi to Ohope	230
EC	**East Cape**, Opotiki to Kaiaua Bay	258
GS	**Gisborne**, Tolaga Bay south to the Waipaoa River	286
MA	**Mahia**, Mahanga to Nuhaka	308
HB	**Hawkes Bay**, Wairoa south to Waimarama	330
WA	**Wairarapa**, Cape Palliser north to Castlepoint	350
WL	**Wellington**, Houghton Bay to Cape Palliser	372
KP	**Kapiti**, Otaki Beach to Titahi Bay	392

SOUTH ISLAND

NB	**Nelson Bays**, Ruby Bay to Whangamoa	402
WC	**West Coast**, Greymouth north to Farewell Spit	412
KI	**Kaikoura**, Robin Hood Bay to Oaro	438
CH	**Christchurch**, Conway Flat south to Timaru	462
DN	**Dunedin**, Oamaru to Papatotara	496

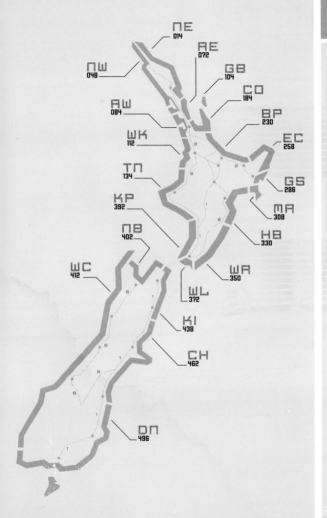

Wavetrack New Zealand Surfing Guide

ISBN 0-476-00942-1

SURF2SURF.com

First published November 2004
Greenroom Surf Media Limited
www.newzealandsurfingguide.com
www.surf2surf.com
Copyright © **Greenroom Surf Media Limited**
All rights reserved. No part of this publication may be
reproduced, stored in a retrieval system or transmitted in any
form by any means, electronic, mechanical, photocopying,
scanning, internet, e-mail, recording or otherwise, without
the prior permission of the publishers. Infringers of copyright
render themselves liable to prosecution.
Copyright © Greenroom Surf Media Limited
Greenroom Surf Media Limited asserts
it's moral rights in the work.
Some maps, descriptions, break names, place names, locations
have been altered for use in this guide.

Writing and content: Peter B Morse, Paul Brunskill
Info & spot data: 50+ New Zealand Locals
Book design: www.notionlab.co.nz
Art direction/design: Paul Brunskill
Designer: Chris Brunskill
Cover photo: Cory Scott (8ft Otama Bay)
Editing/proofing: Ellyn Brunskill, Phil Smith, Toni Spiers
Printing: Everbest, China
Special thanks to: Linda, Murphy, Ellyn and Luke

No liability or responsibility is assumed for errors and
omissions or damages resulting from the use of this book.
New Zealand surf breaks can be dangerous, surf within your
limits and stay safe. If in doubt don't go out.

INTRODUCTION

When we initially thought about creating this book, it was our intention to produce a quality, detailed and highly functional New Zealand surfing guide that would be as inspirational as it was useful. After putting our heads together for a while, we set aside a few months to get the breaks together, and a couple more to design something user-friendly for surfers. Two years and 550 pages later here we are.

During the past twenty-four months we have come to appreciate just how complex, volcanic and reef-lined New Zealand's coastline is. Working on the area and spot maps really brought to light how many excellent breaks there are out there. Kiwi surfers are down right spoilt!

So how does surfing in New Zealand rate, and how good are the waves? Well, we don't have a G-Land, we don't have a Teahupoo or a Cloudbreak, but we do have an array of world-class breaks providing incredible consistency. New Zealand is one the last few remaining surf destinations able to offer large, uncrowded water to surfers. Not only this, but the scenery is spectacular and the unique shape of the land presents many options to those wishing to take advantage of all it has to offer - one of which is that the drive from coast to coast rarely takes longer than three hours.

This guide only scratches the surface of all that is available in this beautiful country. New Zealand is still wide open for exploration and with a little effort and a sense of adventure you are sure to find the waves of your life.

Finally, we'd like to take this opportunity to sincerely thank the fifty local surfers who each shared a lifetime of local knowledge to help create this book. We are eternally grateful to them for giving us their knowledge so that we may share it with others.

Pete Morse

READING OUR SICK LITTLE MAPS

Use our detailed spot maps to navigate your way to surf breaks. Maps show the general layout of the surfing area, walking tracks and obstacles. Note: Break locations and takeoff areas change with swell direction, size, tide and sand bank location. Use the maps as a general guide to get the best out of your surf session.

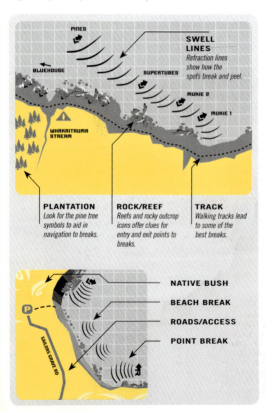

SWELL LINES
Refraction lines show how the spots break and peel.

PLANTATION
Look for the pine tree symbols to aid in navigation to breaks.

ROCK/REEF
Reefs and rocky outcrop icons offer clues for entry and exit points to breaks.

TRACK
Walking tracks lead to some of the best breaks.

NATIVE BUSH

BEACH BREAK

ROADS/ACCESS

POINT BREAK

KEY TO USING ICONS

Break Type

 Left and right reef break

 Left river bar break

 Right-hand point break

 Left point - sand bottom

 Beach break

Swell Direction

 E

 W

 N

 SE

 SW

Best Wind

 NW

 W

 SE

 SW

 NE

Optimum Tide

 Good on all tides

 Best surfed mid to low tide

 Best high tide

 Best low tide

 Best low to mid tide

 Best

 Spot X Alert

 Heavy Shore break

 Sharky Spot

 Worst

 Caution: Ledge

 Caution: Backwash

 Caution: Seals

 Shortened Beach

 Parking Area

 Caravan Park

 Camping Area

 Left-hand Break

 Right-hand Break

 State Highway

 Jetski Tow-in

 Boat Access

STOKE RATING

The Wavetrack New Zealand Surfing Guide rates surf breaks on their quality when a swell is running. Breaks are not rated on their areas swell consistency. This is to ensure that this guide offers an accurate appraisal of each breaks potential when optimum conditions are present.

WEATHER AND WAVE BASICS

WIND MAKES WAVES
In it's simplest form the atmosphere is made up of areas of high pressure and areas of low pressure. In nature, air will always flow from high pressure to low pressure. This process creates wind. As wind blows over the ocean surface an energy transfer occurs. Friction from wind on water creates ripples, then chop, and then fully developed ocean swells. The strength, duration and distance which wind blows in a general direction will determine the size of the swell.

HIGH PRESSURE SYSTEMS
The high pressure system or anticyclone, is an area where the air pressure increases towards the centre of the system. High pressure systems rotate anti-clockwise (Southern Hemisphere) and are often associated with fine, settled weather and light winds.

LOW PRESSURE SYSTEMS
The opposite applies to the low pressure system or cyclone. It's air pressure decreases toward it's centre, and the system rotates in a clockwise direction (Southern Hemisphere). Lows are violent systems which bring strong winds, rain and stormy conditions. Lows are the primary system for swell generation.

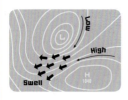

FETCH - THE SYNOPTIC CHART
Fetch is the distance component of the wave making equation. It is also a great indicator for surfers that swell may be on the way. On the synoptic chart look for tightly packed bands of isobars which stretch over great distances. Isobars are lines which join areas of similar pressure. The longer the isobars and more tightly packed they are, the stronger the winds and the bigger the waves will be. Low pressure systems below 990 hPa produce the best swells. If the pressure gets as low as 940 hPa and the fetch is pointing directly at your beach, make sure you have sick days available at work.

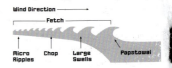

NEW ZEALAND WEATHER

WIND SWELLS
Wind swells are created by weather systems close to the coast. These systems generally produce messy waves which lack power as the fetch has been interrupted and the swell hasn't fully developed.

GROUND SWELLS
Ground swells are what all surfers are looking for. Large swell generating systems off the coast send waves thousands of miles to shore. These powerful swells cover approximately 500 miles per day. During this time they clean up and straighten as they travel. Because the low pressure system may be a thousand miles offshore, local beach conditions can be calm and glassy, or even offshore.

SQUASH - TURBOCHARGE THE SYSTEM
Low and highs can combine to form squash zones. This is like hooking a turbo charger on to a low pressure system. The low doesn't need to be deep or powerful to produce a strong swell, as the low and high meet, the clockwise spinning low and anti-clockwise spinning high combine to pump out serious wind and swell.

PERIOD AND DECAY
Long period swells are created when the wind is successful in transferring substantial energy into the ocean. Long period swells are able to retain their energy more efficiently over vast distances of open ocean because the distance between individual waves is greater and they carry their energy lower. This allows them to duck under the radar of opposite winds and swells. Short period swells carry their energy high, and are prone to losing their energy over vast distances.

OCEAN FLOOR BATHYMETRY
As ocean swells approach the coast they are influenced by the shape of the sea floor and coast. Areas which have deep water canyons offshore, like Kaikoura, Wairarapa, the Catlins produce powerful waves as swells hit reefs and beaches without slowing significantly. This allow breaks to hold and harness larger waves than other areas. As swell hits the coast, it focuses more energy towards shallow areas and refracts. The ultimate example is the Raglan point breaks as they bend 90 degrees around the headland.

UNDERSTANDING THE PATTERNS OF CHAOS

New Zealand weather is dictated by activity in the Intertropical Convergence Zone, the area for equatorial easterlies, South Pacific Convergence Zone, Southern Hemisphere Trades, Roaring Forties Flow, Madden Julian, plus more than our fair share of El Nino and La Nina events. It just so happens that our clean, green little land is positioned right between the giant southern ice block Antarctica and the steaming tropics. So what happens? A heck of a lot.

Instead of boring you with tons of technical weather info, we've created the sickest synoptic chart you'll ever see. Every break in New Zealand is pumping with overhead waves -all at the same time. Although this arrangement of systems is physically impossible, weather maps similar to this have occurred.

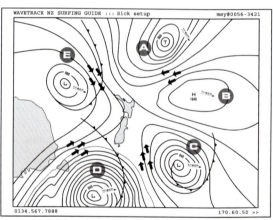

A - TROPOS

November through to March is cyclone season. Cyclones descend from the tropics and track southeast delivering solid ground swells to the northeast coast. Their unpredictable nature means that the swell could last for hours, or days. As they move south these systems transform into sub-tropical depressions delivering east/southeast swells to both islands. Hitting cold air and water their intensity decreases rapidly.

NEW ZEALAND WEATHER

B - SQUASH ZONE - HIT THE TURBO

During summer high pressure systems dominate the weather charts between Norfolk and Raoul Islands. A low pressure system descends from the north and combines with stationary high to produce a squash zone. Wind speed increases and long duration fetch produce clean swell for the east coast. Local beaches enjoy light onshores and clean pumping waves.

C - CHATHAMS WAVE FACTORY INC

A Low pressure system which may have dropped from the East Cape, or tracked east from the southern Tasman Sea stalls when it meets a large blocking high. The system sits and grinds away gaining intensity. As it pushes through the high, it dispatches long straight wrapping lines to the South Island's East Coast through to Gisborne - even The Barrier picks up some swell.

D - THE ROARING FORTIES

Winter brings a barrage of endless low pressure systems complete with lashings of sleet and snow. As they tear through 50-60 degrees south, they churn out long duration mega-swells firing them north. Three to five days later these swells wrap around the North Island's points and barrel on it's West Coast beaches. During spring deep southern ocean systems are forced north by the Antarctic fridge door opening. Fierce howling onshore winds turn the west coast of New Zealand into a giant wind-blown washing machine. During the summer months the southern systems keep a low profile. Below 60 degrees south they creep east sending clean sneaker swells to the west coast.

E - NORTH TASSIE WEATHER BOMB

Warm Queensland tropical air hits the colder air of the southern Tasman Sea. Low pressure systems develop into moisture bombs around Lord Howe Island and quickly intensify. From here they can move quickly through central New Zealand. Look for blocking highs over the North Island. These provide light offshore winds to West Coast beaches as all northwest angle breaks come to life. This offers a refreshing change for West Coast surfers pounded by southwest swells 300 days a year. Kapiti and Nelson surfers dust off their boards for epic sessions.

Find real time surf forecasts and surf cams at -

ABOUT NEW ZEALAND

GEOGRAPHY

New Zealand is located in the South Pacific east of Australia, and features two large Islands the North Island and South Island. While each is vastly different than the other, they both feature spectacular landscapes and rugged coastline. Throughout you will find lush rainforests, active volcanos and large mountain ranges. New Zealand is comparable in size to Great Britain, but only features a population of 4 million people. So it's not difficult to get away and find a place to yourself.

THE CLIMATE

New Zealand's North and South Island feature quite different climates. The north is sub-tropical offering mild weather year round and warm Summers. North Island winters are cold but mild. A 4/3 steamer and booties will keep you warm anywhere in North Island waters. Further south things start to cool down. Southern summers are pleasant, winters are extremely cold. If you are planning to surf the South Island during winter be prepared with a quality wetsuit, booties and hood.

DRIVING

New Zealand roads are narrow and windy and most do not feature median barriers. Driving around New Zealand should be approached with caution, especially if you're used to driving on the right side of the road (Kiwis drive on the left). Because the roads are windy, driving times can increase substantially. Remember if you hit the back roads, make sure you have a full tank of gas.

SAFETY PRECAUTIONS

New Zealand doesn't really feature any nasties. Shark attacks are very rare. We don't have snakes, spider bites are rare. The main concern to travelling surfers is sunburn. New Zealand's clean, unpolluted atmosphere and low latitudes produce stonger sunlight than the Northern Hemisphere. Getting burnt can take as little as 15 minutes exposure.

SURFING NEW ZEALAND

LOCALISM IN NEW ZEALAND

New Zealanders are some of the friendliest people on the planet. Kiwi surfers are no exception. When visiting their local surf breaks show respect and you will have a great time. Some areas of New Zealand feature pockets of local aggression. Listed are a few techniques to enhance your Kiwi surf sessions.

NEVER DROP IN

There is no excuse, ever, to drop in. Warning: In some areas of New Zealand dropping in will be met with serious consequences.

TALK

A smile and a hello can transform the vibe of a break. It may also open the doors to other experiences and breaks. It's simple and it works - try it.

SHARE

Surfers who try to dominate, or snake, cause tension in the line-up which can erupt into abuse and violence. Chill out and take a moment to share this amazing sport with others.

RESPECT

Many New Zealand surf breaks have to be accessed through private land. Dropping rubbish or barging through without permission could close this access. Show respect and we will be able to continue to access these amazing breaks. If the land you wish to cross is Maori, Koha is often a thoughtful gesture. Koha is a gift to show respect.

QUIVER

New Zealand generally produces waves in the 1-8ft range. A small wave short board, and something a little longer will see you through an enjoyable Kiwi surf trip. There are several big wave breaks in the North and South Island, so if you're chasing the big surf bring a gun too.

For more information about surfing in New Zealand, visit - **SURF2SURF.com**

Northland East Coast

Northland's east coast comprises 250 kilometres of complex coastline featuring dozens of beautiful bays, islands, reefs and beaches. We start at Tawharanui, an hour and a half north of Auckland, and continue to the northern-most tip of New Zealand, North Cape. The surfbreaks receive swell from a variety of directions and feature excellent scenery.

Access to some breaks can be difficult but all it takes is a 4WD or a pair of feet, and permission from the land owner, and you could experience superb surfing at truly isolated spots. A road map will make discovery easier: once off the highway the roads are narrow and winding. Check the weather maps. East Coast breaks can accommodate swell from northwest through to southeast. The swells which roll on by the Bay of Plenty, Coromandel and Auckland, can produce epic surf at certain Northland breaks. Sheltered from the south westerlies the region has New Zealand's warmest climate and during summer it gets hot and humid enough for boardshorts. This also means high rainfall and travel plans are sometimes disrupted by flooding. If the Pacific surf is flat you'll be no more than an hour or so from the West Coast. This will double your chances of finding surf. Usually, when one coast is onshore the other is offshore.

The main city is Whangarei and the area includes numerous towns and settlements from which food and accommodation are always available.

A depression moves to the east from the Tasman Sea. Short period swells pour south providing waves for breaks exposed to the north angle swells.

The summer cyclone season brings a tropical depression from the Islands. Grunty swells travel 1000's of miles. Northland's bays fire with calm winds and epic waves.

Classic squash setup. A depression and anticyclone combine to fire east and southeast swells into Northland's many reefs and beaches.

ΠE 015

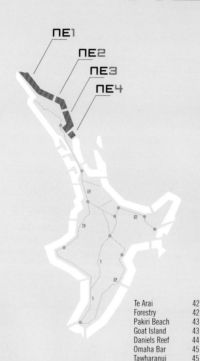

ΠE1	17
Tapotupotu Bay	18
Spirits Bay	18
Tom Bowling	19
Rarawa Beach	19
Great Exhibition	19
Henderson Bay	20
Houhora Heads	20
Raupo Bay	21
Puwheke Beach	21
Tokerau Beach	22
Taipa Beach	22
Motukahakaha	23
Paradise Bay	23
Taupo Bay	23
ΠE2	26
Matauri Bay	27
Takou Bay	27
Russell	28
Elliot Bay	29
Bland Bay	29
Oakura Bay	30
Helena Bay	30
ΠE3	32
Mimiwhangata	33
Okupe Beach	33
Moureeses	34
Whananaki Nth	34
Sandy Bay	36
Ngunguru Bar	36
Pataua Bar	37
Ocean Beach	37
Marsden Point	38
Waipu River	38
Waipu Cove	39
Laings Beach	39
ΠE4	40
Mangawhai	41
Black Swamp	41
Te Arai	42
Forestry	42
Pakiri Beach	43
Goat Island	43
Daniels Reef	44
Omaha Bar	45
Tawharanui	45
INFO	46

O'NEILL — AREA SEASONAL WETSUIT RECOMMENDATIONS

SUMMER
BOARDIES-SPRINGY

AUTUMN
SPRING SUIT

WINTER
3/2 or 4/3 STEAMER + BOOTIES

SPRING
SPRINGY-STEAMER

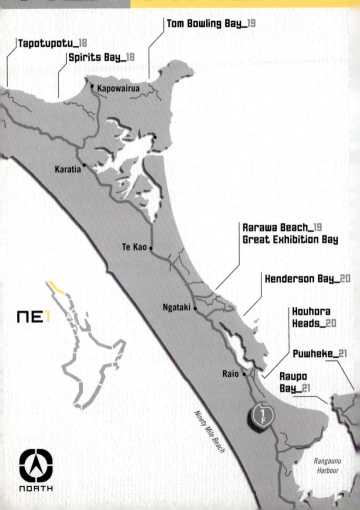

017

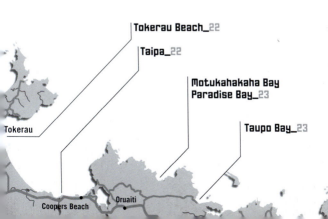

Tokerau Beach_22

Taipa_22

Motukahakaha Bay
Paradise Bay_23

Taupo Bay_23

Tokerau

Coopers Beach • Oruaiti

018 NE1

Tapotupotu Bay

Head north from Kaitaia on HWY 1 to Cape Reinga. Take a right to Tapotupotu Bay, New Zealand's northern-most surf break.

Tapotupotu consists of a sheltered bay offering beach break waves. A pristine, isolated spot, it is located at the point where the Tasman Sea meets the Pacific Ocean. The bay is prone to stong currents and extremely shifty sand banks. Find variable peaks along the beach and a left breaking off the rocks at the west end. Uncrowded and very isolated. Good for surfers of all levels.

Spirits Bay

Drive north from Kaitaia (111km). Take a right at Waitiki Landing to Spirits Bay. Spirits Bay Rd will take you to the east end of the beach. Access the western end by foot - a hike of several kilometres.

Area features a range of beach breaks producing left and right peaks over shifty bars. The bay is offshore east through southwest. Watch for strong tidal currents and shifty banks. Picks up northwest through northeast swells. Isolated and uncrowded.

NE1 019

Tom Bowling Bay

Head to Spirits Bay. Getting to Tom Bowling is a difficult, arduous tramp over rough country. Talk to the locals first, the land is Tribal, so check before embarking.

Bay consists of several kilometres of beach breaks, and peaks around rocky outcrops. Area is rarely surfed. Uncrowded and isolated.

Rarawa Beach

Take HWY 1 north from Kaitaia. Turn off to Rarawa Beach after passing Ngataki.

Rarawa Beach is located at the southern end of Great Exhibition Bay. Great Exhibition features pristine, pure white sand beaches which stretch 20km north to the Parengarenga Harbour. You'll find a range of beach breaks and river/stream mouths which offer fun peaks. Access is very difficult.

Rarawa Beach, which has easier road access and features a quality beach break, produces a range of left and right peaks depending on banks. Optimum size 3-6ft (1-2.5m). Good for surfers of all levels.

020 NE1

Henderson Bay

Take HWY 1 north from Kaitaia. Pass the Houhora Harbour. Then take a right after Waihopo to the Bay.

Bay offers a quality beach break producing grunty peaks which peel through to a shallow shorebreak. Find good banks around many of the rocky outcrops. Sand/reef combos break on inner and outer bars. Expect sucky takeoffs and good barrels. Break holds 6-8ft (2-3m). Offshore S/SW winds. Competent surfers only.

Houhora Heads

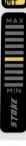

Head north from Kaitaia, pass the Rangaunu Harbour and Motutangi. Take a right on Houhora Heads Rd to the harbour entrance where you can check the waves.

To find the break paddle out a long way towards Stanley Point. Here you'll find a short right and longer left which breaks around the point. Length and angle is dependant on swell angle and sand location. Best surfed with a northeast swell or a wrapping solid east swell. Offshore west/southwest. Optimum wave size 3-6ft (1-2.5m). Competent surfers only - heavy tidal currents.

NE1 021

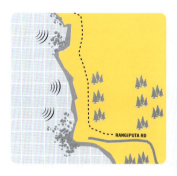

Raupo Bay

From Coopers Beach, take HWY 10 west to Inland Rd. Head out towards Cape Karikari, take a left to Rangiputa and Raupo Bay.

Area has several bays featuring beach, reef and sand/reef combos. Find a range of breaks in the area. Access is by hiking north towards Motuara Bay. Competent surfers.

Puwheke Beach

From Coopers Beach, take HWY 10 west. Take the right at Inland Rd out to the Karikari Peninsula. Turn left at Rangiputa then right on Puheke Rd.

Long bay featuring a range of variable beach breaks and peaks breaking around rocky outcrops. Break is sheltered from east swells by Cape Karikari. Best surfed on a north swell. Good for surfers of all levels.

022 NE1

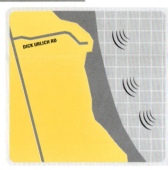

Tokerau Beach

Take HWY 10 west from Coopers Beach. Turn right on Inland Rd. Access the beach via Ramp Rd or Dick Urlich Rd.

Long beach stretches from Taipa north towards the Karikari Peninsula. Find a range of beach breaks which pick up east/southeast swells. Look for the indicators at Knuckle Point Blowhole (100ft plumes of spray), and Fairway Reef in the middle of Doubtless Bay. Fairway features a mega-left reef with big wave tow-in potential. Tokerau best surfed with an easterly swell. Good for surfers of all levels. Uncrowded and isolated.

Taipa

From Kerikeri, Take HWY 10 north to Coopers Beach and Taipa.

Area features a beach break and river mouth with a very narrow swell window. Sheltered break, it needs a solid 6-8ft (2-3m) swell to work. Caution: sewerage problems during storms. Water is murky from clay cliffs. Expect mellow, lazy beach break waves. Offshore south/southwest. Good for surfers of all levels. Good learners wave.

NE1 023

Motukahakaha Bay

From HWY 10, take Taupo Bay Rd east. Getting to Motukahakaha Bay is a long hike over private land. Ask permission first.

Bay features a beach break with peaks breaking around various rocky outcrops. Walk east past Bird Rock - heaps of reef potential, who knows what you may find. Isolated.

Further west find *Paradise Bay*. Get there via a private access track (4WD only.) A beautiful secluded bay, it offers various beachies breaking around rocky outcrops. Expect peaky A-frames. Break is sheltered from strong offshore winds. Check with the landowner for access. Good for surfers of all levels.

Taupo Bay

Take Taupo Bay Rd from HWY 10.

Bay features a beach break and sometimes a right point setup at southern end. Best in northeast and east swells, you'll find consistent A-frame peaks peeling through to a heavy shore break. Be ready for sucky takeoffs and hollow tubes. Bay is offshore west/southwest and is sheltered from strong offshore winds. Bay holds a solid 6-8ft (2-3m) swell. Good for surfers of all levels.

TAUPO BAY. PHOTO: NZ SURFING MAGAZINE

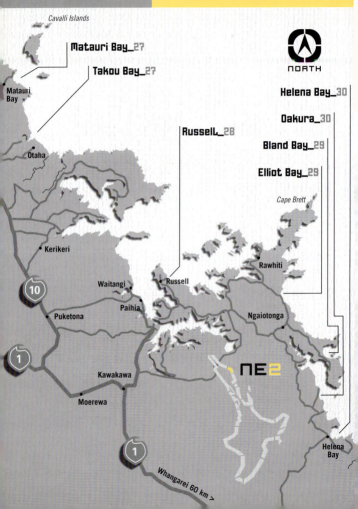

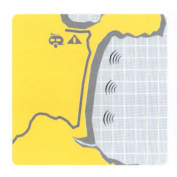

Matauri Bay

From HWY 10 and Kaeo, head northeast on Martin Rd, then Matauri Bay Rd.

Bay features a variable beach break producing mellow peaks - good longboard wave, great for learners. Break is always smaller than other exposed bays. Optimum wave size 2-4ft (1-1.5m). Good for surfers of all levels.

Takou Bay

From Kerikeri take HWY 10 north to Takou Bay Rd. Drive to the end of the road. From here access is over private land - ask permission.

Takou Bay features a river bar and beach break. The banks are shifty and constantly change due to floods. Break is best surfed on east swells. Good for surfers of all levels.

028 NE2

Spot X

Several quality breaks during large north/northeast swells. Cowshit Point, right point break. The Ledge, square and heavy. Reef and outer bombies. Let the Tapuaetahi lead you to the bounty. Locked gate - ask a friendly local.

Russell-Ocean Beach

From Paihia, take the ferry across to Russell.

Find a beach break which needs a very large swell to penetrate the Islands and break. Expect a mellow wave breaking over shifting sand bars. Optimum wave size 2-4ft(1-1.5m). Also of interest are various reefs around Waitangi. These also need a big swell to break, and make for an interesting option when the exposed coast is maxed out.

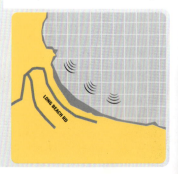

NE2 029

Elliot Bay

From Russell, take Russell Road east. Take a left on Rawhiti Rd and head north. Elliot Bay is located at the point Rawhiti Rd heads inland. From here you cross farmland to the bay. Look for the honesty box on the fence.

Elliot Bay is the first in a series of beautiful bays which feature pristine white sand beaches and crystal clear water. Here you will find a range of beach breaks which pick up east and southeast swells. Breaks can be 3-4ft when the rest of the coast is flat. Be adventurous, head north on foot. A series of incredible bays offer a range of isolated breaks. Good for surfers of all levels.

Bland Bay

Take HWY 1 south from Oamaru. At Maheno, take the turnoff to Orore Point.

Stretch of coast features a range of variable beach breaks. Quality depends on location of sand. At the southern end of the beach you'll find a right reef break peeling around Orore Point.

Beach picks up swells from the northeast through south. Southern point is sheltered from winds. Optimum wave size 4-6ft (1-2m). Good for surfers of all levels.

030 NE2

Oakura Bay

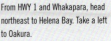

From HWY 1 and Whakapara, head northeast to Helena Bay. Take a left to Oakura.

Bay features a breach break producing a range of peaks breaking over a combination of reef and sand. Bay is semi-sheltered and needs a solid east/southeast swell to work. Find a good reef peak in front of the shop. Good for surfers of all levels.

Helena Bay

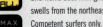

Head north from Whangarei on HWY 1. Turn right at Whakapara.

Helena Bay has several breaks. Find a steep profile beach break producing left and right peaks. Also find good waves around the various rocky outcrops along the beach. Bay picks up north and northeast swell and works best with grunty cyclone swells from the northeast. Competent surfers only.

NE3 033

Mimiwhangata Bay

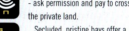

From Helena Bay take Webb Rd east to Ngahau Bay Rd and Mimiwhangata Rd. Difficult access - ask permission and pay to cross the private land.

Secluded, pristine bays offer a beach break and a range of peaks breaking around rocky fingers and outcrops. Bay is a swell magnet even though it does feature a narrow swell window. Also, to the north find Paparahi Point offering various reef peaks. Bay is best surfed with a north/northeast swell at 3-5ft (1-1.5m). Good for surfers of all levels.

Okupe Beach

Find Okupe Beach east of Mimiwhangata Bay.

Area features a range of beach breaks producing left and right peaks on inner and outer banks. Quality depends on sand location. Beach faces east and picks up sneaky southeast and east angle swells. Good for surfers of all levels.

034 NE3

Moureeses

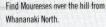

Find Moureeses over the hill from Whananaki North.

Secluded, sheltered bay features a beach break. Find various left and right peaks along the beach, with the main peak located at the southern end of the beach. Expect mellow takeoffs and soft walls. Great learners wave and good for longboards. Optimum wave size 3-4ft (1-1.5m). Good for surfers of all levels.

Whananaki Nth

From HWY 1 take Marua Rd from Hikurangi. Drive northeast to Whananaki South. Take Hailes Rd inland and around to the north side.

Area features a left-hand bar break. Expect long peeling lefts, and easy workable walls with various sections. Break picks up east and southeast swells. Optimum wave size 3-5ft (1-2m). Break tends to close out over this size. Good for surfers of all levels.

036 NE3

Sandy Bay

Drive north from Whangarei on HWY 1. Turn right after Hikurangi. Take Marua Rd to Matapouri Rd and Sandy Bay.

Bay features a beach break offering various peaks along the beach. Quality depends on sand location - shifty banks. Expect grunty waves which can produce hollow barrels. Break handles a solid swell and is best surfed with swells from the northeast, east and southeast. The southern end of the beach offers shelter from southeasterly winds. Optimum wave size 3-6ft (1-2.5m). Break gets crowded on weekends. Good for surfers of all levels.

Ngunguru Bar

Get to Ngunguru by heading south from Sandy Bay on Matapouri Rd. Access the break by paddling across the estuary.

Break consists of a left bar breaking over shifting sand banks. The bar works best with big northeast and east swells on all tides. Banks constantly change, so quality depends on sand build-up. Competent surfers only.

NE3 037

Pataua Bar

From Whangarei take Whareora Rd east to Horahora. Then continue on Pataua Rd.

Here you'll find a classic right-hand river bar break. Banks constantly shift from flow and flooding. If it's on, expect sucky takeoffs followed by long hollow walls breaking over a shallow sand bottom. Look for the barrel. Good for intermediate to expert level surfers.

Ocean Beach

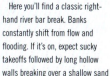

Head east from Whangarei out to the Whangarei Heads.

Area features a beach break and various peaks breaking around rocky outcrops. Always picks up more swell than other breaks. Works on swells from east and southeast angles. Quality beach break producing solid peaks breaking on inner and outer banks. Optimum wave size 3-6ft (1-2.5m). Will handle 8ft (3m.) Break gets crowded on weekends. Head north to Procters for uncrowded waves. Good for surfers of all levels.

038 NE3

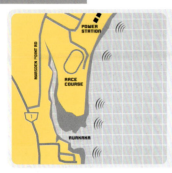

Marsden Point

Head north from Waipu on HWY 1. Take a right on Marsden Point Rd.

Area features a beach break with left and right peaks breaking on various inner and outer bars. Find longer waves and walls after harbour dredging. Beach picks up east and southeast sneaker swells. Also find a river bar break at the mouth of the Ruakaka River. Expect shifty banks with shape of bars changing constantly. Fun waves - good for surfers of all levels.

Waipu River

From HWY 1 take the turnoff to Waipu Cove. Take a left when you reach the river.

Check surf from across the river NB: if it looks 1-2ft, it will be 2ft bigger. Mouth of the river features a right-hand bar break depending on sand bank location. Banks are shifty and constantly changing. Be ready for a sucky takeoff and short hollow wall. Optimum wave size 3-5ft (1-2m). Break is offshore northwest, west and a light southwest. Competent surfers only.

Waipu Cove

From HWY 1, head southeast from Waipu on Waipu Cove Rd.

Here you'll find a variable beach breaks which is sheltered from large east and southeast swells. Find a range of peaks along the beach and a right-hand point located at the southern end. The right breaks with a large wrapping east swell and features a mellow wall which peels through to a sucky shore break. Waipu Cove picks up swells from the north, northeast and east. Good for surfers of all levels.

Langs Beach-Ding Bay

Drive southeast over the hill from Waipu Cove.

Another stunning tree-lined bay. Find Ding Bay at the northern end. Can have quality left and right peaks, Bay is sheltered from strong northwest and west winds. Further south you'll find two streams which usually create good banks, especially after heavy rain. Expect to find a range of shifty peaks along the beach. Best mid to low tide, watch the backwash at high tide. Bay holds 6-8ft (2-3m). Find a bombie which breaks on macca swells at the south end of the bay. Further around the headland there are two other bays offering assorted breaks.

NE4 AREA

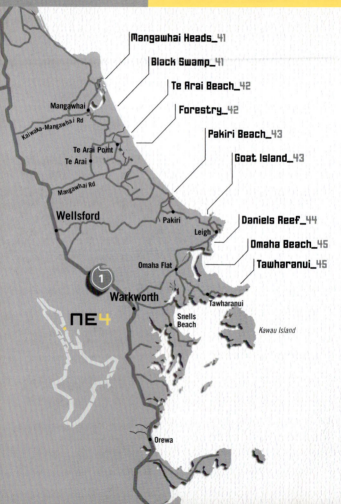

NE4 041

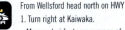

Mangawhai Heads

From Wellsford head north on HWY 1. Turn right at Kaiwaka.

Mangawhai features a range of breaks. In front and to the north of the parking lot and surf club find a beach break producing a range of left and right peaks. The harbour entrance features a right, reef/point peeling through to a grunty shorie.

Mangawhai Bar features a gnarly left-hander, and occasionally a short hollow right. The bar is constantly changing with dredging having a major effect on its shape and quality. Expect a jacking takeoff and hollow wall which can peel for 100-150m on a good day. Best 4-6ft (1.5-2m). Extreme tidal rips - competent surfers only.

Black Swamp

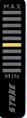

From Mangawhai, take Black Swamp Rd east. Access is via several forestry tracks.

A good place to escape the crowds. Find various beach breaks to the north and south. Breaks often close-out, but can occasionally produce good left and right peaks. Good for surfers of all levels.

042 NE4

Te Arai

Head south from Mangawhai. Take Black Swamp Rd to Te Arai Pnt Rd.

Te Arai offers a range of beach breaks and various peaks breaking around rocky outcrops at the southern end. Break is a swell magnet, picking up swells ranging from north through to east. Te Arai holds a solid swell and it can be difficult to get out when it's over 6ft (2.5m). Gets very crowded on weekends. Sometimes worth a walk up the beach to get a wave to yourself.

Forestry

Head south from Te Arai Point. Sometimes difficult access.

Area features a quality beach break and a left-hand point break at the northern end. Forestry picks up a range of swells from north through to east.

The left point works best with swells from the northeast or east angle and holds up to 6ft (2.5m). Any larger and it tends to close out. Be ready for a sucky takeoff and hollow first section. A mellow workable wall peels through to the shorey for up to 80m on a good day. Gets crowded on the weekends, but you can usually find plenty of peaks down the beach. Good for surfers of all levels.

NE4 043

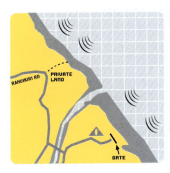

Pakiri Beach

Head south from Te-Arai on the loose metal road towards Cape Rodney. Turn left before Pakiri Hill.

Beautiful long, white sandy beach with pure white, fine grained sand. Sand dredge can often be seen working which affects the quality of the banks. Here you'll find a range of beachies producing sucky peaks up and down beach. Find a river/estuary half a km down the beach. Sometimes features a left and right bar break. Area picks up swells north through east and is good on all tides. Good for surfers of all levels.

Goat Island

Drive south over the hill from Pakiri. Take a left and head towards Cape Rodney.

Sheltered Bay which features a right-hand reef break. Break only works on big swells. Needs to be 6-8ft (2-3m) to break. Swell wraps and changes angle and hits the reef producing a gnarly, sucky right. Expect an intense takeoff followed by a hollow barrel section and fat shoulder - heaps of power and grunt. Heavy crowds and intense takeoff area. Reef picks up northeast and east swells and is best surfed mid to high tide. Experts only.

044 NE4

Spot X

Boulders at Leigh. Secret reef. Ask a freindly local

Daniels Reef

Head south from Leigh, turn left at Wonder View Road.

Area offers a twin peak left and right reef break. Break holds solid swell 8-10ft (4m). As the swell size increases, shifty peaks move further out. Best surfed on a solid east tropo swell. Expect long hollow lefts off the peak. Gets heavy and offers square-hollow barrels. The right is fat and thick and features a tricky late takeoff. Tricky access - paddle out through the rocks and gnarly shorey. Clay access track makes for slippery feet. Intermediate to expert level surfers only.

NE4 045

Omaha Beach - Bar

Drive south from Leigh, turn left at the Point Wells turnoff.

Beach break with occasional quality left and right bar at the north end harbour entrance. With solid east swells Omaha Bar becomes a swell magnet. Swells wedge through the Colville Channel. Straight, long lines result in a long winding left-hander. Break gets very crowded. Holds 3-6ft (1-2.5m). The beach break offers fat mushy waves and a dumping shorebreak. On solid 6+ft (2.5m) swells it pays to check out reef at southern end - can get good. Good for surfers of all levels.

Tawharanui

Head east from Omaha Point to the Tawharanui Regional Park.

Area features a range of reef and beach breaks. Picks up north, northeast and east swells. Sheltered on south and southeast winds. Last chance on the coast for clean waves with these winds. Breaks hold solid wrapping east swells. Expect good left and rights in sheltered bays. Short rides. Gets very crowded. Good for surfers of all levels.

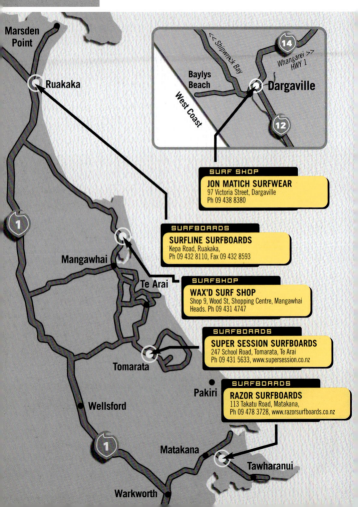

NORTHLAND

Aqua Pulse Surf Shop
41 - 51 Commerce St, Kaitaia
Ph 09 4083020

Good Vibrations Surf Camp
Masters Access Rd, RD 1 Kaitaia
Ph 09 409 4009,
www.surfcoaching.com

High Voltage Fashions
84 Main Rd, Kerikeri
Ph 09 4077140

Jon Matich Surfwear
97 Victoria St, Dargaville
Ph 09 4388380

North Point Surf
88 Keri Keri Rd, Ph 09 407 7399

Rebel Surf N Denim
Cinema Plaza, James St, Whangarei
Ph 09 4387740

Sessions
47 Queen St, Warkworth
Ph 09 4259384

Razor Surfboards
113 Takatu Rd, Tawharanui
PH 09 4229728
www.razorsurfboards.com

Super Session Surfboards
247 School Rd, Tomarata, Te Arai
Ph 09 4315633
www.supersession.co.nz

Surf Adventure Surf School
Steve Tyne, RD 3 Sandy Bay,
Whangarei, Ph 09 434 3443

Surfline Surfboards
Kepa Rd, Ruakaka
Ph 09 432 8110
Fax 09 432 8593
email: surflinenz@yahoo.co.nz

Surf N Beach
Barrington One Ltd, Paihia
Ph 09 4027317

Tribal Surf
RD 1 Hikurangi, Northland
Ph 09 4337119

Wax'D Surf Shop
Shop 9, Wood St, Shopping Centre, Mangawhai
Heads, Ph 09 431 4747

Viv Treacy Surf Design
Agent Surftech Surfboards
RD 4 Ocean Beach, Whangarei
Ph 09 434 0884,
email: vtsurf@actrix.co.nz
www. surftech.com

Northland West Coast

Two enormous beaches make up most of the West Coast of Northland. Exposed to the Tasman Sea and the powerful weather systems of the Southern Ocean, this coast is known for rough seas and more wind and rain than the sheltered eastern side. Ninety Mile Beach is more than 80 kilometres long while Ripiro Beach, between the Hokianga and Kaipara Harbours, is more than 100 kilometres. Both are designated roads but should only be driven on during the lower half of the tide. Between these two beaches is a remote area of huge headlands, isolated harbours, sand hills that can be seen from space, dense rainforest, and one of the world's best left-hand point breaks, Shipwreck Bay. Located at the southern end of Ninety Mile Beach in the lee of the Tauroa Peninsula, Shippies is accessed from Ahipara. For those with a 4WD a selection of nearly eight kilometres of exceptional point breaks awaits their inspection. Large southerly swells wrap round Tauroa Point to create long-walled waves that decrease in size with distance. Rides of a kilometre or more have been recorded. Camping next to the surfbreaks is allowed.

Western Northland includes the famous Waipoua Forest, home to the giant Kauri. South of this, below the spectacular Maungunui Bluff, the road leads on to Ripiro Beach. With an offshore wind and a clean swell both Ripiro and Ninety Mile beaches can offer mile after mile of hollow, deserted beachbreak conditions. But be warned, the West Coast of New Zealand, can be treacherous and lives have been lost in its strong currents and powerful waves.

A deep southern ocean system creates a massive fetch delivering huge southwest swells to the west coast. The Shipwreck Bay points fire.

Equinox - Roaring 40's deliver a hideous westerly onshore flow. 30-60kt onshore winds produce an 8-10ft West Coast washing machine.

A depression tracks east from the Tasman Sea delivering swell. A high pressure system over the country provides offshore winds.

NW 049

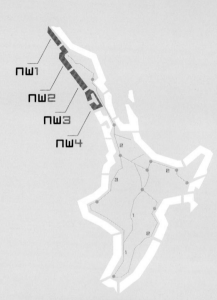

NW1	50
Twilight Beach	51
Scott Point	51
Te Paki	52
The Bluff	52
NW2	54
90 Mile Beach	55
Ahipara Beach	55
Wreck Bay	58
Peaks	58
Mukie 1	59
Mukie 2	59
Supertubes	59
Pines	59
Bluehouse	62
The Box	62
Tanutanu	63
Hokianga	63
NW3	66
Waimamaku	67
Waipou Reefs	67
Kawerua Reefs	68
Aranga Beach	68
Baylys Beach	69
Glinks Gully	69
NE4	70
Ripiro Beach	71
Pouto	71

O'NEILL — AREA SEASONAL WETSUIT RECOMMENDATIONS

SUMMER
BOARDIES-
SPRINGY

AUTUMN
SPRING
SUIT

WINTER
3/2 or 4/3 STEAMER
+ BOOTIES

SPRING
SPRINGY-
STEAMER

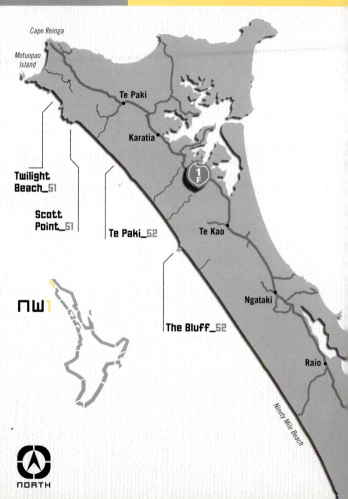

NW1 051

Twilight Beach

Access Twilight Beach from Cape Reinga Rd. Take the Cape Walkway (long walk) down the hill to the beach below.

Isolated beach break offering a range of left and right peaks. Typical beachie with shifty sand banks. Break is always bigger than it appears from car park. You can be assured of a wave to yourself. Optimum wave size 3-5ft (1-1.5m). Sheltered from strong offshore easterly winds. Good for surfers of all levels.

Scott Point

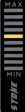

Head north from the Bluff on Ninety Mile Beach (low tide only), alternatively head north from Kaitaia on HWY 1F. Turn left at Te Paki stream - tricky and interesting access for adventurers.

Area is a swell magnet featuring a beach break and a fickle right off the headland. Expect a range of left and right variable beach break waves. Banks constantly change. Watch for serious rips. Optimum wave size 2-4ft (.5-1m). Isolated and uncrowded. Good for competent surfers only.

052 NW1

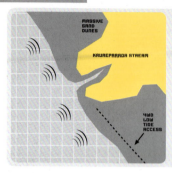

Te Paki

Drive north from Bluff on Ninety Mile Beach (1 hour either side of low tide). Look out for a stream with massive sand dunes either side.

Break features a range of variable beachies which only work on small swells. Find a variety of left and right peaks along the beach. The best banks are usually near the stream. Break is exposed to strong offshore winds. If the surf is bad, try sandboarding the 100-200ft high dunes. If the East Coast has waves, follow the stream for a short cut to the other side. Good for surfers of all levels. Isolated.

The Bluff

Head north from Ahipara along Ninety Mile Beach (low tide only).

The Bluff consists of a large rock and sand outcrop. A swell magnet, it features a range of peaks either side of the outcrop. Break will only handle a small swell, it's a good option if the Shipwreck Bay points are flat. Caution serious currents and rips. Usually lots of fisherman in the area. Exposed, uncrowded and isolated. Competent surfers.

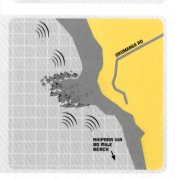

New Box Packaging

Smaller Harder Nipples

Protection & Pleasure for Your Board

www.palmerssurf.com.au

Dealer inquiries: Shorethings Ltd
Ph 09 360 2701, email: shorethings@xtra.co.nz

NW2 AREA

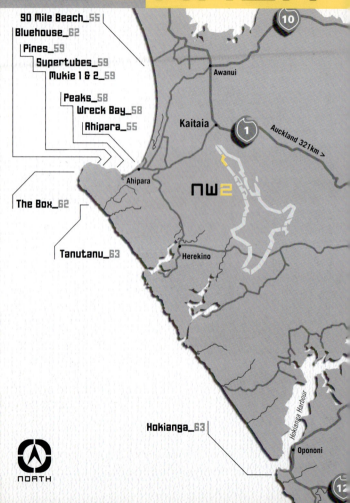

- 90 Mile Beach_55
- Bluehouse_62
- Pines_59
- Supertubes_59
- Mukie 1 & 2_59
- Peaks_58
- Wreck Bay_58
- Ahipara_55
- The Box_62
- Tanutanu_63
- Hokianga_63

Awanui
Kaitaia
Auckland 321km >
Ahipara
Herekino
Hokianga Harbour
Opononi

NORTH

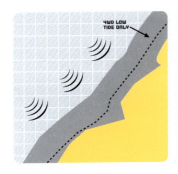

90 Mile Beach

From Kaitaia, take the Kaitaia Awaroa Rd to Ahipara and Ninety Mile Beach.

Long beach stretches north to Scott Point. Take your 4WD up the beach. Caution: watch for soft sand. Ninety Mile Beach is classified as a national highway and it's the perfect place to head off on an adventure. You'll find variable beach breaks which work on smaller clean swells all the way until you hit The Bluff. Isolated. Good for surfers of all levels.

Ahipara Beach

Head southwest from Kaitaia to Ahipara.

Area features a variable beach break producing fat, soft beach break waves. Usually plenty of close-outs. Slow mellow wave which can be fun. Great spot to learn to surf. Optimum size 2-4ft (.5-1m). Good for surfers of all levels.

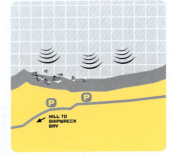

CORY SCOTT PHOTOGRAPHY Ph : (0274) 326 180, e: cozza@ihug.co.nz, **www.coryscott.co.nz**

Peaks - Shipwreck Bay

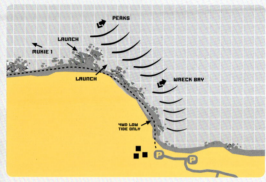

Get to Ahipara by heading west from Kaitaia on Kaitaia-Awaroa Rd. Drive over hill to parking and Shipwreck Bay. From here you can either walk or take a 4WD around the point (only at low tide).

Area features two distinct breaks. The first is Shipwreck Bay which peels from the headland in the first Bay. Expect classic left-hand peaks breaking over sand. Often shifty, it features a mellow, fun wave. Large southwest swells wrap 180 degrees sending waves into Wreck Bay. Break is offshore south through southwest.

Peaks is next. It breaks west of Shipwreck Bay. Get there by continuing on foot or by 4WD. A legendary break, Peaks can produce long, perfect lefts with the right conditions. Get out by paddling through rocky outcrops or launch from the rocks at the headland. Expect a big sucky takeoff followed by a long hollow barrel section. If the banks are good, you can expect a long workable wall which peels and grinds all the way through to Wreck Bay. Be ready for leg-burning rides which can be as long as 500m. Peaks is best surfed at low tide during big southwest swells. Optimum wave size 4-6ft (1-2.5m). Be ready for strong currents with heaps of sweep along the point. Tricky paddle on big days. Experienced surfers.

Pines - Supertubes - Mukie 2 - Mukie 1

Shippie's left-hand madness continues. Head west from Peaks. From here you'll find a range of awesome points.

First you'll hit Mukie 1. Best on low tide, it features a short left-hander (peels 70-80m) which can produce sucky barrels on occasion.

Further west is Mukie 2. A good wave on all tides, M2 produces longer lefts which peel over a sand bottom. Break features more of a suck-up during takeoff and can offer good tubes.

Next is Supertubes - a combo reef/sand bottom left. Be ready for a big heavy takeoff (how deep do you wanna go?) followed by a long hollow barrel section.

Make it out and you'll be greeted with a long wall which peels 200-300m. Supertubes is good on all tides. Optimum size 4-6ft (1.5-2.5m.) Difficult paddle.

Outside Supertubes is Pines. Look for the ridge with a line of pine trees. Pines is Supertube's mellow neighbour. Break works best on a smaller swell and tends to close out on the outer ledge when big. Expect a mellow takeoff and first section (which can sometimes be hollow). Wave bowls into a fat shoulder then a long workable wall. Look for the barrel on the inside. Pines is best surfed at low tide at 3-5ft (1-1.5m). All breaks are offshore south, southwest and southeast.

SUPERS. MUKIE 2. PHOTO: CORY SCOTT

062 NW 2

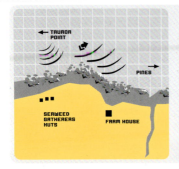

Bluehouse

Head along beach from Pines. Look for the farm house.

Left-hand point setup which picks up more swell. Break is exposed producing heavy, solid waves with ledgy takeoffs. A hollow first section fades before wedging and sucking top to bottom, then peels off with a long workable wall. Hollow barrel to be had. Caution: shallow reef. Difficult paddle, watch out for sharp mussel-encrusted rocks. Optimum wave size 4-6 ft (1-2.5m). Handles 6-8 ft (2.5-3m). Expert level surfers only.

The Box

Head southwest around the point from Blue House. Go past the seaweed gatherer's huts.

Swell magnet right reef break. A beast of a wave, it is best surfed when the points are flat. Be ready for an extreme ledge takeoff and pitching square barrel. Short but intense wave for experts only. Handles 4-6ft (1-2.5m). Isolated and spooky wave.

Tanutanu

Difficult access over old gumfields. Alternatively 4WD access around Tauroa point. Head south from the lighthouse.

Isolated beach break produces a range of left and right peaks. Find the best banks near the many rocky outcrops. Shifty banks with heavy currents. Tanutanu is best surfed on smaller clean swells. Good for surfers of all levels.

Hokianga

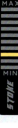

Head north from Waipoua Kauri Forest on HWY 1. Turn left at Omapere.

Hokianga Harbour entrance features a bar/beach break. Find a range of peaks with the better breaks to be found to the south. Break is exposed and prone to strong winds and extreme tides. South Head features a short right-hander producing short, walled peaks on west and northwest swells. Difficult paddle with strong drift. Surfable only 1 hour either side of low tide. Uncrowded. Intermediate to expert level surfers.

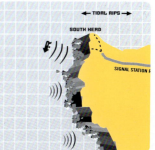

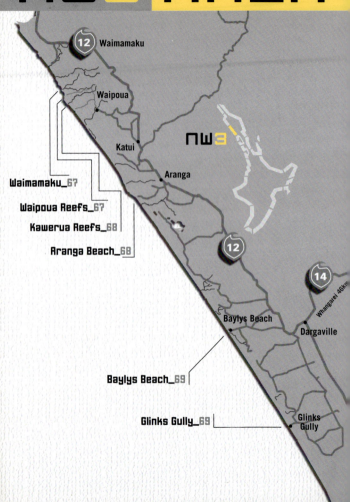

NW3 067

Waimamaku

Drive south on HWY 12 from Opononi. Take a right before you hit Waiotemarama. Head to the mouth of the Waimamaku river.

River bar break features a range of left and right peaks. Bars constantly changing. Optimum 3-5ft (1-1.5m). Good for surfers of all levels.

Tombs - Waipoua Reefs

Head north from Dargaville on HWY 12 to the Waipoua Forest. NB: Get a friendly local to guide you through the maze of forestry tracks. Many tracks have gates which are locked. Alternatively, drive to the Wairau River and walk from there. Reefs are a 1 hour hike south.

Range of powerful reef breaks. Serious big wave spots, home to NZ's own Shark Island. Expect heavy, gnarly waves. Explore the area and you may be rewarded. Reefs hold 8-10ft waves. Expert level surfers only. Isolated and uncrowded. Don't get lost!

068 NW3

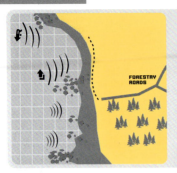

Kawerua Reefs

Hike south from the Waipoua Reefs or get a friendly local to guide you through the forestry tracks.

Area features a variety of reef breaks including a solid left-hander which holds 8-10ft waves. Heavy exposed break. Be ready for ledgy takeoffs and big barrels. Also reports of a big wave right which holds solid 14ft waves. Isolated break, experts only.

Aranga Beach

Take HWY 12 north from Dargaville, past the beautiful clear Kaiiwi Lakes. Turn left at the Aranga Beach turnoff.

Another exposed beach on wild west coast. Uncrowded and raw, Aranga is best surfed on a small swell. Find the odd right-hander off the headland, along with various beach break peaks to the south. Best surfed at high tide with light winds. If the waves are bad, check out the Tuatuas at low tide - a local seafood delicacy.

nw3 069

Baylys Beach

Head west from Dargaville through Mangatara. Wind down valley, find parking on the beach. Beware of soft sand and surging tides.

Area features a huge expansive beach. Only surfable on small swells, it is usually wind-swept and prone to treacherous rips. Expect changeable left and right peaks with shifty banks. Optimum wave size 2-4 ft (.5-1m). Can produce quality waves if conditions are right. Good for surfers of all levels.

Glinks Gully

Drive southwest from Dargaville through Te Kopuru. Turn right and wind down to the beach

Exposed wind-swept beach. Suits small swells and best surfed with light offshores. Optimum wave size 2-4 ft (.5-1m). Find various peaks which break on inner and outer banks. Uncrowded. Good for surfers of all levels. Use caution when it's maxing, beach prone to rips and severe undertow.

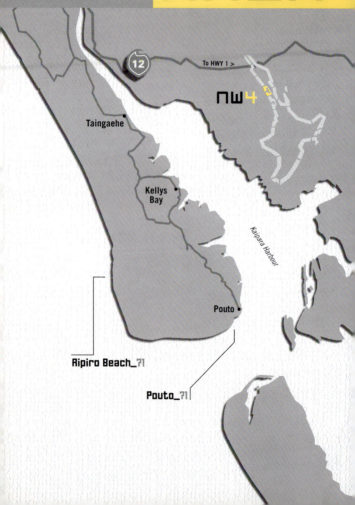

Ripiro Beach

Head south from Dargaville, follow the Wairoa River through Aratapu south towards Kellys Bay. From here it's rough tracks and a long hike to the coast.

Area features a very long beach break stretching to the north. Find variable left and right peaks with shifty peaks and strong currents. Best surfed on high tide with a small clean swell and light or offshore winds. Optimum 3-5ft (1-1.5m). Competent surfers.

Pouto

Travel south from Dargaville. Follow the Wairoa River through Taingaehe to Pouto.

Here you'll find a fickle right-hand point bar break which peels along Kaipara Head. Mythical - needs a 6-10ft southwest swell with a low to incoming tide. Extreme tidal movement and currents. When it's working expect a long wrapping right-hand wall. Competent surfers only.

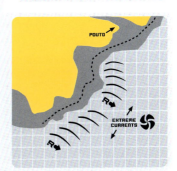

Auckland East Coast

Auckland's east coast beaches have to be one of the most unreliable stretches of coast for surf in New Zealand. Ironically, the area also contains the country's largest urban population.

The shallow, sheltered beaches of Auckland's North Shore generally have flat bottom profiles, with headlands and reefs at each end. While the area has the breaks to produce good waves if there is swell, Great Barrier Island and the Coromandel Peninsula block any swells from the east. It takes a rare scenario when a tropical cyclone tracks southeast or a storm pushes solid north to northeast swell directly into its sheltered bays and beaches.

When the surf is up, word spreads quickly through the local beach beat and every surfer, kayaker, goatboater, flutter boarder, windsurfer and jetskier will head straight to the best peaks. Etiquette is replaced by survival of the fittest and it's every surfer for him or herself. The frenzy is fueled by the fact that swells to the area will only last a few hours due to heavy tidal changes.

Most of the sizable swells arrive with storms. With the rapid expansion of the city, water quality becomes sketchy from polluted stormwater runoff. Auckland surfers are experiencing more ear and stomach infections than ever before so avoid swallowing the water.

A low pressure area moves southwards towards the trade wind belt. Isobars bunch creating an easterly gale and 2-3m swells to the east coast.

A powerful Tropical Cyclone descends southeast from the tropics. As it enters the zone, massive swells pump towards the city beaches.

A depression moves east from the Tassie sending pure north swells and a tonne of rain to the coast. North exposed breaks fire.

AE 073

AE1	74
Waiwera Reef	75
Orewa Beach	75
Orewa Bar	76
Red Beach	76
Fishermans Reef	77
Long Bay Reef	77
Milford Reef	80
O'Neills Reef	80
North Reef	81
South Reef	81
INFO	82

O'NEILL — AREA SEASONAL WETSUIT RECOMMENDATIONS

SUMMER
BOARDIES-
SPRINGY

AUTUMN
SPRINGY

WINTER
4/3 STEAMER
+ BOOTIES

SPRING
SPRINGY-
STEAMER

AE1 AREA

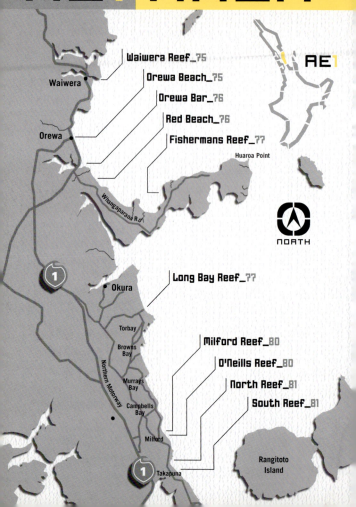

AE1 075

Waiwera Reef

From Auckland take HWY 1 north past Orewa to Waiwera. Turn right at Waiwera before the bridge. Follow the road past the hot pools to the estuary entrance. Access the break by paddling across the river (short paddle).

Break features a left and right peak with a sucky takeoff followed by short hollow walls.

Spot needs solid 6ft plus swell on exposed coasts to work. Optimum wave 3-5ft (1-1.5m). Competent surfers.

Orewa Beach

Head north from Auckland on the Northern Motorway. At the end turn right off the highway, head east to Orewa beach.

Bay features a range of lazy/fun beachies producing long easy workable walls. Find various peaks along the beach. Great learners wave - the wave rolls for a great distance, constantly reforming. Good for surfers of all levels. Optimum wave size 2-4ft (.5-1m).

076 AE1

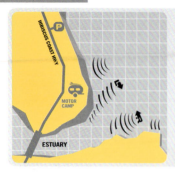

Orewa Bar

Head south through Orewa shops. When you reach the bridge turn left past camping ground.

River bar break features various left and right peaks either side of the river mouth. Banks constantly change due to river flow. Sometimes you'll find a long, soft left peeling up the harbour entrance. Fun wave for mals, easy soft makeable wave. On the south side you can occasionally find a right offering a little more punch. Heavy tidal rip on outgoing tide. Optimum wave size 2-4ft (.5-1m). Good for surfers of all levels.

Red Beach

Drive over the hill from Orewa. Turn left opposite shops, follow road southeast, turn left towards the surf club - car park located in front. Beach features various left and right peaks breaking on inner and outer banks (when big). Mellow, soft wave. Fun for learners. Break works well during onshore conditions. Sometimes you'll find shifty peaks off the rocks at the north and south end of the beach. Optimum wave size 2-5ft (.5-1.5m). Good for surfers of all levels - excellent learners spot.

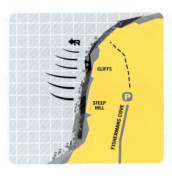

Fishermans Reef

Head east along Whangaparaoa Peninsula. Turn left before hill and Shakespear Park car park and toilet, walk down cliff.

The end of the peninsula at Huaroa Point you'll find a right hand, sucky, short reef. Expect a steep sucky takeoff and quick wall which fades into deep water. Fickle break. Needs solid mega-swell to work. Optimum size 4-5ft (1-1.5m). Competent surfers only.

Long Bay Reef

Head to Long Bay on the North Shore. Car park located along top of cliff overlooking Long Bay.

Fickle break, but sometimes quality left and right peaks depending on swell angle and size. Sucky mellow takeoff turns into a short, fat shoulder - fun hot dog waves. Optimum wave size 2-4ft (.5-1m). Sheltered from strong offshores. Good for surfers from all levels. Gets crowded.

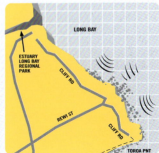

080 AE1

Milford Beach/Reef

     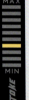

Head to Milford on Hurstmere Rd. Take a right on Saltburn/Ocean View Roads.

Beach features two distinct reef breaks separated by a channel. They feature lefts and rights which sometimes get hollow. Expect sucky peaks with the occasional quick tube section. The rights tend to offer longer workable walls. On lower tides the reefs tend to close out, making the beach a better option. Caution: shallow rocks and poor water quality at times. Further south is Tiri Rd. Break can produce a short fast right at mid tide. Optimum size 3-5ft (1-1.5m). Good for surfers of all levels.

O'Neills Reef

From Takapuna head north to Milford, turn right onto O'Neills Rd.

Fast left-hand reef. Features a bowling wave which wraps down O'Neills Point. Expect a sucky takeoff, followed by a short workable section (which sometimes shuts down). From there a second section can wind down the point for another 50m. Watch out for sharp oyster covered rocks. Crazy crowds. Competent surfers only.

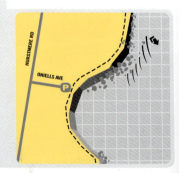

AE1 081

North Reef

Head to Takapuna Motor Camp located at the northern end of Takapuna Beach. The car park is in front of reef.

Classic left and right peak on solid north and northeast swells. Tricky takeoff complete with rock boil-ups. The right is flatter and offers a short workable wall. The left is a sucky little beast, and watch out for the marker pole. Easy paddle out around break. Max crowd and hungry pack. Keep eyes peeled for very rich men with jet skis putting wetsuits on backwards! Optimum wave size 3-5ft (1-1.5m). Intermediate/expert level surfers.

South Reef

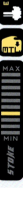

From Takapuna city, turn down any street on the left heading down to Devonport from the shopping centre.

Beach offers a fun wave for local surfers. Works on strong northerly onshores, and with a quick southwest wind change, quality peaks can be had. At south end find various left and right peaks which stand up on hidden rock shelves. Break gets super crowded. Poor water quality after heavy rain. Optimum wave size 2-4ft (.5-1m). Good for surfers of all levels.

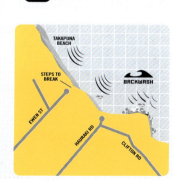

AUCKLAND EAST COAST LISTINGS

Amazon Glenfield
Shop 317 Upper Level, Glenfield Shopping Center
Ph 09 442 2485

Barracuda
Shop 111, Milford Shopping Centre
Ph 09 489 2918

Crossover Sports Distribution
Ph 021 1445 740
www.crossoversports.co.nz

Notionlab
Advertising, Marketing, Book Design, New Media
Designers of the Wavetrack New Zealand Surfing
Guide - lets talk Ph 021 529 599
www.notionlab.co.nz

North Beach Surf n Skate
Store 19 Albany Mega Centre, Don Mckinnon Drive
Ph 09 415 0331

Saturdays of Takapuna
Westfield Shore City, Takapuna
Ph 09 486 1370

Primal Surf Ltd
46 Barrys Point Rd, Takapuna
Ph 09 488 0165,
www.primalsurf.com

Proshapes
70 B Target Rd, Glenfield
Ph 027 416 3680

7th Wave Wetsuits
34 Barrys Point Rd, Takapuna
Ph 0800 843 928,
www.surfallday.co.nz

Surf Reports - Nationwide - Online
www.surf2surf.com

Surf Reports - Phone
Wavetrack 0900 99 777 (Calls 99c/min)
Groms ask your parents first

The Longboard Shop
Unit KL 5 Miro Place, Albany, North Shore
Ph 09 415 7277

Ultimate Surf co nz
Ph 09 480 0821

Wayne Parkes Surfboards
77 Barrys Point Rd, Takapuna
Ph 09 486 1395

XT Sea Surf Shop
40 Hurstmere Rd, Takapuna
Ph 09 489 9755,
www.xtsea.co.nz

wavetrack™   SURF2SURF.com

Auckland West Coast

Auckland's closest wilderness, the West Coast, is 40 minutes easy drive from New Zealand's cosmopolitan metropolis. Starting north of Muriwai and ending 40 kilometres south, at the turbulent Port Waikato beaches, the coastline offers consistent, quality surf, amid awesome volcanic scenery and vast, black sand beaches.

Drive over the bushclad Waitakere Ranges and you'll enter a rugged and beautiful world. The winding road leads to spectacular views of the Tasman Sea and deep blue lines of swell which quicken a surfer's pulse.

Prevailing south westerlies, and the El Nino influence ensure that the coast is never starved of wind, swell and rain.

Winter brings constant southwest swells with rain that can last for a week. Ferocious storms can displace huge areas of sand. Many of the beaches are notorious for their dangerous rips and currents and the lifeguards are kept busy during the holiday months.

Summer offers smaller, cleaner swells with occasional solid, pulsing sets from the southwest. Offshore winds, from the northeast, are more frequent in summer, offering all-time, hollow conditions. Now and then a northwest low pressure system will pump out peaky short-period swells, bringing life to reefs and points that don't normally break.

The West Coast's proximity to Auckland means breaks will be crowded at popular beaches like Piha and Muriwai. But the coast is in no way limited to the big name spots; a short drive and a hike can often reward you.

A deep southern ocean system creates a massive fetch delivering huge southwest swells to the west coast.

Equinox - Roaring 40's deliver a hideous westerly onshore flow. 30-60kt onshore winds produce an 8-10ft West Coast washing machine.

A depression tracks east from the Tasman Sea delivering peaky northwest A-frames. A high to the east provides clean offshore winds.

AW 085

AW1	86
Rimmers	87
Muriwai Beach	87
Maori Bay	88
Bethells	89
O'Neills	89
AW2	90
Anawhata	91
Whites	91
Piha	92
Karekare	93
Whatipu	93
AW3	96
Karioitahi	97
Sunset Beach	97
Port Waikato	98
INFO	98

O'NEILL — AREA SEASONAL WETSUIT RECOMMENDATIONS

SUMMER
BOARDIES-
SPRINGY

AUTUMN
SPRING
SUIT

WINTER
4/3 STEAMER
+ BOOTIES

SPRING
SPRINGY-
STEAMER

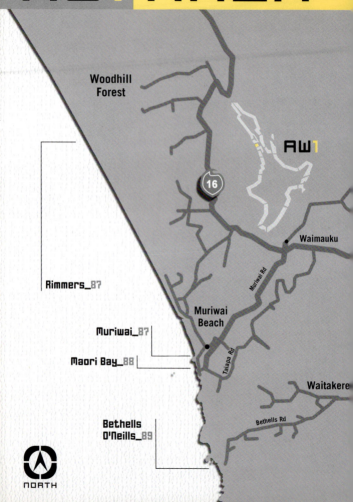

Muriwai - Rimmers

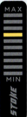

Head northwest from Auckland on HWY 16. Go past the Muriwai turnoff, turn left at Rimmers Rd. Take the forestry road to the beach. You can also drive on the beach from Muriwai - it is classified as a national highway.

Rimmers is a good beachie on a small swell with light offshores. Break is always bigger than Muriwai. Shifty peaks break over outer banks. Semi-reforms can produce hollow waves on the inside. Optimum wave size 1-3ft (0.5-1m). Isolated and uncrowded. Good for surfers of all levels.

Muriwai Beach

Located northwest of Auckland - take HWY 16 through Kumeu, turn left at the Muriwai turnoff.

Long expansive beach, good quality beach breaks featuring left and right peaks- shifty banks, quality depends on sand location. Also find a left-hand point break at the southern end of the beach. Point is prone to backwash from rocks as powerful west coast swells pulse through Muriwai Heads. Caution: beach features serious rips and sweeping currents. Staying in the lineup can be tricky. Optimum 3-5ft (1-1.5m). Gets crowded on weekends. Competent surfers especially when 5-6ft+ (2.5m+).

088 AW1

Maori Bay

Get to Maori Bay by heading over the hill from Muriwai. As you drive over the top look for the right turn to the car park. Walk down the hill to the breaks.

Sheltered spot from strong offshores due to steep cliffs. Find grunty peaks with tons of power in the middle of bay. Oaia Island (offshore) helps to break up the deep southern ocean swells producing shifty, hollow peaks. Expect heavy grinding barrels on the head which peel through to a gnarly double-up shore break.

Further down the beach is Shag Rock. A good big wave spot, it features a long left-hand wall - Shut-downs are common. Optimum size 3-5ft (1-1.5m). Holds a solid 5-7ft (2-3m). Intermediate/expert level surfers.

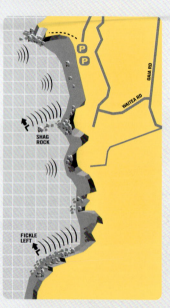

Oaia Island (offshore) helps to break up the deep southern ocean swells producing shifty, hollow peaks.

Bethells Beach/O'Neills

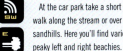

Head northwest from Auckland City though Swanson, then Waitakere to Bethells Beach.

At the car park take a short walk along the stream or over sandhills. Here you'll find various peaky left and right beachies. Beach works on smaller swells. Optimum size 3-5ft (1-1.5m) from any swell angle. Break closes out over 2m. Prone to strong offshores blowing down the valley.

If break is maxing out, check out O'Neills. Get there by heading north over the hill or across the stream and over the sand hills. Best at high tide, it can feature good right-hand reforms. Swift rip at southern end produces sucky double-ups - fun wave. Uncrowded and isolated. Good for surfers of all levels.

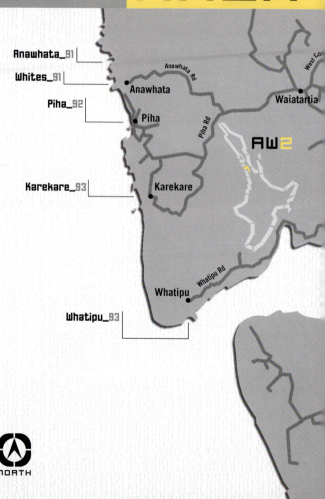

Anawhata

Take the West Coast road towards Piha. Make a right at Anawhata Road. Park at the top of the hill, take the steep track down to the beach (difficult access).

Bay features a variable beach break offering various peaks. Banks are changeable and best on a small swells in the 3-5ft (1-1.5m) range. Bay offers good shelter from strong offshore winds. Isolated and uncrowded. Good for surfers of all levels.

Whites

Whites is a 10 minute bush hike over the hill from the north Piha car park. The walk is scenic offering amazing views.

Beach break which produces good left and right peaks on small swells. Sheltered bay. Sometimes you can find a left and right at the south end of the beach at low tide. Isolated and uncrowded. Good for surfers of all levels.

Piha

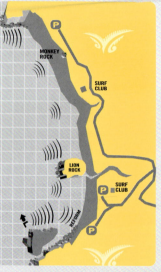

Head northwest from Auckland city through Glen Eden. At top of Waitakere Ranges turn left to the west coast beaches.

Arriving at Piha, you'll be greeted with magical views, rugged cliffs, black sand beaches and bush valleys.

Piha consists of two distinct beaches. South Piha and North Piha with Lion Rock dividing them.

South Piha features a quality left-hand bar break off Camel Rock (or the Beehive). Shifting sandbars produce a sucky wedge takeoff and long workable walls ending with a heavy shorie.

Lion Rock features left and right double-ups formed from backwash off the rocks. You'll find it an easy paddle using the fast current next to the rock. On big maxed out days, there can be a good chunky right-hand re-form next to Patiki Rock.

North Piha features a good left and right on the north side of Lion Rock. You can also find good peaks near the stream mouth and at the caves at the north end of the beach (also offers good shelter to strong NE winds). Piha is best surfed between 3-6ft (1-2.5m). Its location close to New Zealand's largest city means that it will often be crowded. Good for surfers of all levels. When it's big - competent surfers only.

AW2 093

Karekare

Take the West Coast Road over the Waitakere Ranges. Turn left at the Karekare turn-off. Road winds down hill through the bush to the car park.

Karekare features a range of quality beach breaks. At the northern end you'll find a peak offering a fat left and a right wall which peels through to a grunty shorebreak.

Find another peak in front of Watchmans Rock mid-beach. At the southern-end you'll find the Island. Here you can get into a grunty left-complete with wedging double-ups. Be ready for a pitching takeoff and stand-up barrels. Wave peels through to a heavy shorey. Competent surfers.

Whatipu

Head west from Auckland through Titirangi and Laingholm. Follow the Manukau Harbour to Huia then Whatipu.

Long walk over sandhills to the entrance of the Harbour.

The break consists of a big sucky dredging right-hander breaking over shallow sand. Break only works on a solid 6-8ft (2-3m) swell and only on an incoming tide. When it's on, it can produce short, intense sand-sucking barrels. Caution: extreme tidal rip. Isolated and dangerous. Expert level surfers only.

PIHA.PHOTO: NEW ZEALAND SURFING MAGAZINE

AW3 AREA

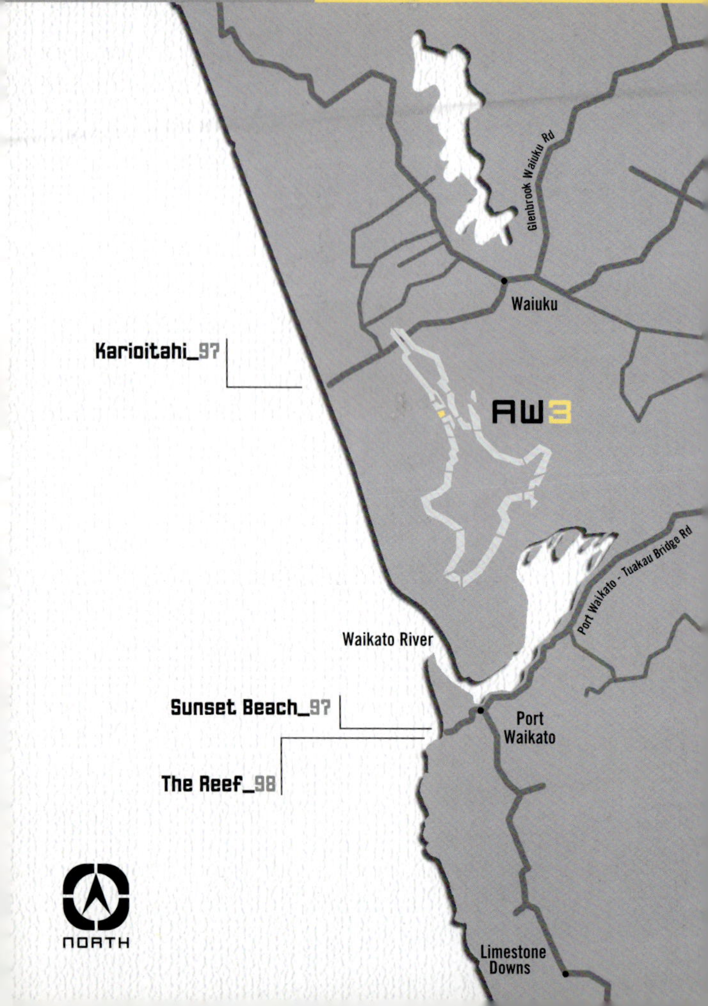

Karioitahi_97

AW3

Waiuku

Glenbrook Waiuku Rd

Port Waikato - Tuakau Bridge Rd

Waikato River

Sunset Beach_97

The Reef_98

Port Waikato

NORTH

Limestone Downs

Karioitahi

Head south from Auckland City on HWY 1. Take a right at Drury. Head west, pass through Waiuku to Karioitahi.

Beach break featuring variable shifty left and right peaks. Will only hold a small swell 2-4ft (0.5-1m). Beach is wind exposed. Uncrowded and isolated. Good for surfers of all levels.

Sunset Beach

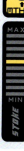

Located south of Auckland City. Take HWY 1 to Pukekohe, continue south through to Tuakau to Port Waikato.

Area features a beach break with good left and right peaks in front of the rocks. Banks are shifty and changeable. During bigger swells when the outer banks are closing out, you may find a right-hand re-form on the inside (needs high tide). Getting out is tricky when big - very deceptive. Heavy water, due to high content fresh water from Waikato River.) Optimum wave size 2-4 ft (.5-1m). Good for surfers of all levels.

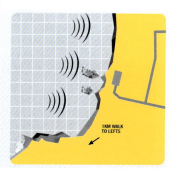

098 AW3

The Reef - Port Waikato

Get there by walking from Sunset Beach at Port Waikato.

Big left-hand reef/point. Holds solid swell 6-8ft (2-3m.) Features a heavy takeoff followed by a long fat wall. Watch for boil-ups over shallow rocks. Heavy paddle, must have good duck diving skills. Experienced surfers only.

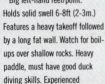

CAUTION
LEDGEY WAVE

1KM WALK FROM SUNSET BEACH

STOKE MIN ▮▮▮▮▮▮▮▮ MAX

INFO

Port Waikato

ACCOMMODATION
Waikatoa Surf Lodge
8 Centreway Rd, Port Waikato, Ph 09 232 9961
www.sunsetbeach.co.nz

Waikato River

Port Waikato   MAIN RD

To Raglan >

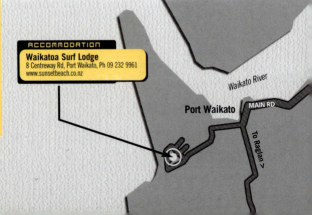

INFO 099

Auckland

SURF SHOP
XT SEA
40 Hurstmere Rd, Takapuna, Ph 09 489 9755
Fax 09 489 9333, www.xtsea.co.nz

SURF TRAVEL
ISLAND HOLIDAYS - Jeremy Shanahon
Surf Holiday Specialists, Ph 64 9 486 1625
email: jeremy @ islandholidays.co.nz
www.islandholidays.co.nz

SURF SHOP
SURF CENTRAL & SKATE
101 Queen Street, Central Auckland
Ph 64 9 377 0822, Fax 64 9 377 0823

SURF SHOP
THE BOARD CO - Engineered Surfboards
24 Centre Street, Freemans Bay, Auckland
Ph 64 9 309 5181, www.theboard.co.net

SURF / SNOW
HOT BUTTERED SURF & SNOW
402 Broadway Newmarket, Round the back
facing Nuffield Street, Ph 64 9 520 4585,
email: hotbutterednz@xtra.co.nz

SURF/SPORT
R&R SPORT
Crn K Rd & Gundry Street, Newton
Ph 64 9 309 6444. www.rrsport.co.nz

Auckland Central

Freemans Bay

VICTORIA ST
COOK ST
QUEEN ST

Parnell

KARANGAHAPE

Newton

Newmarket

KHYBER PASS RD
BROADWAY
REMUERA RD

100 INFO

West Auckland

BOARD BAGS
SURF TUBES BOARD BAGS
62 Patiki Road, Avondale, Ph 64 9 828 3188
info@surftubes.co.nz

SURF SHOP
ARIZONA HENDERSON
West Field Shopping Town, Henderson
Ph 64 9 836 5980, Fax 64 9 836 5525

SURF SHOP
ARIZONA NEW LYNN
Lynn Mall City, New Lynn
Ph 09 827 1637

New Lynn

INFO 101

Muriwai

SURF SCHOOL
Muriwai Surf School - behind the bottom shop at Muriwai Beach, Ph 021 478 734
www.muriwaisurfschool.co.nz

SURFBOARDS
SM SURFBOARDS
16 Woodruffe Ave Henderson, Auckland
Ph 64 9 8377720, email smsurf @xtra.co.nz

Piha

ACCOMMODATION
Piha Beach BB- Quality Accommodation
North Piha, Ph 09 812 8403
www.pihabeachbb.co.nz

TOURS/SCHOOL
SURFIN SAFARIS LTD- Surf Tours/School
P O Box 87, 104 Meadowbank, Auckland
Ph 09 528 2457, www.surfinsafaris.co.nz

TOURS/SCHOOL
ALOHA SURF SCHOOL & TOURS
Brendan Horan, Ph 07 542 3535
www.alohasurfschool.com

SURF SHOP/ACCOM
PIHA SURF SHOP-BACKPACKERS
Custom Surfboards-122 Seaview Road, Piha
Ph 09 812 8723, www.pihasurf.co.nz

TOURS/SCHOOL
AOTEAORA SURF COMPANY
Wayne Glover -Auckland Based, Ph 09 521 2851,
027 250 7906, www.aoteaorasurf.co.nz

AUCKLAND

Amazon Glenfield
Shop 317 Upper Level, Glenfield Shopping Centre
Auckland, Ph 09 4422 485, Fax 09 442 2486

Amazon New Market
252 Broadway, Newmarket, Auckland
Ph 09 520 7916, Fax 09 520 7916

Amazon St Lukes
Shop 261 St Lukes Mall, Auckland
Ph 09 846 4977, Fax 09 846 0604

Arizona Henderson
West Field Shopping Town, Henderson
Ph 09 836 5980, Fax 09 836 5525

Arizona New Lynn
Lynn Mall City, New Lynn, Auckland
Ph 09 827 1637

Cheapskates
15 Khyber Pass Road, Grafton Auckland
Ph 09 379 5048

Hardcore Surf Products
PO Box 344 Kumeu, Auckland
Ph 09 837 1333, 021 991 964

Hot Buttered Surf n Snow
402 Broadway Newmarket, Round the back facing
Nuffield Street, Auckland
Ph 09 520 4585, email hotbutterednz@xtra.co.nz

Island Holidays
Jeremy Shanahon, Surf Holiday Specialists
Ph 09 486 1625. Fax 09 486 1613
email jeremy @ islandholidays.co.nz
www.islandholidays.co.nz

Kiwi Surf Magazine
P O Box 94 Waimauku, Auckland, Ph 09 411 7834
Fax 09 411 7836

New Zealand Surfing Magazine
P O Box 14 - 109 Panmure, Auckland
Ph 09 570 2658, Fax 09 570 2684

Ocean Extreme
Surf Tours / Kite surfing, Ph 027 200 5252
www.oceanextreme.co.nz

R & R Sport
Crn K Rd & Gundry Street, Newton
Surfboards / Wetsuits, Ph 09 309 6444
Fax 09 302 1495

Slide Longboarding Magazine
In Ya Face Images Ltd, 14 Berridge Road Muriwai
Beach, RD1 Auckland, Ph 09 411 7857
Fax 09 411 7859, alan @ slidemagazine.com

Surf Central & Skate
101 Queen Street, Central Auckland
Ph 09 377 0822, Fax 09 377 0823

Surf Tubes Board Bags
62 Patiki Road, Avondale Auckland
Ph 09 828 3188, info@surftubes.co.nz
www. surftubes.com

Snow & Surf Kumeu
Tsunami 7 Weza Lane, Kumeu Auckland
Ph 09 412 7111, www.tsunamiboards.co.nz

Stash It Board Bags
Ph 021 974 186, www.stashit.co.nz

Surfcore Ltd
0800 4 Boards, www.bodyboards.co.nz

The Board Co - Engineered Surfboards
24 Centre Street, Freemans Bay, Auckland
Ph 09 309 5181, www.theboard.net

The Billabong Concept Store
131 Queen Street, Auckland City
Ph 09 307 3314, www.billabong.com

The Quiksilver Boardriders Club
151 Queen Street, Auckland City
Ph 09 359 9412, www.quiksilver.com

AUCKLAND - WEST COAST

Blairs on the Beach
Best burgers in the west, South Piha Car park
Ph 09 812 8309

Aloha Surf School & tours
Brendan Horan, Ph 07 542 3535
www.alohasurfschool.com

Aoteaora Surf Company
Wayne Glover Auckland Based
Surf School / Surf Tours
Ph 09 521 2851, 027 250 7906
www.aoteaorasurf.co.nz

Muriwai Surf School
behind the bottom shop at Muriwai Beach,
Ph 021 478 734, www.muriwaisurfschool.co.nz
email muriwaisurfschool@ihug.co.nz

New Zealand Surf Tours
Surf School Auckland Based
Ph 09 832 9622
email judd@newzealandsurftours.com

SM Surfboards
Custom made NZ surfboards/ longboards
16 Woodruffe Ave Henderson, Auckland
Ph 09 8377720, email smsurf@xtra.co.nz

Surfin Safaris Ltd
Surf Tours Surf School, P O Box 87 104
Meadowbank, Auckland
Ph 09 528 2457, email mark@surfinsafaris.co.nz
www.surfinsafaris.co.nz

Piha Beach BB
Quality Accommodation-North Piha
Ph 09 812 8403, www.pihabeachbb.co.nz

Piha Surf Shop
Custom Surfboards / Backpackers
122 Seaview Road, Piha, Ph 09 812 8723
www.pihasurf.co.nz

Notionlab
Advertising, Marketing, Book Design, New Media
Designers of the Wavetrack New Zealand Surfing
Guide - www.notionlab.co.nz

Surf Reports - Nationwide - Online
www.surf2surf.com

Surf Reports - Phone
Wavetrack 0900 99 777 (Calls 99c/min)
Groms ask your parents first

Great Barrier Island

Great Barrier Island is geologically an extension of the Coromandel Peninsula, separated by the notorious Coville Channel, so it has the same super clean water, deserted beaches with pure white sand, and rocky bushclad headlands jutting out into the endless blue Pacific.

Less than 40 kilometres long and a day's sail from Auckland, the 290 square kilometre landmass is the North Island's largest island. At night the lights of the Auckland metropolis appear 80 kilometres to the southwest, heightening your feeling of isolation.

Getting to the island is an adventure. You need to catch a ferry from Auckland or take a charter flight from a mainland airport. Most of the stunning east coast, from Whangapoua Beach in the north to Kaitoke and Medlands to the south, consists of magical sheltered beaches, estuary bars, and reefs, all picking up swells from differing angles.

The island works well on any swell from the northeast through to the southeast and the wave size is generally bigger than the Coromandel surfbreaks. Thanks to the remoteness of the island it's breaks rarely get crowded.

Getting around can be a problem. Two of the airstrips are only fifteen minutes walk from excellent surf breaks. However the roads are rough and if you're staying more than a few days it could be worth taking your own vehicle. There are plenty of motels and backpackers to choose from, and places to camp close to the surf.

A sub-tropical depression combines with a high pressure system producing a classic squash - Barrier cranks.
As the swell moves southeast, the islands swell magnets continue to pump.

A low pressure wave factory holds to the east. Massive fetch fires solid swells into Great Barrier's exposed beaches and reefs.

Great Barrier Island sits north of the Coromandel Peninsula. Its position is perfect to pick up sneaky southeast swells.

GB 105

GB1	107
Whangapoua	108
Awana Bay	110
Palmers	110
Kaitoke	111
Medlands	111
Shark Alley	111

O'NEILL — AREA SEASONAL WETSUIT RECOMMENDATIONS

SUMMER
BOARDIES-
SPRINGY

AUTUMN
SPRING
SUIT

WINTER
3/2 or 4/3 STEAMER
+ BOOTIES

SPRING
SPRINGY-
STEAMER

GB1 AREA

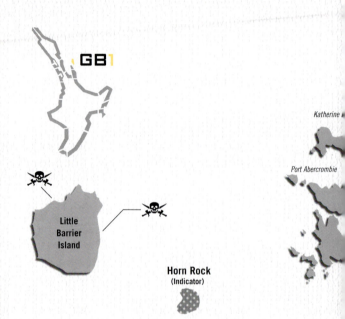

107

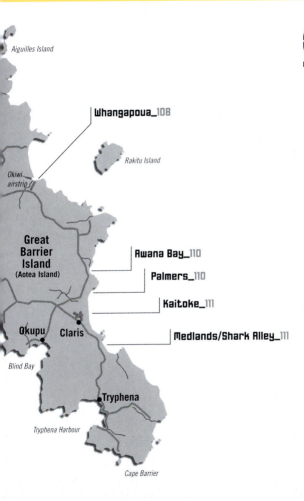

Whangapoua/Okiwi

The best way to access Whangapoua is via light aircraft. Fly into Okiwi airstrip, you'll see the break as you approach to land. Pilots - use caution when landing during strong southerly winds - strip is prone to powerful down drafts from the mountain range. Break is a 1km walk east from the airstrip. Find a camping ground next to the airstrip.

Whangapoua, commonly referred to as Okiwi, features an excellent right-hand bar break. It picks up a wide range of swell from north through to large southeast. Best on north swells, you can expect long lines wrapping for 60 to 100m. The takeoff is sucky and is immediately followed by a short, hollow barrel. The wave continues to rifle off with speedy sections and long workable walls. A fun wave at 4ft, it tends to break wide and fatter on larger swells. The bar handles solid east and northeast swells. Optimum wave size 2 to 6ft (.5 - 2m). The break can get crowded especially during summer. Spot features a good solid local crew. Watch out for stingrays if you have your feet on the sand. Area is known as a shark breeding ground. Competent surfers only.

110 GB1

Awana Bay

Find Awana Bay 5km north of Claris Aerodrome and 12km north of Tryphena Harbour.

Bay features a powerful beach break offering quality peaks along the beach. At the northern end of the bay find a good left which breaks at the river mouth. The southern end is home to solid peaks with longer rights. Expect sucky hollow waves and a beach prone to serious rips. Optimum wave size 2-7ft (1-2.5m). Best for competent surfers with good ocean knowledge. Isolated and dangerous beach.

Palmers

Find Palmers at the north end of Kaitoke Beach, or approximately 10km drive to the north from Tryphena Harbour.

Here you'll find a variable beach break (and reef) which is a magnet for east and south swells. Find a variety of peaks along the beach which handle solid waves. Banks are constantly changing, quality depends on sand buildup. Optimum wave size 3-7ft (1-2.5m). Competent surfers. Watch for rips.

Kaitoke

Head north from Tryphena to Claris. Access Kaitoke off Hector Sanderson Rd or travel further to Palmers. Limited access near Kaitoke Creek - respect private land.

Area features a quality bar break at the mouth of Kaitoke Creek. Banks are constantly changing due to river flow and floods. Heading south down the beach you will find good left and right peaks off the rock island in the middle of the bay. The southern end sometimes features a shifty right-hander. Caution: heavy rips and keep an eye out for sharks during summer. Beach holds solid swells, optimum wave size 3-7ft (1-2.5m). Competent surfers only.

Medlands Beach

Head north from Tryphena towards Claris. Find Medlands Beach south of Kaitoke beach.

Here you'll find a powerful beach break producing various left and right peaks along the beach. Expect grunty top to bottom waves which peel through to a heavy shorie. At the southern end find a big jacking right reef break. Large north swells wedge into *Shark Alley*, peak-up and rifle off right. Be ready for a sucky takeoff and solid, chunky walls. Optimum wave size for the beach 3-6ft (1-2m). Shark Alley handles a solid 6-8ft (3m plus). Intermediate to expert level surfers.

Waikato

This area takes us from Te Akau (northwest of the inland city of Hamilton) south along the coastline through Kawhia to Kiritehere (a small beach settlement near Marokopa). This region is home to New Zealand's most famous surf destination - Raglan.

West of this sleepy little coastal town are a series of excellent left-hand point breaks which peel mechanically over volcanic reef and boulders - each of which offers waves of superb quality. However, it is the consistency of surf at Raglan that makes it remarkable. This is attributed to three main factors. Firstly, the unique shape of the headland allows large, southwest swells to wrap ninety degrees. Secondly, the elevated terrain blocks the prevailing southwest winds, and finally the mountain valleys channel the wind to produce semi-clean waves at the points.

Although Raglan is the undisputable focal point of the Waikato region (and New Zealand for that matter) there are a range of other excellent surfing options around the area. The surrounding beaches to the north and south offer the perfect solution when the swell has dropped on the points as many of them are exposed to swells from the southwest and can provide waist to chest high waves when Raglan is flat. To the south of Raglan things get downright fascinating for the adventurous surfer as the coast is simply littered with small points and inlets which work best on clean, mid-sized swells.

A southern ocean system creates a massive fetch and delivers huge southwest swells to the west coast. Swells wrap around the Raglan points offering wind-protected waves.

Equinox - Roaring 40's deliver a hideous westerly onshore flow. 30-60kt onshore winds produce an 8-10ft West Coast washing machine.

A depression tracks east from the Tasman Sea delivering lots of wind rain and messy northwest wind/ground swells to exposed coasts.

WK 113

WK1	114
Te Akau	115
Mussell Rock	115
Wainui Beach	116
Manu Bay	120
Whale Bay	121
Indicators	124
Ruapuke	125
WK2	130
Albatross Point	131
Kiritehere	131
INFO	133

O'NEILL — AREA SEASONAL WETSUIT RECOMMENDATIONS

SUMMER
BOARDIES-SPRINGY

AUTUMN
SPRING SUIT

WINTER
3/2 or 4/3 STEAMER + BOOTIES

SPRING
SPRINGY-STEAMER

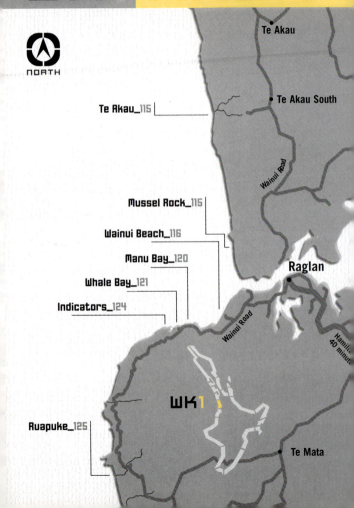

Te Akau

From Wangaro take Te Akau Rd to the coast. Access is through farmland. Permission is required for all spots in the area.

Features a range of left and right beach breaks. Look for rocky outcrops and stream mouths for the best banks/waves. Best on a smaller swell in the 2-4ft (0.5-1m) range at mid to full tide. Typical west coast beachie, heaps of grunt. Uncrowded, isolated. Competent surfers. Heavy rips.

For the adventurous head north and look near Koura. Find reef/sand combo points, bombies and a range of quality beachies on the right tide and swell. Go search. Be rewarded.

Mussel Rock

Mussel Rock is located on the north side of the Raglan Harbour Mouth. Access is by paddling the channel (caution: very strong currents) or by boat (recommended).

Break features a range of variable beach breaks producing left and right peaks around the rocky outcrop. Bank constantly changes due to heavy currents. Spot is best surfed when the Raglan points are in the 2-4ft range. Good for surfers of all levels. Make sure you're up to the long paddle.

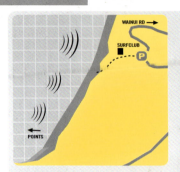

Wainui Beach

Head southwest from Raglan township towards Manu Bay, make a right at Wainui Beach turnoff, drive over hill to the car park.

Good sheltered beach break featuring left and right peaks. Best on small days 3-5ft (1-1.5m) at mid-high tide. Can produce very grunty hollow waves, with the lefts being a little longer and hollower. Good for surfers of all levels. Good learners option at Raglan. Break can get crowded.

SURF2SURF.com
New Zealand Surf Reports - Surfing Guide

INDIES BARREL. PHOTO: TRAM

MANU BAY. PHOTO: TRAM

Manu Bay - The Point

From Raglan township take Wainui road out to the points (5km).

Manu Bay is located west of Wainui Beach. It is the first of three world-class point breaks. Breaking over a boulder bottom, it produces a long winding left-hander which features multiple sections as it peels around past the boat ramp.

Entry is via the rocks located at the western end of the point. Use caution, especially during large swells - experienced surfers only.

The point features a sucky takeoff, followed by an intense ledging section producing good barrels (low tide). Best to takeoff outside of the ledge and look for the barrel on the way through. From there it'll fatten up offering a variety of high performance sections - great for round-house cutties and snaps off the top. Generally the lower tide produces faster waves and more barrels.

In front of the jump-off area you can also find Boneyards. Basically just the outside section of the Manu, it can be another option if the crowd gets out of control on the ledge.

The point holds a solid swell of 6-8ft (2-3m), optimum wave size is 4-6ft (1-2.5m). It can be surfed on a variety of winds, including the prevailing southwest wind - which is why the Raglan points offer some of the most consistent quality surf breaks in New Zealand.

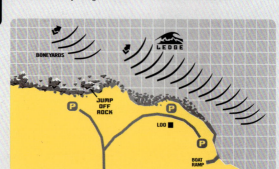

Whale Bay

Drive further out along the Mt Karioi headland to Whale Bay. Look for the turn down the hill to the car park. On the north side of the car park you'll find steps which lead down to Whale Bay and the path to Indicators.

Whale is the mellow break of the three points, but still a great wave in its own right. Expect a takeoff that is a little more forgiving than the Manu Bay ledge. From there you can enjoy a long fat wall peeling down the bay offering a range of sections. Don't get too comfortable at this point as there's a dirty great rock mid-way down the line to avoid at all costs. As you pass the rock the wave comes to life as it sucks, boils and rifles off down the line. At higher tides and small swells the rock will cut the wave in half. If you're not an experienced surfer don't push it, pull out, or wait for a larger set wave so you can make the section. Whale is best surfed at 4-6ft (1-2.5m). It will handle a big swell, but gets tricky when it's huge, as a serious current sweeps the bay.

Access to the break is rocky and tricky.

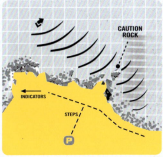

Whale Bay is the mellow break of the three points, but still a great wave in its own right.

Experienced surfers jump off the rocks at the northwest end. If you're unsure best to paddle out at the east end of the bay. Good option for less experienced surfers.

INDIES/WHALE BAY. PHOTO: SURF2SURF.COM

Indicators

From Raglan township take Wainui Rd out to the Whale Bay parking lot. Take the steps down to Whale Bay, follow the path out to Indicators.

If you decide to walk around to the takeoff areas, keep low to the rocks and avoid crossing the private land.

Indicators is the longest and fastest breaking of the three Raglan points. It features a range of high-performance sections with plenty of opportunities to get in the barrel (especially when it's offshore). The wave features two distinct takeoff areas - Outsides and Insides.

Find Outsides at the western point of the headland. It features a sucky takeoff very close to rocks. If you survive the drop you'll be confronted with a top to bottom wall complete with a grunty barrel section. When it's big, Outsides will peel all the way through to the valley and even to Whale Bay on mega-sized swells.

On smaller swells it'll usually out-speed you prior to the next takeoff zone which is Insides.

Insides features a moderate, bowling takeoff followed by a fast wall.

You'll hit speed barrel sections, cutty sections, and eventually end up screaming through towards the valley at Mach 2. At this point the wave can become ridiculously fast, and on lower tides very shallow. It's not unusual to see a few rocks popping up as you speed through. Watch it if you're in the barrel at this stage - if you have to ditch and you see rocks, think flat - don't go headfirst.

The inside section, referred to as the Valley, is a good spot to surf if you're not up to the hustle and bustle of the outside takeoff zones - it gets good too.

Optimum size for Indies is 4-7ft (1.5-2.5m) and handles solid 8-12ft (3-4m).

Usually a staunch crowd. Surf with respect and you won't have a problem. Intermediate to expert level surfers.

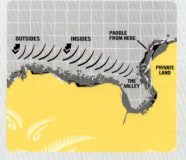

Spot X

Monster left point. Holds 15ft waves. Boat access only. Bribe a fisherman.

Ruapuke

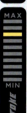

When Raglan is flat, often a good option is to head around the Mt Karioi headland to Ruapuke. From Raglan drive out past Whale Bay. Head up the hill and take the metal road around the coast to Rua's (about 10km from Whale Bay).

Ruapuke is a swell magnet and offers a variable beachbreak. You'll find grunty peaks up and down the beach along with a right breaking out of the rocks in front of the stream. Can produce quality waves and good barrels. Tide sensitive - best mid to high tide. Optimum wave size 3-6ft (1-2.5m). Can be a tough paddle when big. Good for surfers of all levels.

WHALE BAY. PHOTO: TRAM

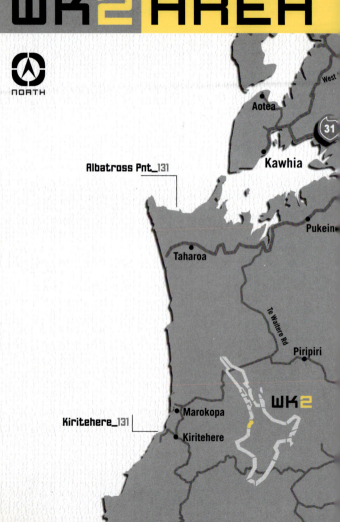

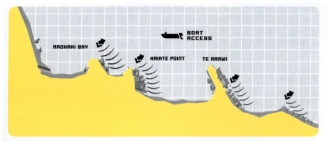

Albatross Point

Find Albatross Point on the southern side of the Kawhia Harbour west of Urawhitiki Point. Permission is mandatory to cross the private land and to access the breaks by boat. Give respect and Koha.

Area features a range of sand/reef point combos and a beach break. Breaks need a 6-10ft+ southwest swell to work - swells need to wrap a full 180 degrees to hit the points. Expect a range of quality left-handers offering multi-section high performance waves. Length and quality of waves depend on sand build-up on the points. Area is offshore south/southeast and is surfable with southwest winds. Isolated. Experts level surfers only.

Kiritehere

From Waitomo take Te Anga Rd to Mangatoa Rd and Kiritehere.

Find an exposed, rugged left-hand point break at the south end of the beach which is best surfed on small swells. Expect a long left breaking around a rocky headland. Find various other peaks to the north near the mouth of the stream.

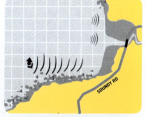

RAGLAN - HAMILTON - PORT WAIKATO

A S R Marine Consulting and Research
Artificial Surfing Reef Design
Ph 07 825 0380, email: kblack@asrltd.co.nz
www.asrltd.co.nz

Backdoor Surf Shop
7 Worley Place, Hamilton
Ph 07 839 0368

Bear Surfboards - Mickey T
Longboards Funboards Retro Style
Hand Crafted Custom Surfboards
Ph 07 825 0544, 0274 460 396
email: mickeytsurf@hotmail.com

Gag Raglan Surf Shop
9 A Bow Street, Raglan
Ph 07 825 8702

Manu Bay Surfers Flat
Overlooking Manu Bay
Earles Place Wainui Road, Raglan
Rates $125 to $150.00. Ph 07 825 8947
0274 111 999, email: jouzzo@clear.net.nz

Notionlab
Advertising, Marketing, Book Design, New Media
Designers of the Wavetrack New Zealand Surfing
Guide - www.notionlab.co.nz

Surfing New Zealand
Raglan, Ph 07 825 0018
www.surfingnz.co.nz

Raglan Surfing Academy
P O Box 80, Raglan
Ph 07 825 8140
www. raglanarea.school.nz

Raglan Surf Co - Surf Shop
3 Wainui Road, Raglan
Ph/Fax 07 825 8988
email: hughsey@raglansurfco.com
www.raglansurfco.com

Raglan Surfing School
Ph 07 825 7873

Raglan Holiday Park
34 Marine Parade, Raglan
Ph 07 825 8283

Raglan Retreat
5 Earles Place, Wainui Road, Raglan
Ph 07 825 0064
www.raglanretreat.co.nz

R&R Sport - Surfboards Wetsuits
943 Victoria Street, Hamilton
Ph 0800 777 767, Ph 07 839 3755
www.rrsport.co.nz

Ruapuke Beach Motor Camp
Ruapuke Beach, Ph 07 825 6800

Surf Reports - Nationwide - Online
www.surf2surf.com

Surf Reports - Phone
Wavetrack 0900 99 777 (Calls 99c/min)
Groms ask your parents first

The Local Surf School
Coach Miles Ratima, Guides Transport to Beach
Ph 0211 064052
email: isurfedraglan@surf.co.nz

Waikatoa Surf Lodge - Port Waikato
Backpackers & Budget Accommodation
8 Centreway Rd, Sunset Beach, Port Waikato
Ph/Fax 09 232 0061
email: backpackers@sunsetbeach.co.nz
www.sunsetbeach.co.nz

Taranaki

From Awakino in the north, around a spectacular volcanic peninsula, past Opunake, and southeast down to magical Wanganui, Taranaki's semi-circular coastline contains more epic surfbreaks per kilometre than anywhere south of Oahu. Add to this the fact that it is regularly pounded by consistent southwest swells

The route to take is Surf Highway 45, which follows the curve of the coastline, through New Plymouth, for over 100 kilometres. Radiating from the highway are lots of narrow farm access roads. These lead to innumerable surfbreaks, some of them named after their access road. A few require permission to get to. Show respect and watch for electric fences.

Being shaped like half an island Taranaki has more than 180 degrees of swell aperture and for those who know where to look it provides waves somewhere, on every day of the year. Usually there're a number of uncrowded breaks firing simultaneously. And due to the range of breaks and the relatively small surfer population it's possible to score a perfect reef or point to yourself.

The range from low tide to high tide is nearly four metres so conditions change radically. Most of the coast is hard rock and surfing some breaks means climbing down cliffs and hiking over boulders.

Be prepared for mind-blowing vistas as the 2518-metre Mount Taranaki towers over the landscape. The mountain has a direct affect on the weather as it funnels the wind 360 degrees.

A southern ocean system creates a massive fetch and delivers huge southwest swells to the west coast. Taranaki's hundreds of reefs, points and beaches pump.

Equinox - Roaring 40's deliver a hideous westerly onshore flow. 30-60kt onshore winds produce an 8-10ft West Coast washing machine.

A depression tracks east from the Tasman Sea delivering northwest ground swells to exposed coasts. A high pressure system provides offshore winds.

TN | 135

TN1	136
Awakino	137
Mokau	137
TN2	141
Waitara	142
Bell Block	142
Waiwhakaiho	143
The Groyne	143
Fitzroy	146
Boulder Bay	146
Bog Works	148
Belt Road	148
Back Beach	149
TN3	151
Oakura Beach	152
Ahu Ahu	152
Weld Road	153
Kumera Patch	154
Kumene Road	156
Puniho's	156
Graveyards	157
Rocky Lefts	158
Rocky Rights	158
Stent Road	160
Crushers	164
Fin Fucker	164
TN4	167
Kina Road	168
Arawhata Road	168
Opunake	169
Desperation Point	169
Sky Williams	172
Mangahume	172
Greenmeadows	173
TN5	175
Patea	176
Waverley	176
Wainui	177
The Point	177

Kai-iwi	178
Longbeach Drive	178
Rangiora Street	179
North Mole	179
Whanganui Mouth	180
South Beach	180
INFO	181

O'NEILL — AREA SEASONAL WETSUIT RECOMMENDATIONS

SUMMER
BOARDIES-
SPRINGY

AUTUMN
SPRING
SUIT

WINTER
3/2 or 4/3 STEAMER
+ BOOTIES

SPRING
SPRINGY-
STEAMER

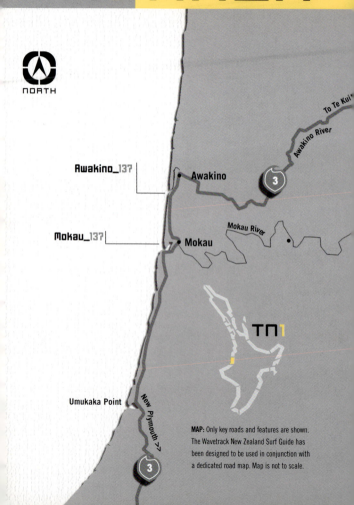

TN1 137

Awakino

Awakino is the first break you'll hit heading southwest from the inland town of Te Kuiti.

Awakino is a great swell indicator for all the Taranaki spots and if conditions are right it can offer a great wave.

The break itself is a river bar and variable beach break. Both can produce high-quality waves if the banks are good. On clean days you'll find lefts and rights on either side of the river mouth, the bars are constantly changing - if you find it firing you're in for a real treat.

Beware of very strong currents. Best for competent surfers.

Mokau

Find Mokau 5km to the south of Awakino on HWY 3.

It consists of a quiet little village next to the banks of the Mokau River Mouth.

Area features a long beach stretching to the north and a river mouth bar break situated at the south end. St Peters is the main break, consisting of a good beachie breaking in front of the St Peter's Church on the hill. Depending on the condition of the ever-shifting sand bars, it can produce quality left and rights with plenty of power. Watch for very strong rips. Best for intermediate to expert level surfers.

ST PETERS, MOKAU. PHOTO: DAISY DAY

TN2 AREA

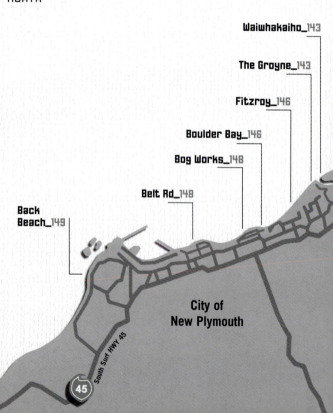

141

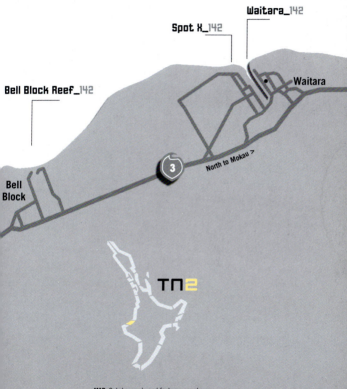

TN2

MAP: Only key roads and features are shown. The Wavetrack New Zealand Surf Guide has been designed to be used in conjunction with a dedicated road map. Map is not to scale.

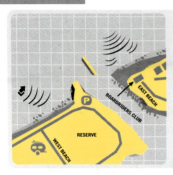

Waitara

From New Plymouth drive north to Waitara. Get to the east side of the river by taking Princess to East Beach from HWY 3.

River bar break produces good lefts and rights depending on banks. Shingle is constantly on the move due to river flow.

Across the river look for the left point - Spot X. Get there by taking McLean to Browne St from HWY 3. The left is a favourite for wind and kite surfers.

Caution: strong currents around the river mouth. Respect the locals when surfing their break. Good for surfers of all levels.

Bell Block

Take HWY 3 north from New Plymouth. Get off at Mangati Rd, head 1.5km to Bell Block beach.

The break is an offshore reef located 250m offshore. Be ready for a long paddle out which is worth the effort if the conditions are right.

The reef doesn't break very often, but when it does you can expect a heavy, ledgy wave complete with several barrel sections breaking over a very shallow reef.

The area handles a southwest wind and is recommended for expert level surfers only.

If you're learning, the inner beach is a good spot to work on your skills.

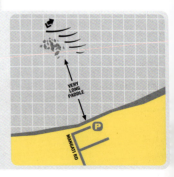

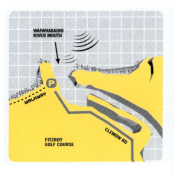

Waiwhakaiho

To get to Waiwhakaiho you can either walk from Fitzroy Beach or take Devon St East to the end of Clemow Rd and park there. You'll arrive at the western bank of the Waiwhakaiho river - paddle across river to the break.

The break consists of a river bar producing a juicy A-frame peak. The rights break steeper and can get hollow (plus crowded) - the lefts offer very long rides. If Waisy's is working you're in for a real treat.

1000m offshore is a bombie which is an excellent indicator for sets. Best for intermediate to expert level surfers. Show locals respect.

The Groyne

Get to the Groyne by parking at Fitzroy and walking east until you find a good peak. Driving, take Devon to Clemow Rd, follow it around Lake Rotomanu to end.

When the Groyne is on, expect short peaky A-frame peaks producing intense barrels. With size it's a wave of consequence offering big thick lips and shifty peaks breaking over a shallow bottom.

Good for all surfers when small - experts when it's overhead. Accommodation - camp at the local Fitzroy Campground.

WAIWHAKAIHO . PHOTO: DAISY DAY

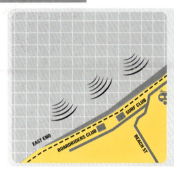

Fitzroy

Get to Fitzroy Beach by taking Devon St to Beach St or Knobs Lane.

Quality beach break. When Fitzroy is overhead and the offshore winds are howling it can get very hollow and produce excellent barrels.

Waves tend to get smaller towards east end of beach. Busy beach with surfers, swimmers and lifeguards - you may find some less crowded waves further up the beach towards the Groyne.

Check out New Plymouth Boardriders Club - the envy of boardrider clubs around the world.

Good for surfers of all levels. Expert only when big. Always respect the locals.

Boulder Bay

Boulters Bay, generally referred to as Boulder Bay. To get there take Devon St to Hobson St or walk from Fitzroy Beach.

Reef break consisting of a left-hand point break producing flat and fat waves with several sections. The wave is suited to longboards and is often better than it looks from the beach. On the inside you'll find a small right re-form which breaks on a sandy beach. The sea breeze doesn't affect the bay at high-tide. As the tide drops, watch out for rocks. Good longboard wave.

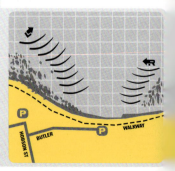

148 TN2

Bog Works

Check Bog Works from Octavius Pl. To get there take Devon St to Hobson. From there take the foreshore walkway to the old sewage pipe.

The wave breaks 300m from shore - paddle out from the sewage pipe. Getting in and out of the water is tricky, use caution. Bog Works starts breaking properly when it's 6ft plus and will hold up to 12ft waves. It consists of a big peak with a good right and some lefts. Expect a steep takeoff then it'll back off and wall up again. Grunty wave with thick lips and plenty of juice. Current will pull you deeper into the pit. Getting caught inside is a given. Expert surfers.

Belt Road

Take Devon St to Belt Rd.

Once in a blue moon the elements come together and the legendary lefts of Belt reel down the line with tubing precision.

More often than not (when it does break) it consists of a fat, sectiony mush-burger type wave.

Belt Rd needs a large southwest swell - it usually starts to break at around 4ft and will hold a solid 8ft. Across the channel you'll find a short right which can be a fun wave. Watch the sharp rocks on entry and exit. Competent surfers.

Back Beach

Take HWY 45 to Beach Rd or St Aubyn St to Centennial Drive.

Good beach break featuring fast-breaking grunty peaks up and down the beach. Big cliffs and the Sugar Loaf Islands form a wind barrier, so spot is often sheltered in strong wind conditions. When checking the surf from the beach wave size can be deceptive - it's usually 2ft bigger than Fitzroy.

Caution: strong rips when big. Good for surfers of all levels.

SURFLINE
0900 47 873
0900 4 SURF

Updated accurate surf reports since 1993
Calls $1.20 per minute - Groms ask your parents first

113 AREA

NORTH

Kumera Patch_154
Komene Rd_156
Puniho's_156
Graveyards_157
Rocky Lefts_158
Rocky Rights_158
Stent Road_160
Crushers_164
Fin Fucker_164

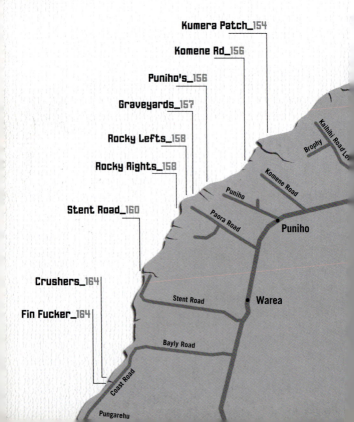

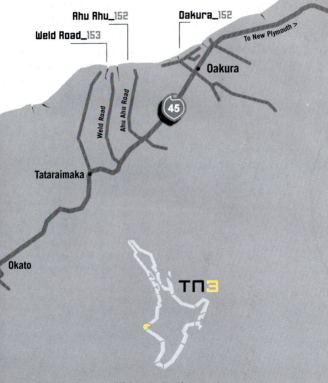

MAP: Only key roads and features are shown. The Wavetrack New Zealand Surf Guide has been designed to be used in conjunction with a dedicated road map. Map is not to scale.

Oakura Beach

Get to Oakura Beach by taking HWY 45 to Dixon St or Wairau Rd.

Typical beach break with constantly changing banks. Look for the best waves near the river mouth and the streams. Oakura offers good wind shelter from southwesterly winds.

Offshore you'll see a bombora - this is the site of the famous ride featuring 13 people on one surfboard. Good for surfers of all levels.

Ahu Ahu Road

Head south from New Plymouth on Surf HWY 45 to Ahu Ahu Rd.

Jekyl and Hyde break. On the west side you have a left-hander which can get fast and hollow, but generally offers a long mellow ride. Break is great for learners who aren't afraid of rocks.

On the east side of the bay are several punchy rights which break hard and fast close to the rocks. Expect ledgy hollow barrels with consequence. Starts breaking at 4ft and will hold 8ft. Beginner to expert depending on which direction you paddle out.

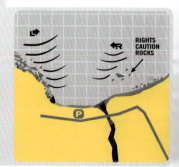

Weld Road

Take Surf HWY 45 to Weld Road.

Weld Road is visible from Ahu's - the two are divided by a rocky spit. Weld features a small sandy section of beach with rocky outcrops to the east and west. You'll find lefts and rights and your own mini Mt Taranaki sitting in the middle of the line-up.

Weld is a good longboard spot and will work in a westerly wind. Good for surfer of all levels.

www.hang20.com

Greg Page - Surf Hiway 45, Oakura, Phone 06 752 7734, Mob 0274 899 232

JUST TO look @

from New ... on surf HWY 45 - ... take a right on ...

Park at the end of the road. From here it's a 20 minute walk southwest along the beach to the break.

Kumera Patch is an awesome left-hander which mechanically peels around a boulder point. The wave features a wide, shifty takeoff zone. From there it's a fast down the line wave complete with a myriad of tubing, bowling, cutback and speed sections. It's a sight to behold when it's firing.

Make sure your fitness is up to peak level - a ride Kumera's can take you between 100-200m+ around the point. Worn-out legs and noodle arms are side effects of indulging in too much Kumera Patch magic.

The wave is best surfed with a southwest swell in the 4-12ft range (1.2-3.6m), and works well on all tides.

After a full days surfing head to the

Worn-out legs and noodle arms are side effects of indulging in too much Kumera Patch.

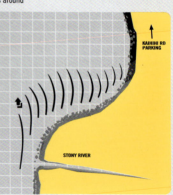

Stony River Hotel to rehydrate and fuel up for the next Kumera session.

Good for intermediate to expert level surfers. Remember to always respect the locals - this is their turf.

KUMERA PATCH. PHOTO: SURF2SURF.COM

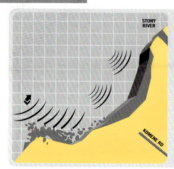

Komene Rd

Take Surf HWY 45 to Komene Rd. From there, walk across the sand hills. Breaks are located between Kumera Patch and Puniho's.

Here you'll find various beach and reef breaks which change in quality with the tides. At the southwestern end of the beach is a left reef. This area is a good place to get a wave to yourself. Optimum wave size 1-4ft (.3-1.2m). Beach tends to close out with bigger swells. Good for surfers of all levels.

Puniho's

Get there by taking Surf HWY 45 to Puniho Rd. Park at the end of the road. Climb over a stile, walk towards the right.

Juicy A-frame peak. Features a short right-hander and a long left. Expect a sucky, hollow takeoff followed by a cutback section. The wave will then speed up down the line followed by more hollow sections. Good high-performance wave. Optimum wave size 2-6ft (1-2m). Competent surfers with high level of ability required - lots of rocks. Respect the locals.

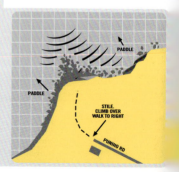

TN3 157

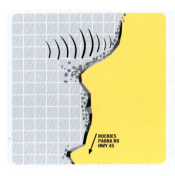

Graveyards

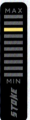

Find Graveyards to the north of Rocky Point. Take Surf HWY 45 to Paora Rd. Walk across the paddock to the headland. Graveyards is visible from Rocky Lefts.

Expect a juicy A-frame peak producing a long, winding left-hander. Starts with a steep ledgy takeoff followed by a flat cutback section. From there it fires off down the line peeling and tubing for up to 150m. Sometimes you'll find a short punchy right off the peak. Competent surfers - lots of rocks. Give locals respect.

Spot X

Big left and right reef break. Holds an 8ft wave. Big barrels. Ask a friendly local.

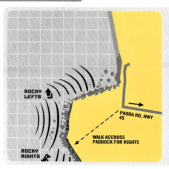

Rocky Lefts

From New Plymouth take Surf HWY 45 to Paora Rd. Access Rocky Lefts off Paora Rd.

North side of the point features a quality/rocky left. Expect a tight takeoff zone and a hard breaking left offering a slalom ride around rocks with names like "Freddo." Watch the locals first - they have it wired pulling into tubes in front of rocks, or popping aerials over them. Expect heavy intense barrels. Competent surfers only.

Rocky Rights

From Rocky Lefts and Paora Rd - access the Rights by parking at the hard right bend in the road. Head over farmland to the south side of the headland.

Rocky Rights features a fast breaking right-hander which rifles-off into the bay. The right works in swells ranging from southwest to northwest and will hold anything up to 10ft. Competent surfers only.

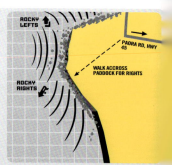

TN3 — ROCKY LEFTS. PHOTO: EVOLVE

Stent Road

Take Surf HWY 45 south from New Plymouth to Stent Rd. Don't be surprised if surfers have snagged the road sign - it's constantly being taken as a souvenir, or de-sign-posted by locals.

Stent Road rates as the premier break on the Taranaki coast. It's the perfect right setup, and like most top spots large crowds are part of the deal.

Stent is a big pumping right point, featuring an intense big, hollow takeoff, followed by a fast wall complete with a range of sections.

Stent is a big pumping right point featuring an intense, hollow takeoff followed by a fast wall complete with a range of sections. Expect everything from full-on barrels to wide cutback bowl sections. Stent has no problem handling the big swells - it all depends on what you're prepared to paddle out in. The break picks up a wide range of swell from northwest through to southwest and works on all tides. Look for the best barrels on the lower tides.

If the break gets too crowded and intense get adventurous and go for a walk. There are five quality breaks in the vicinity - plenty of options for all. Who knows what you'll find just around the corner, you may be rewarded.

A high level of experience and competency is required to surf Stent Rd. Respect the locals at all times.

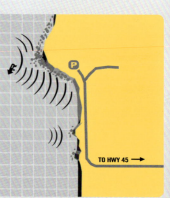

ENT
PHOTO: DAISY DAY

164 TN3

Crushers

Take Surf HWY 45 to Bayly or Pungarehu Road.

Several good reef and beach breaks. All breaks are very exposed and prone to strong winds. However, with a clean swell and calm or offshore winds the reefs can come to life and produce good waves. Competent surfers - lots of rocks and strong currents.

Fin Fucker

Head towards Cape Egmont on Surf HWY 45. Take Pungarehu to the Coast Rd.

Variety of reefs and beach breaks. Fin Fucker is a favourite with windsurfers. No surprise that this spot is prone to very strong winds and prevailing southwest onshore/cross shores. If the swell is clean and the winds are right, this break can produce a long juicy left. The reefs tend to break a distance from the shore - watch for strong currents. Competent surfers.

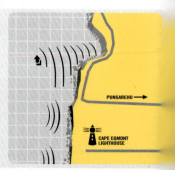

TN4 AREA

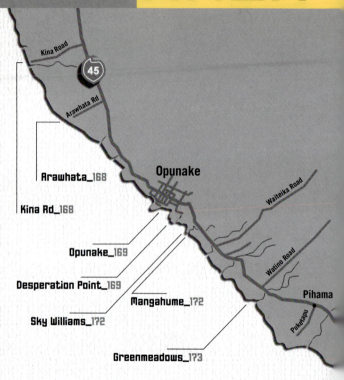

Opunake

Arawhata_168

Kina Rd_168

Opunake_169

Desperation Point_169

Mangahume_172

Sky Williams_172

Greenmeadows_173

NORTH

167

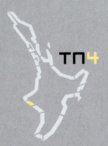

TN4

MAP: Only key roads and features are shown. The Wavetrack New Zealand Surf Guide has been designed to be used in conjunction with a dedicated road map. Map is not to scale.

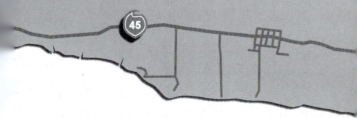

168 TN4

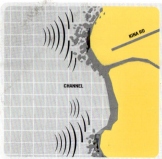

Kina Road

Take Surf HWY 45 south to Kina Rd. Spot features several reef peaks. Holds a big swell - can break between 2-20ft (.5-6m). The north end offers better rights, while the south end offers good lefts. Huge takeoff zone when swell is over 6ft. Good place to escape the crowds if you don't mind taking a few on the head. Good for intermediate to expert level surfers. Break is a favourite of wind surfers.

Arawhata Road

Further south on HWY 45 you'll find Arawhata Rd. Leave the farm gate as you find it.

Bay features a right-hand reef point. Expect a sucky bowling takeoff followed by a cutback section. The wave then steepens and peels down the point - generally a soft wave. You'll find other breaks in the area. Further south in the middle of the bay is a good left hander. Intermediate level surfers and above. Watch out for sharp rocks.

MAYBE

which peels across the bay - swell needs to be in the 3-4ft range.

Bombora on the south side of the bay is surfable - beware of strong currents. The old wharf is the proposed location for an artificial reef. Good for surfers of all levels.

Desperation Point

Take Surf HWY 45 to Opunake. From there take Layard St out to the point.

Point Annihilation, or Dumps as it is often referred to, features a grunty right-hand reef to the south, and a shifty left to the north. The rights produce a workable wall, and start with a sucky takeoff. Both breaks handle a large swell. Watch for strong currents and sharp rocks. Competent surfers only.

172 TN4

Sky Williams

Take Surf HWY 45 2km south to the next headland (past Point Annihilation).

Break consists of a boulder bottom left-hand reef/point combo. Sky Williams is a wave magnet and is best surfed in the 2-4ft range (.5-1.2m). It will hold up to solid 10ft waves. It is usually better than it looks. Expect long rides with the odd tubing section. Good for intermediate to expert level surfers.

Mangahume

Mangahume is located on the southern side of the headland next to Sky Williams. To get there take Surf HWY 45 2km south from the Opunake township.

Big exposed reef break. A swell magnet it can hold very large waves. Expect a juicy A-frame peak with a steep takeoff. Starts working at around 4ft (1.2m), and features a massive takeoff zone. Watch the channel on big days it's a bit dodgy when it's pumping. Getting caught inside on a big day is heavy. Best with a light northeast wind. Expert level surfers only.

Greenmeadows

Take Surf HWY 45 to just south of Watino Rd (approx 8km). Follow the stream to the coast. Check with farmer to access break.

Quality right-hand point featuring long walls complete with speed, barrel and cutback sections. Holds a solid swell. Best surfed above 4ft (1.2m+) with light northeast winds. Expert level surfers.

TN5 AREA

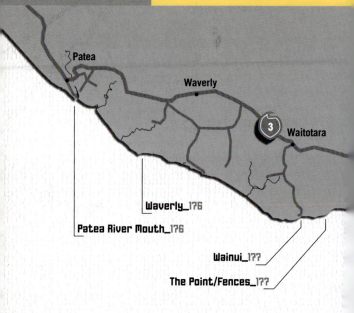

Waverly_176

Patea River Mouth_176

Wainui_177

The Point/Fences_177

NORTH

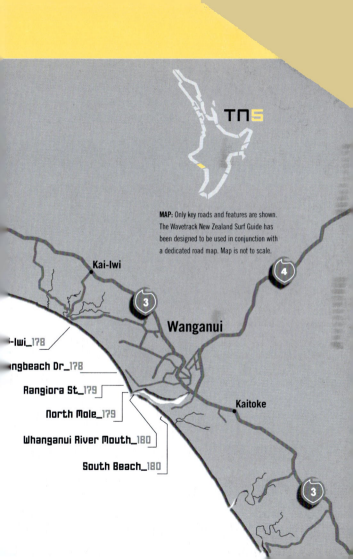

Patea River Mouth

From HWY 3 take Kent St to Beach Rd. This will place you at the mouth of the Patea River.

The best waves are located on the south side of the river - get there by paddling across.

Here you'll find short punchy hollow lefts and longer rights. On big swells the waves will travel up the river producing small rights which peel and wrap, sometimes tubing. The beach break on the north side tends to be shifty. Beware of serious currents. Good for surfers of all levels and abilities.

Waverley

Take HWY 3 south from Patea to Waverley. Take Waverley Beach Rd to the coast.

Shifty beach breaks which sometimes feature good shore-break tubes. The northwestern point offers a right-hand sand point - not much known about this break - go discover.

To the south of the beach check out some of the interesting caves and arches. Good for all surfers.

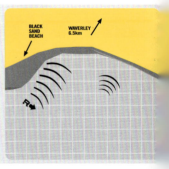

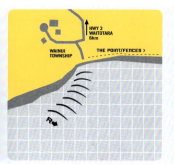

Wainui

Take HWY 3 to Waitotara. Turn off at Wainui Beach Rd.

Wainui features a right-hand sand bottom point setup and a beach break. Spot can produce fun hollow waves on occasion. Good place for learners on small days.

The Point/Fences

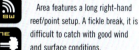

From Wainui take the road east to the point or walk 1km along the beach to the break.

Area features a long right-hand reef/point setup. A fickle break, it is difficult to catch with good wind and surface conditions.

Find The Point closest to Wainui. Break features a sucky takeoff and good barrel section. Inside is Fences - a difficult wave to read, it offers long feathering walls and is prone to breaking wide. Inside Fences is Cabins. Expect a reform on the reef and rifling barrel section over shallow reef. Break offers shelter from strong offshores. All sections link when conditions are right. Experts only.

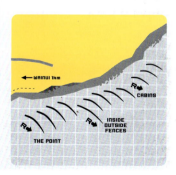

Kai-Iwi

Head south from Waitotara on HWY 3 to Kai-Iwi. Take Kai-Iwi Valley Rd to the coast.

Here you'll find a variable beach break producing a range of left and right peaks. Banks are constantly shifting due to stream flow. Generally an inconsistent break which can occasionally produce an ok wave. Good for surfers of all levels.

Longbeach Drive

From central Wanganui head out towards Castle Cliff Golf Course (approx 3km.) Take Longbeach Dr to the end and park.

Find a long beach break featuring a variety of left and right peaks. The break and banks are constantly changing. Best surfed at high tide with a light northeast offshore. Good for surfers of all levels.

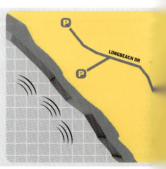

TN5 179

Rangiora St

Head 1km north of the rivermouth to Rangiora St and Seafront Rd.
   Variable beach break featuring a range of left and right peaks. Constantly moving banks, usually a shifty line-up. Good for surfers of all levels.

North Mole

Take Bryce St to Morgan St and the mouth of the Whanganui River.
   Find a variable beachie which breaks near the north mole of the river mouth. Expect a heavy, wedgy beach break which can produce hollow waves. Surfable in most conditions. Break features shifty banks. Competent surfers only.

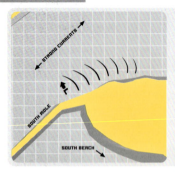

Whanganui Mouth

Head to the mouth of the Whanganui River.

During huge swells find a left-hander breaking 500m inside the Whanganui River mouth. Needs mega swell to break properly. Watch for very dangerous currents. Best surfed on an incoming tide. Competent surfers only.

South Beach

From Wanganui, take Airport Rd to the south side of the Whanganui river. Walk across sand dunes to the break.

Break features a variable breach break and a quality left and right A-frame which breaks in front of an outfall pipe. Expect sucky, powerful left-handers which rifle through to the beach. Break offers good rights also, but not as long as the lefts. Powerful break - competent surfers only.

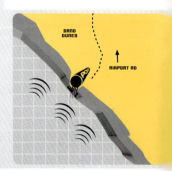

INFO 181

New Plymouth

SURF SHOP
BEACH STREET SURF SHOP
Lost in the 60s - 39 Beach St New Plymouth
Ph 06 7580400, www.lostinthe60s.com

SURF SCHOOL
LEARN TO SURF - DAISY DAY
The Beach Street Surf Shop, Ph 06 758 0400
Mob 0274 414 3654

SURFBOARDS
SEASONS-CHEAPSKATES - Cnr Gover & Leach St, Ph 06 759 4609, email seasons@xtra.co.nz, www.seasonssurfboards.co.nz

SURF SHOP
SURF SKATE & SNOW- Del surfboards
Home of Taranaki Hardcore, 454 Devon St East
Ph/Fax 06 7581757, www.delsurf.co.nz

Oakura

TANDEM SURFING
TARANAKI TANDEM SURFING
Greg Page, Surf Hiway 45, Oakura Ph 06 752 7734, 0274 899 232, www.hang20.com

SURF SHOP
VERTIGO SURF
605 Surf Hiway 45, Oakura
Ph 06 752 7363, email vertigosurf@xtra.co.nz

SURF SCHOOL
SURF SCHOOL TARANAKI
Heather Dent, Oakura Beach, Ph 0274 508 283
email surf@blackdiamondsafris.co.nz

ACCOMMODATION
WAVEHAVEN BACKPACKERS
1518 South Road, Oakura, Surf Hiway 45
Ph 06 752 7800, email wavehaven@winz.co.nz

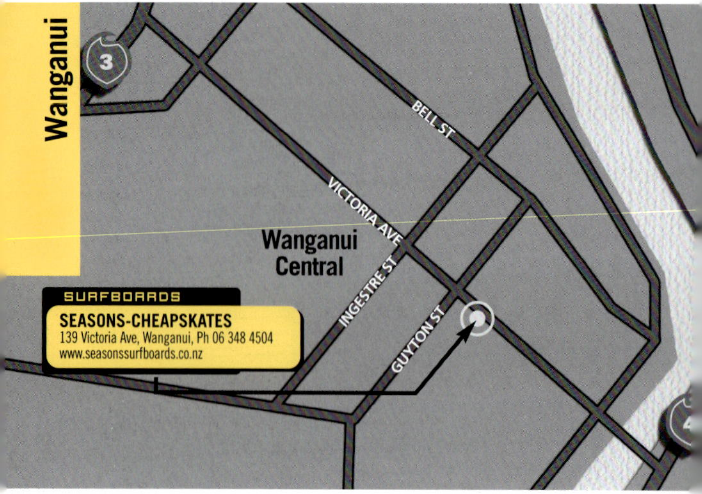

182 INFO

Wanganui

Wanganui Central

SURFBOARDS
SEASONS-CHEAPSKATES
139 Victoria Ave, Wanganui, Ph 06 348 4504
www.seasonssurfboards.co.nz

SURF2SURF.com
New Zealand Surf Reports - Surfing Guide

TARANAKI

Beach Street Surf Shop-Lost in the 60s
39 Beach St New Plymouth
Ph 06 7580400, email beachstreet @xtra .co.nz
www.lostinthe60s.com

Coastal Taranaki - Surf Camp
Beach Front Cabin Accommodation
Guided Coastal Surf Tours
Ph 0274 305 443

Del Free N Easy
34 Devon St East, New Plymouth
Ph 06 758 8480

Dingle Repairs
102 Tasman St Opunake, Ph 025 446 148

Learn To Surf
Daisy Day -New Plymouth, The Beach Street Surf Shop, Ph 06 7580400
0274 414 3654

Monsta Surfboards
www.monsta.net.nz

Reach the Beach Surf Shop
Centre City Gill St, Ph 06 758 1889

Seasons / Cheapskates - Surfboards
Crn Gover & Leach St, New Plymouth
Ph 06 759 4609, email seasons@xtra.co.nz
www.seasonssurfboards.co.nz

Sirocco Surf
605 Surf Hiway 45, Ph 06 752 1363

Surf Skate Snow
Del surfboards
Home of Taranaki Hardcore
454 Devon St East New Plymouth
Ph / Fax 06 7581757
www.delsurf.co.nz

Surf School Taranaki
Heather Dent, Oakura Beach Taranaki
Ph 0274 508 283
email surfblackdiamondsafris.co.nz

Taranaki Tandem Surfing
Greg Page - Surf Hiway 45, Oakura
Ph 06 752 7734, Mob 0274 899 232
www.hang20.com

Tom Smithers Surfboards
905 Surf Hiway 45, Oakura
Ph 06 752 7562

Vertigo Surf
605 Surf Hiway 45, Oakura, Ph 06 752 7363
email vertigosurf@xtra.co.nz

Wavehaven Backpackers
1518 South Road Oakura, Surf Hiway 45
Ph 06 752 7800, Fax 06 752 7080
email wavehaven @ winz.co.nz

WANGANUI

Seasons - Cheapskates
139 Victoria Ave, Wanganui, Ph 06 348 4504
www.seasonssurfboards.co.nz

Coromandel

The Coromandel Peninsula offers some of the finest coastal scenery in the North Island. Pouhutakawa fringed beaches of fine white sand, reefs and rocky outcrops, harbour bars, points and headlands pick up Pacific swells from a range of different angles.

From Auckland it is two or three hours drive across the Hauraki Plains and around the Firth of Thames. Highway 25 winds its way over the ranges and up the eastern side, where quality waves are found all the way from Whiritoa, in the south, through to Port Jackson in the remote north.

An incredible array of islands, some with their own excellent reef breaks, is a feature of the Coromandel coast. The main surf town is Whangamata, which has a solid surf community, surf shops, board manufacturers, and all other services. Summer holidays boost Whangamata's population to over 40,0000 people, all out to party, surf and sunbathe.

Central to the peninsula is the mountain range which divides the weather; on the west side there's often wind and rain, whilst the east is bathed in sunshine, with offshores. Nothing quickens a surfers pulse more than motoring over the hills and seeing a lined up swell stacked to the horizon knowing that their favourite surf break will be cranking and probably uncrowded.

During the summer a cyclone descends from the Tropics. It combines with the trade wind belt producing a classic fetch. Swells push towards Coromandel covering about 500 miles/day.

A low pressure wave factory holds to the east. Massive squash fires swells towards the Coromandel's coast. Time for pumping, clean waves.

A large low sits off the east coast. Big southeast swell pump and wrap into Coromandel breaks.

CO1	186
Waikawau	187
New Chums	187
Whangapoua	188
Matarangi	188
Rings	189
Kuaotunu Reef	189
Black Jacks	190
Opito Bay	190
Whitianga	192
Hahei	192
Hotwater Beach	193
CO2	196
Sailors Grave	197
Tairua	197
Pauanui	199
Opoutere	199
Onemana	201
Whangamata Bar	204
Whanga Beach	208
Whanga Estuary	208
Whiritoa	210
INFO	211

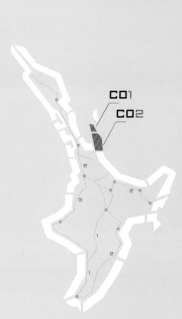

AREA SEASONAL WETSUIT RECOMMENDATIONS

SUMMER
BOARDIES-
SPRINGY

AUTUMN
SPRING
SUIT

WINTER
3/2 or 4/3 STEAMER

SPRING
SPRINGY-
STEAMER

CO1 AREA

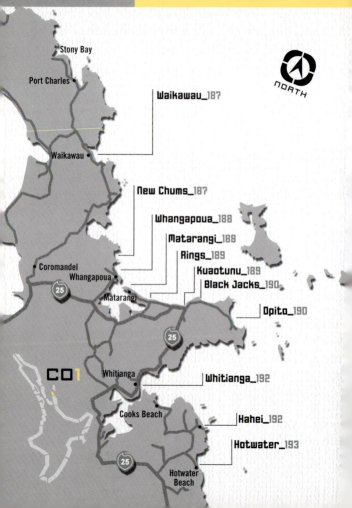

Waikawau

From the town of Coromandel, head north past Kennedy Bay to Waikawau Bay.

Area features a beach and reef/point which works on all tides. It is best surfed on a solid east or northeast swell. Spot often closes out over 4ft (1.5m). Uncrowded and isolated. Offshore is northwest, west and southwest. Suitable for surfers of all abilities.

Look for another fickle reef/point when conditions are right. It starts with R but is surfed by Bart.

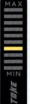

New Chums

Head north on HWY 25 from Whitianga. When you reach Te Rerenga, take a right and head up the western side of the Whangapoua harbour. From Whangapoua, the break is a 10 min walk north to Wainuiototo Bay.

New Chums features a small cove with a peaky right peeling around the rocky outcrop, plus a beach break in the centre of the beach. The bay needs a decent swell to break, as it is sheltered from the Mercury Islands offshore.

Great spot to get a wave to yourself. Wind protected. Good for surfers of all levels.

Whangapoua

Drive north on HWY 25 to Te Rerenga (over the hill from Whitianga Beach). Take a right and head north to Whangapoua.

Bay is swell protected and needs a solid north, northeast or mega-east swell to work.

The southern end of the bay features a semi point break which can produce hollow rights. Further up the beach a rocky island outcrop breaks up swells and can produce fun A-frame peaks. The north end of the beach can produce a peeling left point break on occasions. Optimum wave size 3-5ft (1-3m). Uncrowded. Good for surfers of all levels.

Matarangi

Located 14km north of Whitianga - Matarangi is a luxury beach development built around the local golf course.

Here you will find a beach break, plus left and right bar break at the northern end of the beach. Quality of breaks depend on sand movement and location.

On the right swell Matarangi can produce good waves. Beach needs solid north/northeast swell to break. Suitable for all surfers. Airstrip located at the east end of the golf course.

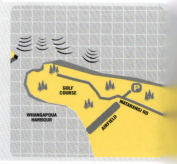

Rings

Get to Rings by taking HWY 25 north from Whitianga past Kuaotunu.

Rings breaks when the Coromandel Coast is 6-8ft (3m). A sheltered spot. When it's on, it features numerous peaky rights and lefts through the change of tides. Optimum wave size 2-4ft (1m). Good learners wave.

Kuaotunu Reef

Get there by taking HWY 25 15km north from Whitianga. Take the Opito Bay turnoff, look for the road to the boat ramp.

Grunty right reef break producing fast barreling rights. Can get shallow on lower tides. Needs a big north or northeast swell to break. Competent surfers.

BLACK JACK RD
OPITO BAY >>

Black Jacks

From Whitianga, head north to Kuaotunu and take a right towards Opito Bay.

Black Jacks consists of a left peeling around the Motuhua Point. Like all the breaks in this area, it is sheltered from swell by the Mercury Islands. Black Jacks needs a big north or northeast swell to break. If it's working you can expect long winding lefts featuring barrel, cutty and speed sections. Good for surfers of all levels.

Opito Bay

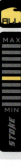

Take HWY 25 north from Whitianga. Take a right at Kuaotunu to Opito.

Swell sheltered bay features a range of variable beach breaks. Narrow swell window, picks up large east swells. Find numerous peaky rights and left through the change of tides. Optimum size 2-4ft (1m). Good for surfers of all levels.

Also worth a look is Otama - a grunty swell magnet/beach break. Find this break north of Opito around Tokarahu point.

BLACKJACK RD

Whitianga

Whitianga is located 30km north of Pauanui on HWY 25.

Spots include a beach break - Buffalo beach, and a right hander breaking in the harbour entrance. All spots require a mega 6-8ft (3m) east/northeast swell to break. Beach is good for learners - soft and mushy.

Hahei

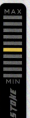

Take HWY 25 north. Turn right at the turnoff for Hotwater/Cooks beaches.

Hahei is classic Coromandel. Its beautiful sheltered beach features a right hand reef break which will only work with a solid 6-8ft (3m) east/south east swell. Sucky rock/reef takeoff, closes-out over 3 ft (1m). Competent surfers.

Hotwater Beach

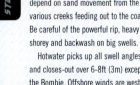

Hotwater Beach is located 14km north of Tairua. Take HWY 25 north, turn right at the Cooks Beach turn-off, head towards the coast for 5km.

Voted one of the top ten most beautiful beaches in the world, Hotwater Beach is great place to stay and surf.

Its steep-profile beach produces a range of waves. At the north end you'll find a left-hand point break, at south end you'll find a right-hand reef break and outer-bombora. The beach itself features a variety of powerful peaks, producing grunty sand sucking barrels. The banks depend on sand movement from the various creeks feeding out to the coast. Be careful of the powerful rip, heavy shorey and backwash on big swells.

Hotwater picks up all swell angles, and closes-out over 6-8ft (3m) except for the Bombie. Offshore winds are west through southwest. Check the central car park, it'll give you the best indication of what is working on a particular swell.

At low tide in front of the banks and rocky outcrop are natural hot water pools.

Voted one of the top ten most beautiful beaches in the world, Hotwater Beach is great place to stay and surf.

Just look for kids and tourists digging in the sand or sitting in their own hottie. After a chilly winter session, soak in your own natural hot pool. Good for surfers of all levels.

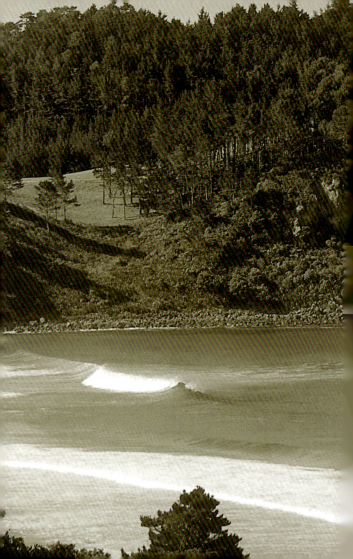

CO2 AREA

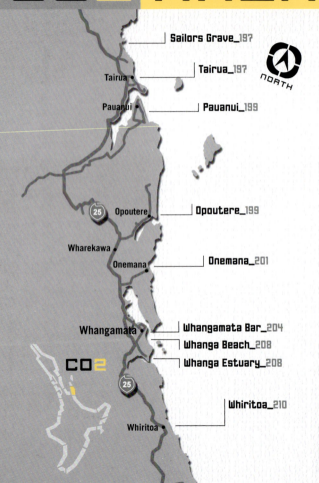

Sailors Grave

From Tairua (HWY 25) take a right hand turn off the main road to Te Karo - Sailors. Find the carpark at the end of the road. Walk down the track to the beach. To the left is the grave of seaman William Simpson, who drowned in the surf while loading Kauri onto the HMS Tortoise in 1842 (British naval ships used to visit the bay to collect spars for their masts). The bay features a beach break and two reef breaks. The reefs at each end of the bay feature sucky rights and lefts and hold a 4-6ft (2m) swell. The beachies tend to close out. Good for competent surfers only.

Tairua

Located across the estuary from Pauanui. Tairua features a powerful dredging beach break. Peaky A-frame peaks peel off down the line to form a gnarly shore break on the inside. Tairua picks up swell from the north and northeast, and can handle waves in the 4-6ft (1.5 - 2m) range. Best surfed at mid to low tide. Offshore south/southwest. Intermediate - expert surfers.

Pauanui

From Whangamata take HWY 25 north for 22km, then take the right to Pauanui.

Features three different breaks. At the north end of the beach is home to a left bar break featuring a peaky left with a hollow takeoff and long wall. It has a tendency to shut down if the banks aren't quite right. The middle of the beach is home to a beach break, and at the southern end you'll find a good right-hander, which works best with an east/southeast groundie wrapping around the point. A sucky takeoff eases into a softer shoulder down the line. Break good for surfers of all levels.

Opoutere

You'll find Opoutere 15km north of Whangamata. Take HWY 25 north, make a right at the Opoutere turnoff - the road follows the Wharekawa Harbour to the coast.

It features a beach break and right point bar. Beach picks up all swells - north through to southeast. Quality of banks depend on size and angle of the swell. Optimum wave size 3-5ft (1.5-2m).

To get to the breaks you have a long scenic walk across the estuary. Secluded and uncrowded. Good for surfers of all levels.

Onemana

Drive north from Whangamata on HWY 25. Take a right to Onemana and Whitipirorua Pt.

Beach break featuring left and right peaks. A good option to escape the crowds of Whangamata. Picks up all swells - north to southeast. Offshore west through to southwest. Good for surfers of all levels.

Spot X

Left and right reef breaks. Look for a mansion on the hill. Bribe a Whanga local for info. Also, offshore island reef breaks - the Coro is littered with them. Stop whinging about your local being crowded - get a boat, get searching. Good luck.

WHANGA BAR: PHOTO:DANIEL DAVIE

CO2

Whangamata Bar

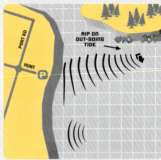

Whangamata is located on HWY 25 mid-way up the Coromandel coast. It's home to one of the finest left river bar breaks in New Zealand.

Paddle out by taking the rip in the channel - watch the strong outgoing tides if you're not an experienced or paddle-fit surfer.

Takeoff is a sucky drop followed by a good barrelling section. When you've spent enough time in the barrel, you can carve up the long workable wall firing off down the line for 150m. The Bar is a high performance wave, offering fast sucky sections perfect for snaps and roundie cutties. It'll pick up any swell northeast through to southeast, and breaks on the lower tides up to 6ft (2.5m).

Along with fine waves comes the crowds. Whangamata is a well-known and popular holiday destination for Kiwi's (and especially Aucklanders). In the peak of summer its breaks can become very crowded, especially the bar when it's firing. Remember to respect other surfers, there are usually plenty of waves for all - a little respect goes a long way.

When you've spent enough time in the barrel, you can carve up the long workable wall firing off down the line for 150m.

Further down the beach you'll find some sweet little beachies which hold up to 5-6ft (2-2.5m). Expect peaky takeoffs and long, fast, workable walls which morph into a heavy (fun) shorebreak. Good for surfers of all levels.

WHANGA BAR. PHOTO: SURF2SURF.COM

WHANGA BAR. PHOTO:DANIEL DAVIE

208 CO2

Whangamata Beach

From the main street of Whangamata, take Ocean to the Esplanade.

Quality beach break producing peaky lefts and rights. Gets sucky and hollow - long workable walls peeling into heavy shore break. Beach can handle up to 5-6ft (2-2.5m). Good for surfers of all levels.

Whangamata Estuary

The estuary is located at the south end of Whangamata Beach.

Depending on the location of sand, the estuary can offer a very good right-hand bar break. When it's on, you can expect a sucky takeoff followed by a hollow right wall producing long rides. Competent surfers only.

WHANGAMATA BEACH. PHOTO:DANIEL DAVIE

Whiritoa

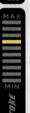

Take HWY 25 from Waihi 14km. Turn right and head out to Whiritoa beach.

Super-grunty hollow beach break, also a reef break (Mataora Reef) located around the cliffs at the southern end of the beach. Difficult access around cliffs. Holds solid 6-8ft (3m) swell. Picks up all swells - north through southeast. Always better on north to northeast swells at mid to low tide. Intermediate - expert surfers only.

COROMANDEL

Anderson Surfboards
Custom Surfboards, Factory / Showroom
308 Aickin Road Whangamata
Ph 07 865 7388, www.surfboard.co.nz

Black Jack Surf Shop
35 Albert Street, Whitianga
Ph 07 866 5800

Inside Out Surfboards
Factory / Showroom
312 Aicken Road Whangamata
Manufacturers Legend Point, Munro longboards
Byrning Spears Hardcase glassing
Ph 07 865 7112, Fax 07 865 9363
email: insideout.surf@actrix.gen.nz

Notionlab
Advertising, Marketing, Book Design, New Media
Designers of the Wavetrack New Zealand Surfing
Guide - www.notionlab.co.nz

Offshore Surf Shop Ltd
Rosemount Road, Waihi
Ph 07 863 7992

Paul Shanks - Tubecruiser
Surfboards, Ph 7 865 8119

Reel n Wave
29 Wilson Road, Waihi Beach
Ph 07 863 5859

Salt Water Surf Shop
505 Port Road, Whangamata
Ph 07 865 8668, Fax 07 865 8666

Sunshine Surf Coaching - Waihi Beach
8 Scarborough Rd, Waihi Beach
Ph 07 863 45 87, Mob 021 135 7950
email: sunshinesurfcoaching@hotmail.com

Surf Reports - Nationwide - Online
www.surf2surf.com

Surf Reports - Phone
Wavetrack 0900 99 777 (Calls 99c/min)
Groms ask your parents first

Tairua And Pauanui Surf School
Well get you up and riding
Ph Luke 07 864 8979
Ph Alison 07 864 7553
email: lkmillen@xtra.co.nz
email: alisonsmith@xtra.co.nz

The Outback Surf Shop
Ghost & Simon Avery Surfboards
Shop 13 Pauanui Shopping Village
Pauanui Beach, Ph/Fax 07 864 7558
021 241 9710, email: avery1@xtra.co.nz

Whangamata Surf Shop
634 Port Road, Whangamata
Ph 07 865 8252

Gallery 213

Photo: Mark Stevenson

Photo: Karol Strange

Photo: Paul Kennedy

Photo: Cory Scott

Bay of Plenty

Stretching 150 kilometres from Orokawa Bay, near Waihi Beach, to the town of Ohope in the southeast, the Bay was named by Captain Cook who sailed past in 1769.

The area features a range of beach, reefs, points and river bar breaks. Though it gets its share of storms, the Bay of Plenty is on the wrong side of the North Island to get the same regular Southern Ocean swells that places like Taranaki and Gisborne enjoy. The Bay has a limited window for swell and survives on northeast and east groundswells, stormy wind swells and topical cyclones during the summer months. When there is swell it rarely lasts more than a few days: the prevailing winds are from the southwest and while they help create clean hollow waves they also blow the swell back out to sea. But when conditions are right the Bay has many breaks capable of producing superb surf.

For much of the Bay of Plenty the roads run next to the coast making access to spots easy. For the adventurous, the area also offers a range of interesting island breaks which require boat access. Make sure to get some local advice before taking a small boat out into heavy seas.

During the summer the Bay suffers a population explosion. Waihi, Mt Manganui and Whakatane are popular summer holiday destinations for Kiwis who come for surf, sand and sun. Usually there are plenty of waves for all. Each of these towns offer a range of surfshops, surfboard and wetsuit manufacturers, surf schools, and anything else a travelling surfer may need.

During the summer a cyclone descends from the Tropics. It combines with the trade wind belt producing a classic squash. Solid swells hit the Bay.

A low pressure wave factory holds to the east. Massive fetch fires solid swells towards the Bay of Plenty. Breaks exposed to the east pump.

A depression tracks east from the Tasman Sea. As it spins to the north, it pushes a north wind/ground swell on to north exposed spots.

BP 231

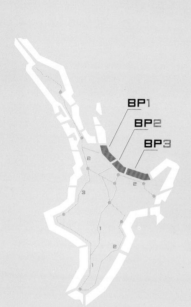

BP1	232
Orokawa Bay	233
Waihi	233
Bowentown	234
Nth Matakana	234
BP2	236
Matakana	237
Main Beach	240
Shark Alley	240
Tay Street	241
Arataki	241
Papamoa	244
Kaituna	244
Motiti Island	245
Maketu	248
Newdicks	248
Little Waihi	250
Pukehina	250
BP3	252
Matata	253
Airports	253
Whakatane	254
Ohope	254
INFO	256

O'NEILL — AREA SEASONAL WETSUIT RECOMMENDATIONS

SUMMER
BOARDIES-SPRINGY

AUTUMN
SPRING SUIT

WINTER
3/2 or 4/3 STEAMER + BOOTIES

SPRING
SPRINGY-STEAMER

BP1 AREA

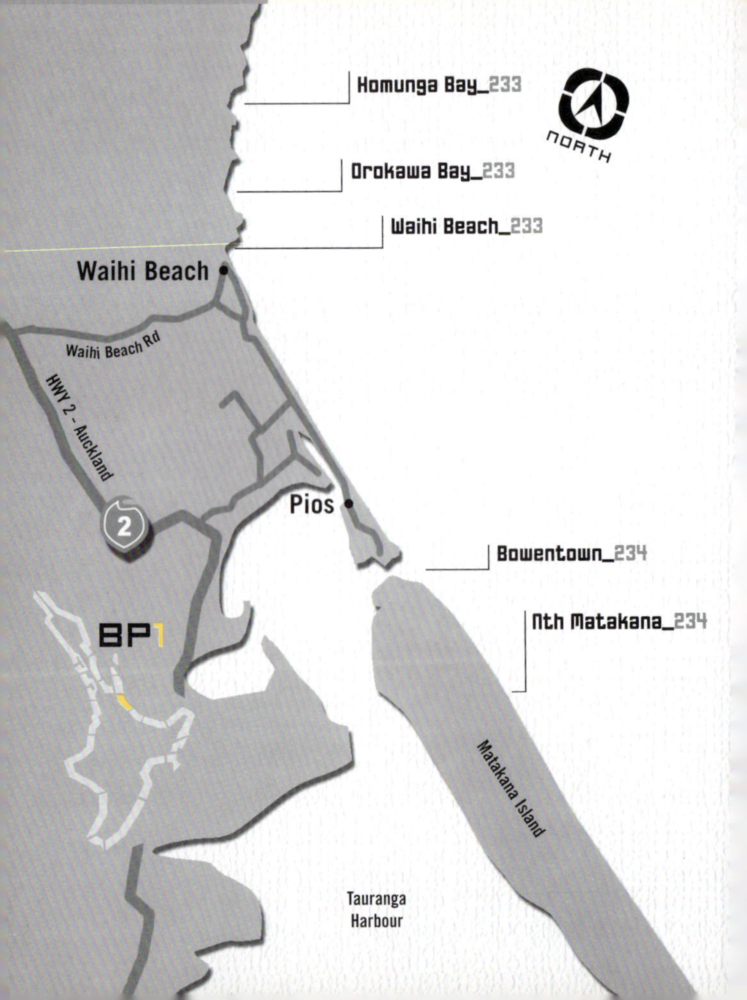

- Homunga Bay_233
- Orokawa Bay_233
- Waihi Beach_233
- Bowentown_234
- Nth Matakana_234

Waihi Beach

Waihi Beach Rd

HWY 2 - Auckland

2

Pios

BP1

Matakana Island

Tauranga Harbour

NORTH

BP1 233

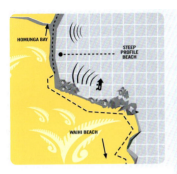

Orokawa-Homunga Bay

Get to Orokawa Bay from the north end of Waihi Beach. Take the walking track north around the point - it's a beautiful scenic hike which takes 30 minutes.

Break consists of a right-hand reef/point at the south end, and beach breaks further north. Spot is secluded and remote. On a solid swell it can produce a very good, grunty right with barreling section and long wall. Competent surfers. Continue north on the track to Homunga Bay. Here you'll find an isolated mega-reef bombie break in the centre of the bay which produces grunty big peaks. Easy track, but very long walk.

Waihi Beach

Head south from Waihi township, take a left at the Waihi Beach turnoff.

Waihi features a good beach break and a fickle left point at the north end. To get good waves on the point the sand needs to be in the right place - when it's working it can produce nice long peeling lefts. Optimum wave size 3-4ft (1-1.5m). Good on all tides and for surfers of all levels.

234 BP1

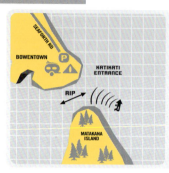

Bowentown

Drive south from Waihi Beach to Athenree and Pio Shores. You'll see Matakana to the southeast across the channel.

Break is located across the channel and breaks off the Matakana bar. Check the tide and rip when you paddle across. Shifty banks with heavy current. Picks up northeast and east swells. Offshore west/southwest. Uncrowded and difficult access. Competent surfers.

North Matakana Island

Northern-end of Matakana Island. Get there by boat or by Matakana Ferry (take your car and go exploring). Various beach breaks of similar quality to Mount coast. Quality depends on the state of banks, sand movement and swell size. Can be a difficult paddle out over 4-5ft (1.5-2m). The outer banks hold solid swells. Uncrowded and isolated, this spot is rarely surfed. Optimum wave size 3-4ft (1-1.5m). Competent surfers.

BP2 AREA

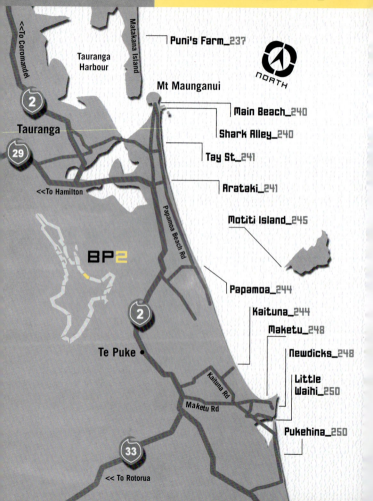

BP2 237

Matakana - Puni's Farm

Getting to Matakana used to involve a mad-dash paddle across the harbour entrance, which often meant battling very strong currents. After many close calls with in-bound container ships, it is now illegal to paddle across.

Access the breaks by boat or by taking the ferry from Tauranga's Sulphur Point.

The Island is legendary for producing hollow left and right beach break peaks of supreme quality. Outer sand banks break up ocean swells, which in turn re-form on the inside to produce sand sucking A-frame peaks.

Be ready for very sucky takeoffs, long barrels and a gnarly shorie. At low tide it can get extremely shallow.

Surfing from a boat can be heaps of fun. It's a great way to check out and choose the peak you want to surf. Take some lunch, if the Island is epic heading back to Mt Maunganui for some tucker may be the last thing you'll want to do.

Camping on the Island is prohibited, as is lighting fires on the beach.

The Island is legendary for producing hollow left and right beach break peaks of supreme quality.

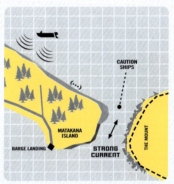

Optimum wave size 3-6ft (1-2.5m) with a northeast or east swell. The Island usually breaks a foot bigger than the Mount coast. For classic hollow Island, you'll want low to mid tide with a stiff offshore (12-15kt+ SW). Best for intermediate to expert level surfers.

240 BP2

Main Beach

From Tauranga, take the Harbour Bridge to the base of Mount Maunganui.

Area features a beach break and a right-hand sand bar point located at the southeastern end. The right, commonly known as the 'Blow Hole' can produce a peeling right-hander with a fat wall up to 50-80m long. It then peels through to a sucky shore break. You'll find various other peaks north towards the surf club. When it's big, the rip is a great way to get out the back with minimum effort. Good spot for onshore winter storm days - swirling winds help make crappy conditions ok. Surfers of all levels.

Shark Alley

Shark Alley is located southeast of the Main Beach.

It features a beach break which has improved over the years thanks to harbour dredging. It can produce fun peaks for longboarding and learning to surf.

The Alley will sometimes pick up swells which other breaks miss and offers wind protection from northwesterlies.

Rabbit Island features two breaks - a mega right-hand reef which is one of the few surfable big wave spots in the BOP (breaks on a 10-15ft+ northeast swell). Also, the eastern side of Rabbit features a reef break producing a fat left. Access the break by boat.

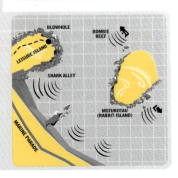

BP2 241

Tay St - Omanu

From the base of Mt Maunganui, take Marine Parade southeast down the coast.

Here you will find a range of beach breaks to choose from. If the swell is on, it's just a matter of finding a peak to yourself. Tay St, Clyde St and Omanu tend to offer the best banks - all feature fun peaky waves breaking on inside and outside sand banks. On large swells it can be a tricky paddle out and in most cases there will be a strong easterly drift. The coast holds up to 6ft (2m) and optimum size is 3-5ft (1-1.5m). Good for surfers of all levels. Good beach for learning to surf.

Arataki

Get to Arataki from Mt Maunganui Rd by taking Girven Rd northeast to the coast.

Arataki is beach break featuring a slightly steeper profile beach when compared to the rest of the coast. The breaks offer a little more grunt and can produce nice hollow peaks when the conditions are right. Arataki is a good option to escape the crowds on the Mt Maunganui coast. Good for surfers of all levels.

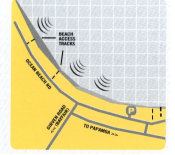

244 BP2

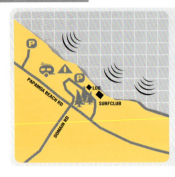

Papamoa Beach Park

Papamoa is located 8km to the southeast of Mt Maunganui. Take State HWY 2 southeast to Domain Rd and head to the coast.

Beach break featuring peaky waves on the inner and outer banks. Generally a foot smaller than the Mt Maunganui coast due to swell blanketing from offshore Motiti Island. Find nice banks in front of the boat ramp, Pony Club and domain parking lots. Holds 4-6ft (1.5-2m). Picks up north swell. Good for surfers of all levels. Great beginners spot.

Kaituna Cut

Take State HWY 2 southeast through the town of Te Puke. At Rangiuru take a left on Maketu Road. Take Kaituna Rd to the mouth of the river.

Bar break - sometimes produces a very hollow left and right-handers. Very fickle spot which can produce heavy, Kirra-like right-hand screamers. Needs a strong true southerly wind for epic conditions (which is a rare wind direction for area).

Also, various beach breaks in the area. Picks up north, northeast and east swells. When it fires, expert surfers only. Popular fishing spot for locals - watch out for lines.

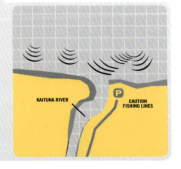

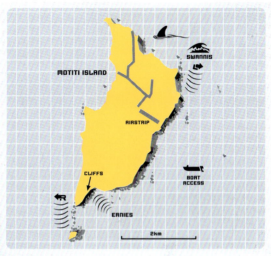

Motiti Island

Motiti Island is located 22km from the Tauranga Harbour entrance or 10km northeast of Papamoa. Get to the Island by boat or air. Caution: the boat trip is a serious ocean voyage when the swell is running. Don't take small boats - you will be swamped before you make it half way. For aerial charters, contact Tauranga Aero Club, tel 07 575 3210. Permission is required before flying out to the Island.

The Island features several breaks. At the northeastern tip find Swannis, a powerful left-hander breaking over a weed covered rock shelf. Expect ledgy, sucky waves which can peel for 300m. Break works on northeast and east swells and is prone to cross shore surface lump.

To the south is Ernies. Break features a range of peaks which work on east and southeast swells. Grunty A-frames peel in towards the Island, large cliffs offer good wind protection and clean surface conditions. West of Ernies find a long peeling reef which fires on large northeast swells - not much known about this break, go discover.

Motiti is a spooky, sharky place to surf. Expert level surfers only.

ERNIE. PHOTO: KAROL STRANGE

Unit 5, 15 Portside Drive, Mt Maunganui
Ph: 07 575 9133 - www.mountsurfshop.co.nz

248 BP1

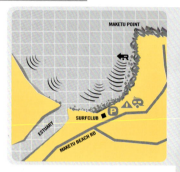

Maketu

Take State HWY 2 southeast through Te Puke. Turn left at Maketu Road near Rangiuru.

Beach break and right hand reef break. Both offer good shelter from south to southeast winds. Southern end features a sucky right reef break. Works on solid swells, best surfed on high tide. You can also find good peaks in front of the motor camp and shop, with a right peeling towards the estuary mouth. Heaps of inward drift on the incoming tide. Picks up north, northeast and east swells. Best for intermediate level surfers and above.

Newdicks

Head to Maketu. Take Town Point Rd up the hill to Newdicks Rd. It will curve around and down to Newdicks Beach which is located on the eastern side of the Maketu point.

The beach is private access - pay to surf (look for the honesty box).

Newdicks features a massive array of beach breaks, rocky outcrops and reefs. Peaky suckie lefts and rights break over submerged rocks. Sand build-up around the rocks can make for interesting peaks. Great wind-protected spot from dreaded west and northwest winds. Uncrowded. Competent surfers. Maketu pies are legendary!

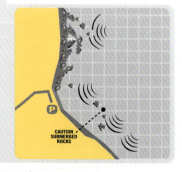

MAKETU POINT. PHOTO: KAROL STRANGE

250 BP2

Little Waihi

Access to Little Waihi is via Maketu. Take Maketu Beach Rd to Little Waihi Rd. At the top of the hill take a right on Arawa Rd. Take the first left, Bledisloe Rd down the hill. Parking is in front of the shop.

Check the waves by walking through the motor camp or climbing the hill. Access the break by paddling across the river.

Grunty river bar break producing hollow peaks. Predominant left-hander peels through, long rides and barrels at low tide. Find more peaks to the east. Experts only.

Pukehina Beach

Get to Pukehina by taking HWY 2 southeast from Mt Maunganui through Te Puke to Pukehina Beach Rd.

Here you'll find a steep profile beach break producing left and right peaks. Find the best banks towards the Little Waihi Bar.

Good for surfers of all levels.

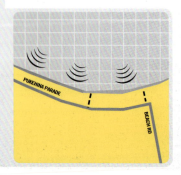

BP3 AREA

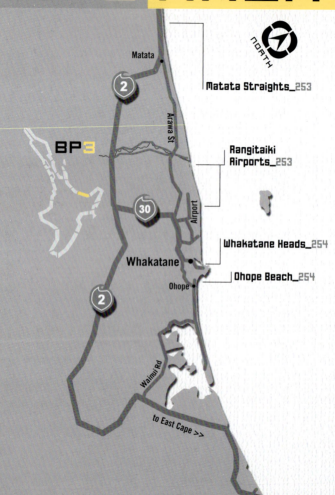

Matata

Matata is located on HWY 2 between Te Puke and Whakatane. You can check the surf while you drive - the highway runs parallel along to the coast for 10km.

At Matata you'll find beach break peaks up and down the beach. Waves break on the inner and outer banks. Various streams create better banks in areas. While Matata is not the crown jewel of the coast, it can produce nice waves in the right swell and conditions. Good for surfers of all levels.

Airports/Rangitaiki

From HWY 2, take Gow Rd to Thornton and the mouth of the Rangitaiki River.

Here you'll find a river bar break and a range of variable beach breaks which stretch back to the Whakatane Airport.

The Rangitaiki Mouth features constantly shifting bars due to heavy river flow. Bar produces a variety of good left and rights which can get hollow. Uncrowded waves. Competent surfers.

254 BP3

Whakatane Heads

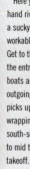

Whakatane is a little over an hours drive from Mt Maunganui on HWY 2. Drive through Whakatane township to the Heads.

Here you'll find a quality right-hand river bar break. Expect a sucky takeoff, followed by a fast workable wall peeling for 100m. Get to the break by paddling across the entrance. Watch out for fishing boats and heavy rips on the outgoing tide. Consistent break - picks up north, northeast and wrapping east swells. Offshore south-southwest. Best low through to mid tide. Crowded and intense takeoff. Competent surfers.

Ohope

Head over the hill from Whakatane. At the bottom of the hill take a left to the west end.

Beach break and occasional left point break at the northern end of the beach. Quality of left point depends on sand build-up. Combination of peaks and occasional long-walled beach break. Mellow fun waves up to 4ft (1.5m). Picks up east and southeast swells. Great learners wave.

256 INFO

Mt Maunganui

SURF SHOP
MOUNT SURFSHOP
96 Maunganui Rd, Mt Maunganui
Ph 07 575 9133, www.mountsurfshop.co.nz

SURF VIDEO
SLIPPERY STICK - VIDEO
Commercial Video Specialists
Ph 07 572 2603, Mob 025 435 664

SURF SHOP
ASSAULT BOARDRIDERS
24 Pacific Ave, Mt Maunganui,
Ph 07 575 7831, www.assault.co.nz

SURF SHOP
ISLAND STYLE
227 Maunganui Rd, Mt Maunganui
Ph 07 575 3030

SURF SCHOOL
NEW ZEALAND SURF SCHOOL
Marine Parade, Tay St on da beach, Mt Maunganui
Ph 021 477 873, www.nzsurfschool.co.nz

SURFBOARDS
HIGH VOLTAGE-SUNSHINE
crn Mark Rd & York St, Mt Maunganui
Ph 07 575 8478, www.highvoltage.co.nz

WETSUITS
BODYLINE WETSUITS
135 Totara St, Mt Maunganui
Ph 07 575 8518, www.bodyline.co.nz

SURFBOARDS
THE BOARD CO
139 Totara St, Mt Maunganui
PH 07 574 0076, www.theboardco.net

SURF COACHING
SURFING BAY OF PLENTY
Coaching, Mentor, Coordinator
021 252 3243

MUSEUM / BOARDSHOP
MOUNT SURF MUSEUM
Uit 5, 15 Portside Dr, Ph 07 575 9133
Mob 027 295 6262, www.mountsurfshop.co.nz

SURFBOARDS
HANDS SURF BOARDS
19/ Unit 14 McDonald St, Mt Maunganui, Ph
07 574 1905, 021 733 687, www.handssurf.co.nz

SURF SHOP
EVOLVE SURF & SKATE
37 Jellico St, Te Puke, Ph 07 573 6009

The Mount
Pilot Bay
GROVE
MARINE PDE
TAY
MAUNGANUI
HULL
TRITON
TOTARA ST
MAUNGANUI RD
GOLF RD
HEWLETTS ROAD

<TAURANGA

Tauranga Airport

TAURANGA - MT MAUNGNUI

Assault Boardriders
108 Devonport Rd, Tauranga, Ph 07 577 0017

Assault Boardriders
24 Pacific Ave, Mt Maunganui, Ph 07 575 7831
www.assault.co.nz

Boardwalk Denim Surf Skate
Red Square, Tauranga, Ph 07 578 7477

Bodyline Wetsuits - The Wetsuit CO Ltd
135 Totara St, Mt Maunganui, Ph 07 575 8518
www.bodyline.co.nz

CC Foils - Hand Made Fins
PO Box 4414, Mt Maunganui, Ph 021 255 2171

Evolve Surf & Skate
37 Jellico St, Te Puke, Ph 07 573 6009

Hands Surfboards
19/ Unit 14 Mc Donald St, Mt Maunganui
Ph 07 574 1905, 021 733 687,
www.handssurf.co.nz

**High Voltage Surfboards -
Sunshine Design & Surf Ltd**
Cnr Mark Rd & York St, Mt Maunganui
Ph 07 575 8478, www.highvoltage.co.nz

Island Style Surf & Skate Shop
25 years at the Mount - 227 Maunganui Rd
Mt Maunganui, Ph 07 575 3030

Lovely Planet Surf School
Main Beach, Mt Maunganui, Ph 07 572 3399

Ministry of Surf
Shop 2, Tower 1 Marine Parade, Main Beach
Mt Maunganui, Ph 07 574 9283

Mount Surf Shop
96 Maunganui Rd, Mt Maunganui, Ph 575 9133
www.mountsurfshop.co.nz

Nevada Denim Surf Skate
Bayfair Shopping Centre, Girven Rd
Mt Maunganui, Ph 07 575 0069

New Zealand Surf School
Marine Parade, Tay St - on the beach
Mt Maunganui, Ph 021 IS SURF (477 873)
www.nzsurfschool.co.nz

Notionlab
Advertising, Marketing, Book Design, New Media
Designers of the Wavetrack New Zealand Surfing
Guide - lets talk Ph 021 529 599
www.notionlab.co.nz

Sunshine Surf Coaching - Waihi Beach
8 Scarborough Rd, Waihi Beach
Ph 07 863 45 87, Mob 021 135 7950
email: sunshinesurfcoaching@hotmail.com

Surfing Bay of Plenty
Surf Coaching/Mentor/Coordinator
Ph 021 252 3243

Surf Reports - Nationwide - Online
www.surf2surf.com

Surf Reports - Phone
Wavetrack 0900 99 777 (Calls 99c/min)
Groms ask your parents first

Tauranga Aero Club - Charters/Flight Training
Charter Flights to Great Barrier, Motiti, Raglan,
Shippies, Gisborne, Pauanui
Ph 07 575 3210, www.flytac.co.nz

The Board CO - Engineered Surfboards
139 Totara St, Mt Maunganui, Ph 07 574 0076
www.theboardco. net

The Garden - Surf, Skate, Snow
80 A Devonport Rd, Tauranga, Ph 578 2323

New Zealand Homestay Adventures
Surf Adventures - Call 07 575 83 86
www.nzhomestayadventures.co.nz

WHAKATANE

Epic Surf & Skate
150 The Strand, Whakatane, Ph 07 308 6817

Salt Air Surf Co
190 The Strand, Whakatane, Ph 07 308 8807

East Cape

The East Cape of the North Island can be split in to two unique surfing destinations - the northern facing coast and the east coast.

The area east from the town of Optotiki to Cape Runaway features a range of mythical breaks which are very difficult to catch with optimum swell and wind conditions. Geographically speaking all the ingredients are present to produce quality waves, but sadly the swells are not. To get these breaks working a solid northwest, north or mega northeast swell is required. Tropical cyclones can sometimes offer the best conditions but only if they are positioned far enough offshore.

Head east from Waihau Bay and you'll hit the eastern facing coast. This is where it gets very interesting as the area stretching south to Gisborne is home to hundreds of quality breaks. Many of these are located miles from the highway and require access across private land so remember to show respect and get permission before crossing. The coast picks up a range of swells from northeast through to south and is generally pretty consistent. Here you'll find points, reefs, river bar breaks and powerful beach breaks accompanied with spectacular scenery.

When hitting the Cape for a surf mission, be prepared with a few supplies to keep you going. The area is fairly remote although there are general stores and accommodation in the various small towns.

During the summer a cyclone descends from the Tropics. It combines with the trade wind belt producing a classic squash. Massive swells hit the Cape.

A low pressure wave factory holds to the east. A large fetch fires solid swells towards the East Cape. The coast pumps.

A depression from the Tasman Sea brings life to the East Capes north exposed river mouths and points. While the BOP is 1-2ft, east of Opotiki is chest to head high.

EC 259

EC1	261
Opotiki	262
Torere	262
Hawai	263
Maraenui	263
Motu	266
Hariki Beach	266
EC2	269
Waihau Bay	270
Hicks Bay	270
Horseshoe Bay	271
Tokata	271
Te Araroa	274
EC3	276
Waiapu	277
Waipiro Bay	277
EC4	280
Tokomaru Bay	281
Anaura Bay	281
3 Points	284
Kaiaua Bay	284

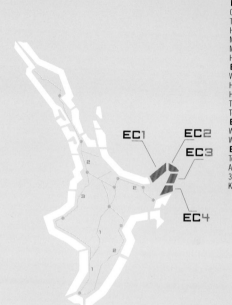

O'NEILL — AREA SEASONAL WETSUIT RECOMMENDATIONS

SUMMER
BOARDIES-
SPRINGY

AUTUMN
SPRING
SUIT

WINTER
3/2 or 4/3 STEAMER
+ BOOTIES

SPRING
SPRINGY-
STEAMER

EC1 AREA

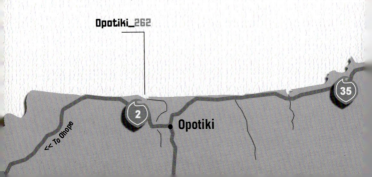

Opotiki_262

Opotiki

<< To Ohope

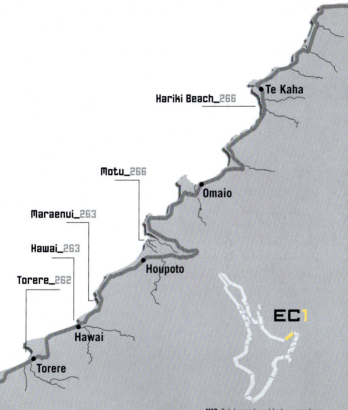

Opotiki

From Ohope take Wainui Rd to HWY 2 east and Opotiki.

The area features a range of beach breaks and river bar breaks along the coast. The Waiotahi Beach features many rivers and streams producing banks of reasonable quality. Storms and river floods are constantly changing the shape of the banks. Area can offer quality waves especially around the river bars. Good for surfers of all levels.

Torere

Torere is located 20km to the east of Opotiki on State HWY 2. When you reach the Torere River, take a left and park on the side of the road.

Fickle and sheltered spot from most swells. Needs a solid north or northwest wind swell of at least 8ft (3m) to work. Mega northeast and east swells can also wrap in to the bay if they are big enough. Mystical quality right-hand reef with a good workable wall. Very inconsistent. Hard to catch working. Uncrowded. Competent surfers only.

EC1 263

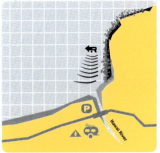

Hawai

Head east from Opotiki on HWY 35. Hawai is the next point east of Torere.

Changeable river bar break. Sand and shingle build-up is constantly changing due to floods.

Good quality wave with sucky takeoff and fast walls which rifle off to the shore. Good barrel sections. Water is often dirty and brown. When it's cranking expect a 60-100m ride. Needs large northwest/north swell or mega northeast swell to work. Wind swells tend to shut down break. Optimum wave size 3-6ft (1-2.5 m). Uncrowded. Best for intermediate to expert level surfers.

Maraenui

Head around the corner from Hawai. Park your car on the side of the road to check the surf. Spot always looks smaller than it really is.

Get to the point via a steep track to the beach.

Fat pushy right-hand point break producing a slow mellow (long) wave. Needs large northwest/north swell, or mega northeast swell to work. When it's on, expect long rides with multiple sections. After each ride walk back along beach to the point. Maraenui is normally surfed when Hawai is blown out. Isolated. Suits intermediate level surfers.

PHOTO: KAROL STRANGE

Motu River Mouth

The mouth of the Motu River is located 35km east of Opotiki on HWY 35. Cross the Motu Bridge, on the left is a lookout and parking area.

Amazing long right-hand peeling point. With the right swell and all sections linking up, the Motu can peel for hundreds of metres. As it sucks and grinds down the shingle/river stone point, expect hollow barrels and ballistic sections. Caution: gets shallow in areas. Can hold an 8ft wave. Bay is exposed and prone to gusty offshores sweeping down the flat river plain. Optimum size 3-6ft (1-2.5m). Murky water conditions. Shark breeding ground.

Hariki Beach

Find Hariki Beach about 1km south of Te Kaha. Park on the side of the road near the stream.

Hariki is basically a low quality beach break producing fat waves which often close out. Occasionally it can get reasonable with a large northwest swell and is better with offshore winds.

It's true value is as an indicator for the Motu. If there are waves at Hariki the Motu will be pumping. Good learners wave.

EC2 AREA

NORTH

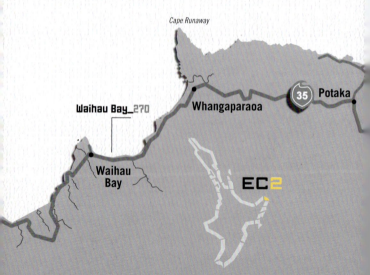

Cape Runaway

Waihau Bay_270

Waihau Bay

Whangaparaoa

35 Potaka

EC2

MAP: Only key roads and features are shown. The Wavetrack New Zealand Surf Guide has been designed to be used in conjunction with a dedicated road map. Map is not to scale.

269

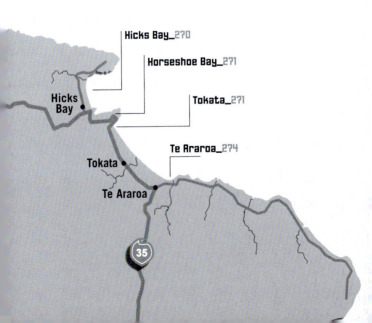

- Hicks Bay_270
- Horseshoe Bay_271
- Tokata_271
- Te Araroa_274

270 EC2

Waihau Bay

Find Waihau Bay 30km east of Te Kaha on HWY 35.

Bay consists of a surfable beach break. Usually waves are small and wind affected but it can get good. Reports of possible reef options around the northern point - go searching, the rewards may be high. Good learners wave. Uncrowded.

Hicks Bay

Take HWY 35 east from Whangaparaoa inland to Hicks Bay.

Beach break which always looks smaller from top of hill - when it looks like it's 2ft, it will be solid 4ft (1m). Find nice peaks in middle of bay, soft mellow wave. Great wind-protected spot, very sheltered from gusty westerlies. Great learners wave. Uncrowded.

EC2 271

Horseshoe Bay

From Hicks Bay take Onepoto Rd to Horseshoe Bay.

Left and right peaky beach break which handles small to moderate swells in the 3-5ft range (1-1.5m). Wind protected spot, extremely scenic. At the south end of the bay is a good right breaking under the cliffs - needs low tide and a northeast swell. Good spot for surfers of all levels.

Tokata

From Hicks Bay take HWY 35 over the hill to Tokata.

Long stretch of coast featuring left and right beach break peaks and a left point below the cliffs. Beach breaks get sucky and can produce hollow waves - expect backwash on the higher tides. Good for surfers of all levels.

EC RIVERMOUTH.PHOTO: KAROL STRANGE

274 EC2

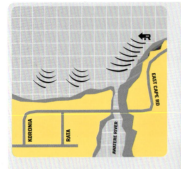

Te Araroa

From Hicks Bay take HWY 35 10km to Te Araroa.

Te Araroa features quality beach breaks with an abundance of right-handers. Find the best waves in front of the Marae.

South of the river mouth is a right point break. It is often disjointed and needs a larger swell than the beach to work. Expect solid walls, sections and good barrels grinding through to the shallow shorie. Advanced surfers only. If flat, take the road to the East Cape lighthouse - great views.

SURF2SURF.com
New Zealand Surf Reports • Surf Guide

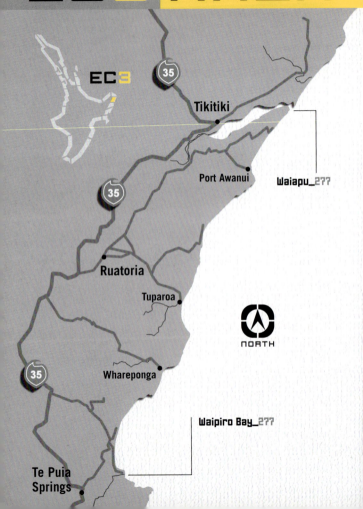

EC3 277

Waiapu

Take HWY 35 south from Te Araroa 18km to Tikitiki. Take a left on the Tikitiki/Rangitukia Rd, drive for 6km, take the first right to the mouth of the Waiapu River.

Quality peaky breaks around the river mouth. Moving banks depend on shingle movement. Break is exposed and can get wind-blown.

At the northern end, with the right swell, the point can produce long winding lefts. Three points can link up in a larger swell. Intermediate and expert level surfers.

Waipiro Bay

From Tokomaru Bay head north on HWY 35. Take a right at Te Puia to the coast. Difficult access, check with a local first.

Waipiro is sheltered from south and southeast winds, and features numerous reef/beach/point options. At the southern end find Creeks. Expect a tricky sucky takeoff and speed-wall barrel. Difficult access through the rocky foreshore - very good wave. Close by is Frog Rock, a short punchy right reef which breaks into rocks. Expect longer rides on big swells. The middle of the bay features reef beach combos. The north-end features left point options - go explore. Expert surfers.

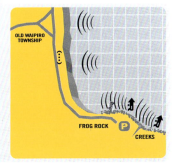

EC4 AREA

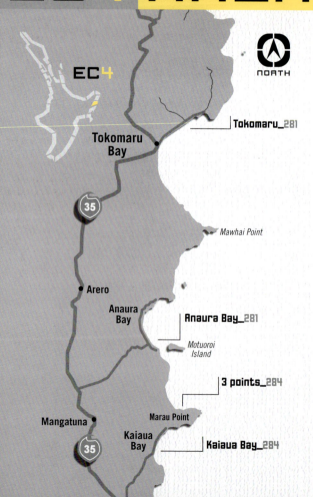

EC4 281

Tokomaru Bay

Take HWY 35 north 30km from Tolaga Bay. Drive along the beach side road past the pub and over the small bridge. Take the track right to the beach.

Right-hand reef break close to shore. Features a sucky takeoff zone with hollow sections on the inside. Needs a 2m plus southeast swell to work. Also, reasonable beach breaks in front of the township in the right conditions. Competent surfers.

Anaura Bay

Take HWY 35 north from Tolaga Bay to Mangatuna. Travel another 2km, then take a right to Anaura Bay.

Various beach breaks which work on north to northwest swells. Motuoroi Island offshore features reef breaks and picks up south swell. Isolated and uncrowded. Competent surfers.

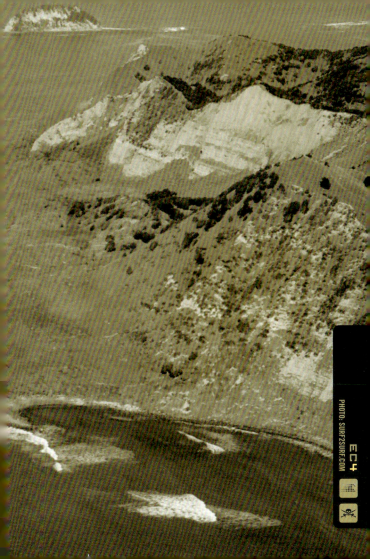

EC4 284

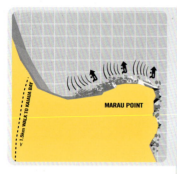

3 Points

Head north from Tolaga Bay. Take the Kaiaua Bay Rd 6km to the end. Walk northeast over the Marau headland (1.5km). Permission is required from the farmer. Difficult access and a very long walk.

Breaks consist of beach break stretching up Marau Beach, and you guessed it, three point breaks hugging the headland. Points need a macca southeast/east swell to fire. If it's 10ft at Wainui, the Points will be 3ft. Break is isolated and exposed. Expert level surfers.

Kaiaua Bay

Drive 3km north from Tolaga Bay. Take a right on the gravel road to Kaiaua Bay (5km to the coast).

Exposed and isolated beach break. Variable quality depending on banks. Can get good. Get a wave to yourself. Intermediate level surfers.

Gisborne

This hard core surfing city of 32,000 people located on the east coast of the North Island is famous for its high quality, stress-free waves.

Check out any weather map and there's a good chance you'll see isobars fresh from the east or south pushing three or four metre swells on to the rugged Gisborne coastline.

In spite of being off the beaten track (six and a half hours from Auckland, four from Napier) Gisborne has been a magnet for surfers since the sports birth. It's remoteness means a lack of crowds and a more relaxed attitude. It's not unusual to find yourself sharing a quality break with just a handful of others.

Promoting itself as First To See The Light, Gisborne is also known for the number of brilliant competition surfers it's spawned over the decades.

The reputation for quality surf is based on the coast's exposure to a 180 degree swell window. Factor in an assortment of reefs, beaches, points and bars which face different directions and you've got more options than you can surf. The region is also one of the sunniest parts of New Zealand, the Gisborne area has mild winters and hot, Mediterranean summers; an ideal climate to go with the perfect waves.

Gisborne offers everything a travelling surfer needs on a mission. You will find all you'll need in town including a range of accommodation, surf shops, board manufacturers and places to eat.

During the summer months cyclones descend from the Tropics and combine with the trade wind belt producing a classic squash. Gissy pumps.

A depression holds and churns to the east. A large fetch fires solid swells to Gisbornes many reefs, beaches and points.

A deep mega-low holds near the Chatham Islands. Massive fetch sends solid swells to Gisborne breaks.

GS 287

GS1	288
Tolaga Bay	289
Cooks Cove	289
Loisells	290
Whangara	290
GS2	292
Pouawa Beach	293
Makorori Reef	293
Nth Makorori	293
Makorori Centres	294
Makorori Point	294
Whales	296
Pines	296
Stock Route	296
Sponge Bay	298
The Cliff	298
The Island	299
GS3	302
Waikanae	303
Midway/Pipe	303
Waipaoa River	306
INFO	307

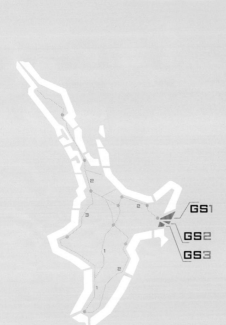

O'NEILL — AREA SEASONAL WETSUIT RECOMMENDATIONS

SUMMER
BOARDIES-
SPRINGY

AUTUMN
SPRING
SUIT

WINTER
4/3 STEAMER
+ BOOTIES

SPRING
SPRINGY-
STEAMER

GS1 AREA

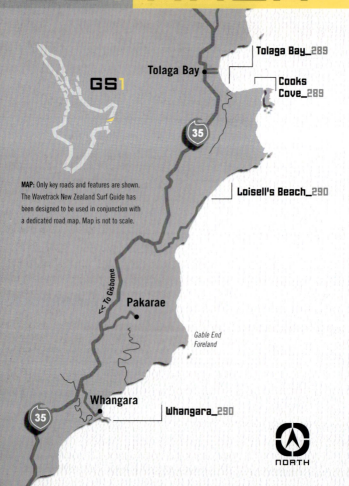

GS1 289

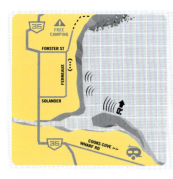

Tolaga Bay

Get to Tolaga Bay by taking HWY 35 north from Gisborne (50km).

Tolaga features an average beach breaks which closes-out most of the time. The river bar break located at the south end of the beach offers quality lefts and rights when conditions are favourable. Expect hollow takeoffs and workable walls. Shape and quality depends on sand location. Tolaga is one of the few bays around Gisborne that is surfable in a southerly wind. The southern end of the bay features an old wharf providing easy access on big days. Good for surfers of all levels.

Cooks Cove

Get to Cooks Cove by taking Wharf Rd to the Cooks Cove walkway car park. Breaks are a 25 min walk from the car park to the cove.

Quality breaks which handle solid swells. Chunky right reef break complete with heavy 'Island Style' takeoff and full-on stand up wall. Length of ride varies depending on angle and size of the swell. Find other reef breaks and outer bombies at Pourewa Island and surround Mitre Rocks. Isolated spot for expert level surfers only.

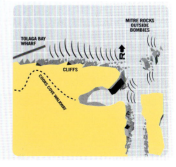

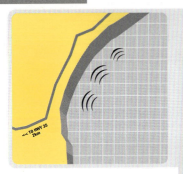

Loisell's Beach

Waihau Bay or Loisell's as it is commonly known is located 40km to the northeast of Gisborne on HWY 35. Access is by taking a 6km gravel road from the main highway to the coast.

Vast, open ocean bay featuring a range of beach breaks and rocky outcrops. Fun waves - beach picks up all swell angles. Good for surfers of all levels.

Whangara

Travel north from Gisborne to the Whangara turnoff. Take Pa Rd to the coast.

Whangara gained international notoriety as the location for the film 'Whale Rider'.

On the surf riding front, it offers variable beach breaks to the north and south and a left-hand reef break offshore on the south side of Whangara Island. The reef offers a long peeling wave with multiple sections. Good for surfers of all levels.

GS2 AREA

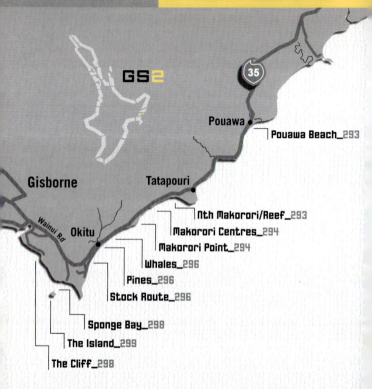

GS2

Pouawa
Pouawa Beach_293

Gisborne
Tatapouri
Nth Makorori/Reef_293
Makorori Centres_294
Wainui Rd
Okitu
Makorori Point_294
Whales_296
Pines_296
Stock Route_296

Sponge Bay_298
The Island_299
The Cliff_298

NORTH

Pouawa Beach

Take HWY 35 north from Gisborne for 13km.

Pouawa is a sheltered beach break featuring short, punchy lefts and rights. The bay is offshore northwest through to a very light southwester. It picks up a variety of swells from northeast to southeast. Great place to get some uncrowded waves. Good for surfers of all levels.

North Makorori

Get to Makorori from Gisborne on HWY 35 north.

Two breaks located at the northern end of Makorori - occasional fat left point break which is a good longboard wave when it's on. Also, a reef break/bombie off the tip of the Turihaua point which rarely gets good but has gained mythical status among local surfers when it fires. Can hold solid swell, gets big and mean when it's huge. The inside is good for learners, outsides intermediate to expert surfers only.

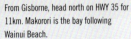

Makorori Point / Centres

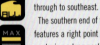

From Gisborne, head north on HWY 35 for 11km. Makorori is the bay following Wainui Beach.

Makorori features a variety of surf breaks. Complex reef/sand systems offer plenty of break options and like most Gisborne surf breaks Makorori features a wide swell window spanning northeast through to southeast.

The southern end of the bay features a right point break producing a long peeling wave over reef. A fat wave, the point requires continuous cutbacks to stay in the pocket. It's a fun spot and is especially suited to longboarding when conditions are small. When the swell picks up from the northeast the point can liven up providing a sucky takeoff followed by a firing first wall section which bends around towards you. When it's real big, Makorori loses all of its fat, lazy characteristics and can be a mean proposition.

Further north up the beach you'll spot Centre Break, Red Bus and Creeks. All feature shifty peaky lefts and rights

A 'fat' wave, the point requires continuous cutbacks to stay in the pocket. It's a fun spot, and especially suited to longboarding when conditions are small.

breaking over sand and reef. Many of the breaks are tricky to access, especially at low tide due to the pointed rocks and jagged reef.

After a long surf, head north to Tatapouri for a cold-one at the Tatapouri Hotel. Good for surfers of all levels.

Wainui - Stock Route, Pines, Whales

From Gisborne, take Wainui Rd (HWY 35) 4.5km to the coast. Find parking areas off Oneroa Rd (Stock Route), Wairere Rd and at the Lysnar Reserve for Pines.

Long beach stretches from Tuaheni Point to the Makorori Headland. Within this stretch are a range of high-quality beachies breaking over a mixture of reef and sand.

Find Stock Route by taking the first right off HWY 35. It got its name from the cattle drovers who used the beach to move stock before roads were built.

Stock Route is home to excellent beach break peaks which rival those found in Mexico or France. Expect sucky takeoffs and fast, pitching barrels. The bigger it gets, the heavier the wave. Double-ups produce 'Indo-like' square pits. High-performance wave, great for fine-tuning your tube riding skills. Can be a tough paddle when big. Holds up to 8ft (2.4m) waves.

Find more variable lefts and rights in front of the Wainui School. Further up the beach is Pines near the mouth of the stream. Here you'll find parking areas above and behind the surf club. The wave

Expect sucky takeoffs and fast, pitching barrels. The bigger it gets the heavier the wave. Double-ups produce gnarly square pits.

is similar to Stock Route, producing sucky, hollow waves. Find more peaks at Whales located at the north end of Wainui. Whales is near the site of a Sperm Whale Grave. Optimum size for Wainui breaks is 3-6ft (1-2.5m). All swell angles produce fast top to bottom barrels. Sea breezes can be strong in summer. Good for surfers of all levels.

GS2
THE ISLAND.PHOTO: SURF2SURF.COM

GS3 AREA

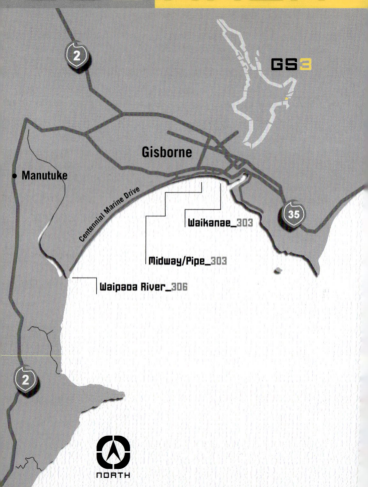

WAINUI BEACH. PHOTO: CORY SCOTT

298 GS2

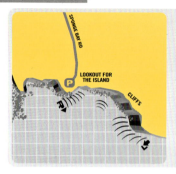

Sponge Bay

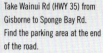

Take Wainui Rd (HWY 35) from Gisborne to Sponge Bay Rd. Find the parking area at the end of the road.

Variety of breaks to choose from. All need a south swell to work.

Find a left reef break at the eastern end of the bay - swell bends from various angles forming a peak and left-hander. In the middle of the bay is a beachie breaking over a sand/reef combo. The small point below the parking lot features a short right reef. All spots offshore northwest/north. Good spot for learners.

The Cliff

From the main street of Gisborne, take the Esplanade to Kaiti Beach Rd. Drive past the Yacht Club to the end of the road.

Area features a left-hand reef break which needs a large south/southeast swell to work. Holds an 8ft (2.4m) wave. Competent surfers when big.

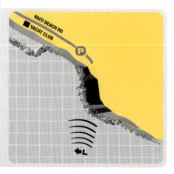

The Island

Take Wainui Rd (HWY 35) from Gisborne to Sponge Bay Rd. Parking is located at the end of the road. There is no view of the break from the parking area so always best to check from Kaiti Hill before driving out for a surf (see the Cliff for directions).

Access the Island by paddling, or walking when the tide is low. Boat is your best option to get the most out of an island session.

The crown jewel of the Gisborne Coast - The Island features a legendary, grinding left reef break with inside and outside sections.

The outside peak features the 'Bowl', a heavy, intense left which pitches, sucks-up and fires through to the inside. The inside section consists of a hyper-speed left-hand barrel which breaks along the side of the Island over shallow reef. Expect long hollow grinding barrels when conditions are on.

Check out Outside Island - an exposed offshore reef producing a juicy right in larger swells 4ft-huge (1.2m - huge.)

The Inside section consists of a hyper-speed left-hand barrel which breaks along the side of the Island over shallow reef. Expect long hollow grinding barrels when conditions are on.

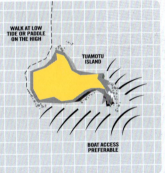

Optimum swell for the Island is south through southeast. Best with north or east offshore winds. Expert level surfers - serious paddle, serious wave.

GS3 303

Waikanae Beach

From the Main Street of Gisborne turn at Clock Tower and head to the beach.

Break consists of a mellow beach break with constantly changing banks. Soft long walls closes out over 4ft (1.5m). Semi offshore on north, northeast sea breezes. Great learners wave. Caution: logs and debris often wash up after a storm.

Midway / Pipe

Head west from Waikanae to Midway. Break located 500m to the west of the Surf Club.

Pipe is a quality beach break peak which breaks left and right. The right is longer and Pipe is legendary for its hollow barrels. Expect a sucky takeoff with a speedy tube section and short workable wall peeling into a rip channel. Break responds best to the south swell angle and holds a solid 8ft (2.4m) wave. Optimum wave size 3-6ft (1-1.8m). Heavy crowds, competent surfers.

PIPE; PHOTO: PAUL KENNEDY

306 GS3

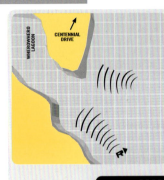

Waipaoa River Mouth

From Waikanae, take Centennial Drive south to the end. Walk to the mouth of the river.

Fickle spot featuring left and right river bar peaks. High volume river creates constantly moving sand and shingle banks. Spot is legendary for producing big A-frames on outside banks when all the elements come together. Tricky paddle when big. Strong currents. Advanced surfers only.

659 Upper Wainui Road - Wainui Beach - P.O. Box 2205 - Gisborne - New Zealand
Email: aardee@clear.net.nz - Ph: 0064 6 867 1684 - Fax: 0064 6 867 9276 - Mob: 0064 0274 453 955

The BOARDROOM is a factory and no nonsense
retail outlet located in Wainui Gisborne New Zealand,
making custom and off the shelf surfboards,
incorporating Lost, Pipedream, Dick Brewer, Aardee and STD

Check out website.. http://www.surfboards.net.nz

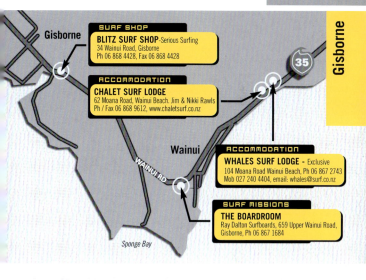

GISBORNE

Action Surf Shop
Custom Surfboards
279 Gladstone Road, Gisborne
Ph 06 868 9591, Fax 06 868 3364

Blitz Surf Shop - Serious Surfing
34 Wainui Road, Gisborne
Ph 06 868 4428, Fax 06 868 4428

Chalet Surf Lodge
62 Moana Road, Wainui Beach
Gisborne. Jim & Nikki Rawls
Ph / Fax 06 868 9612
email: chaletsurf@xtra.co.nz
www.chaletsurf.co.nz

Gisborne Surfboard Rentals
Long / Short Term
Ph 021 154 6656

Mason Surfboards
Custom Surfboards, Gisborne
Ph 06 867 7192

New Wave Surfboards
189 Awapuni Road, Gisborne
Ph 06 867 1439

Surfing With Frank
Surf Coach, Gisborne
Ph/Fax 06 867 0823
email: coach.russel @clear.net.nz

The Boardroom
Ray Dalton Surfboards
659 Upper Wainui Road, Gisborne
Ph 06 867 1684, Mob 0274 453 955
www.surfboards.net.nz

Wainui Beach Motel
34 Wairere Road, Wainui Beach
Gisborne, Ph 06 868 5882
Fax 06 868 8482
email: info@wainuibeach.co.nz
www.wainuibeach.co.nz

Whales Surf Lodge
Exclusive Beachside B & B
104 Moana Road Wainui Beach
P O Box 2047 Gisborne
Ph 06 867 2743
Fax 06 867 3743
027 240 4404
email: whales@surf.co.nz

SURF2SURF.com

Mahia

A vast triangular tableland joined to the mainland by a few kilometres of sand dunes and tidal marshland, the Mahia Peninsula comes close to being an island. If you could design the perfect geographic setup for a surf area it would closely resemble the Mahia Peninsula.

Located an hour south of Gisborne this area can be every surfer's dream – and nightmare! There's a dozen or so well known breaks that produce everything from small and glassy through to huge and horrible. Keep a close eye on the weather maps and you'll know which side of the triangle to head for. Be prepared to drive, there is nearly always a break somewhere offering good clean waves.

The exposed position of the peninsula means it gets its fair share of storms, especially from the south. Some breaks, such as Rolling Stones and Point Annihilation can easily hold waves in the 10ft range.

Mahia's weather is unpredictable and can change suddenly. Winters can be very cold so take adequate warm clothing and thick rubber.

Some of the breaks we have included in this guide require permission to access. Respecting this protocol will reduce tension in the line-up and ensure that visiting surfers will always enjoy a warm welcome.

The area features a few motels, B&B's, farmstays and shops. The area offers a unique surfing and travel experience.

A depression descends from the north combining with the trade wind belt producing a classic squash. Mahia's northern exposed breaks crank.

A depression holds and churns to the east. A large fetch fires solid swells to Mahia's many reefs, beaches and points.

Massive low pressure system pours swell into Mahia and Gisborne. Mahia's southern points light-up. Stones will be heavy with 15/20 wave sets - know your duck dives.

MA1	311
Blacks Reef	314
Blacks Cliffs	314
Rolling Stones	315
Point Annihilation	315
Tracks	318
Opoutama Beach	318
Mahia Reef	319
Last Chance	319
Happy Jacks	320
Mahanga Point	320
Oraka Beach	322
Old Mans	322
The Spit	323
Tuehuru Reefs	323
Boat Harbour	326
Auroa Point	326
Southeast Coast	328
INFO	328

MA1

O'NEILL — AREA SEASONAL WETSUIT RECOMMENDATIONS

SUMMER
BOARDIES-
SPRINGY

AUTUMN
SPRING
SUIT

WINTER
4/3 STEAMER
+ BOOTIES

SPRING
SPRINGY-
STEAMER

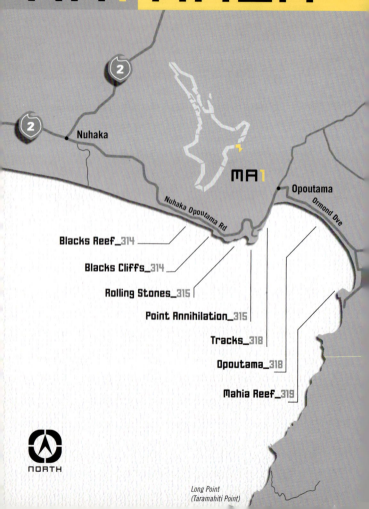

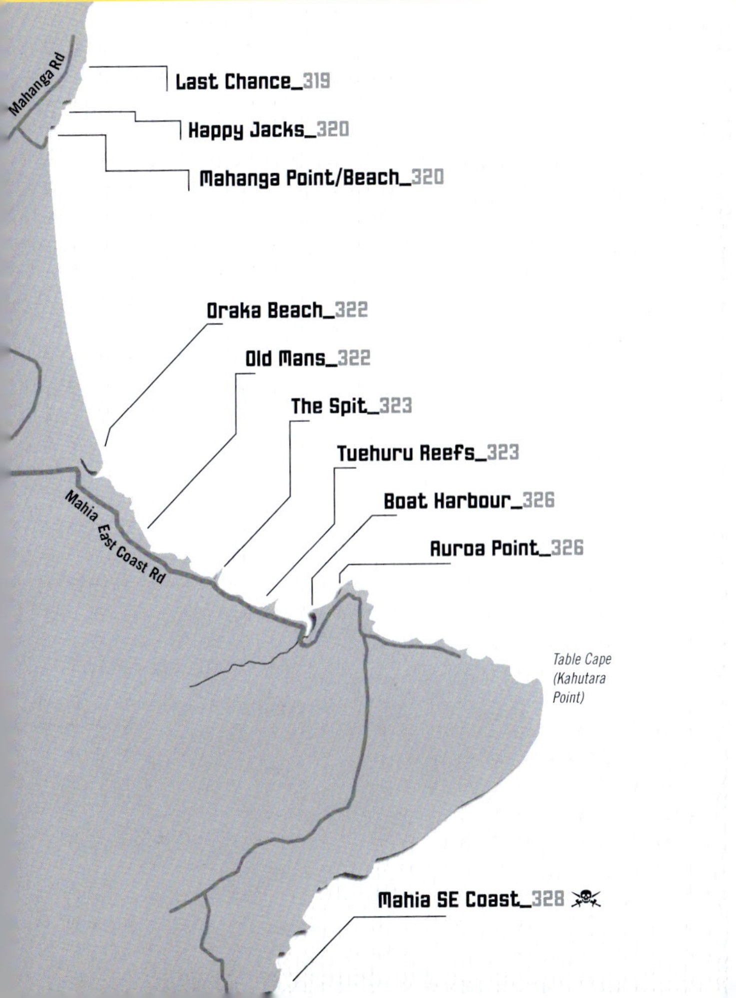

311

- **Last Chance**_319
- **Happy Jacks**_320
- **Mahanga Point/Beach**_320
- **Oraka Beach**_322
- **Old Mans**_322
- **The Spit**_323
- **Tuehuru Reefs**_323
- **Boat Harbour**_326
- **Auroa Point**_326

Mahanga Rd

Mahia East Coast Rd

Table Cape (Kahutara Point)

Mahia SE Coast_328 ☠

314 MA1

Blacks

Find Blacks 6.5km east of the Nuhaka turnoff. Look for two car parks as you reach the coast. The first has succumbed to erosion.

Break consists of a quality peak/reef break. Blacks is a swell magnet. South swells hit the reef at a perfect angle producing long hollow rights. It produces lefts during east/southeast swell angles. Rights are usually better quality. A mellow takeoff is followed by a long wrapping workable wall. Look for the barrel on the inside. Optimum wave size 3-6ft (1-2.5m). Easy paddle. Break can get crowded. Respect the locals - don't drop in. Good for surfers of all levels.

Blacks Cliffs

Take Nuhaka Opoutama Rd to the Blacks parking area.

Find various left and right peaks east of Blacks. The eastern end features a left which breaks outside the rocks on the point. Find long mellow walls which re-form and peel to the inside. Also find various peaks which peel off rocky outcrops - get a wave to yourself. Optimum wave size 3-6ft (1-2.5m). Competent surfers.

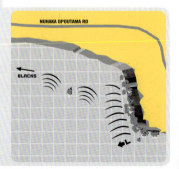

MA1 315

Rolling Stones

Head east from Nuhaka past Blacks. Turn right after the railway bridge to Waikokopu. Parking is near the green shed. From here, walk over the hill to the break.

Here you'll find a big gnarly right-hand reef/wave magnet. Expect an intense takeoff as the fast moving swells hit the reef and jack. Big walls fire off down the line. Look for stand up barrels in solid swells. Don't freak when duck diving, you'll hear stones moving on the bottom during solid swells. Difficult paddle due to gnarly shorey surging over rocks. Needs a solid swell 5-6ft to work. Handles 6-8ft (2-3m). Expert level surfers only. No dogs on the private land - pick up your rubbish.

Point Annihilation

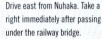

Drive east from Nuhaka. Take a right immediately after passing under the railway bridge.

Break features a grunty right-hand point. Be ready for a heavy takeoff followed by a fast section and big bowl. Find good barrels as it wraps and bowls into the small bay. Handles a solid swell. Optimum wave size 4-6ft (1-2.5m). Works best with large/long-pulse south swells. Easy paddle out, can get crowded. Recommended for intermediate to expert level surfers. Mahia Law: Don't drop in, respect the locals and surf in harmony.

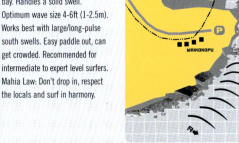

318 MA1

Tracks

Head north of Point Annihilation. Check the wave from the lookout car park off Nuhaka Opoutama Rd. To access the break you can either walk from Point Annihilation or paddle out from Opoutama Beach (long paddle).

Tracks consists of a right-hand point break which wraps and peels along a boulder bottomed point. The break is wind and swell sheltered. To work it needs a large south or southeast swell - look for Point Annihilation to be 6-8ft plus, and Tracks will have good waves. Expect a mellow takeoff and long wrapping, workable walls featuring various sections Fun wave. Good for surfers of all levels.

Opoutama

Take Nuhaka Opoutama Rd east from Nuhaka, turn right at Opoutama. Take Ormond Drive to the beach.

Long beach stretches southeast from Tracks. Here you'll find a variable beach break with constantly changing banks. A great learners wave, Opoutama features mellow left and right peaks which are best in small swells. Good longboard wave. Good for surfers of all levels. Uncrowded.

Mahia Reef

From Opoutama take Ormond Rd east to Moana Dr, past the camp ground to Newcastle Street and the point.

Area features a left-hand reef break and an occasional right, which only works during large south or southwest swells. Break rarely gets good, but is a good indicator for surfers living around the Mahia Beach area. If there's waves here, Blacks will be pumping. Te Hoe reef is another indicator located to the south at Whakatakahe Head.

Last Chance

From Opoutama, head out to Mahanga Beach. Take a left on Mahanga Rd (The Quarters). Drive until you see the lake on the right. Note: permission required to access break. Taking seafood from the area is prohibited.

Down the hill you will find a left-hand boulder point break. A swell magnet, it produces quality, fast left-handers. Expect a sucky takeoff and long high-performance sections. Likes clean long-lined swells. Northeast swells create longer walls. Easy paddle out. Optimum wave size 3-6ft (1-2.5m). Competent surfers only.

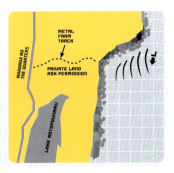

320 MA1

Happy Jacks

From Opoutama take Mahanga Rd north to Mahanga Beach. Access the breaks by paddling around the point from Mahanga.

Small bay features a range of peaks which break off points and a small island. Bay picks up northeast through east swells - can produce good waves. Difficult access, long paddle. Optimum 3-5ft (1-1.2m). Competent surfers. Ask before crossing private land.

Mahanga Beach/Point

From Opoutama take Mahanga Rd north to Mahanga Beach.

Area features a variable beach break and a good left point located at the northern end. Find a range of left and right peaks at the beach with constantly changing banks.

At the northern end of the beach find a left point setup. Breaking over a combination of boulders and sand, it can produce long lefts which peel into the beach.

Fun, mellow wave. Optimum wave size 2-4ft (.5-1m). Uncrowded. Good for surfers of all levels.

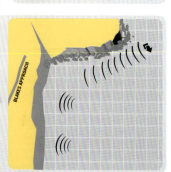

322 MA1

Mahanga/Oraka Beach

Take Mahia East Coast Rd east from Opoutama Beach. Look for the sign to Oraka Beach on the left side before you head up the hill to Mahia.

Here you'll find a range of variable beach breaks producing left and right peaks near the estuary mouth. Banks are constantly shifting due to estuary water flow and flooding. Optimum size 3-4ft (1-1.2m). Good for surfers of all levels.

Old Mans

Find Old Mans by driving over the hill from Oraka Beach. Find the breaks under the cliffs as you come down the hill prior to Mahia.

Area offers a range of mellow left and right peaks breaking over various reefs and rock fingers. Good mal and learners wave. No crowds - good for surfers of all levels.

MA1 323

The Spit

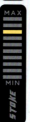

Take Mahia East Coast Rd southeast from Mahia Township. As you head down the hill, you'll have no problems spotting the Spit (especially at low tide).

One of Mahia's classic breaks. A gnarly left and right breaks from a massive reef spit protruding into the ocean. More known for its lefts than rights, the spit is an intense wave especially in sizable swells. Be ready for a pitching takeoff followed by a long, hollow wall which bends towards you. On the lefts, as you fire off down the line, the wave will hit a rock ledge and nearly suck dry. Optimum 4-8ft (1.5-3m). Intense tricky line up. Experts only.

Tuehuru Reefs

Head 200m to 1km southeast from the Spit.

Find various reef breaks producing a range of left and right peaks. Various rocky outcrops and reef fingers produce good waves depending on tides. Best surfed 3-4ft (1-1.2m). Good for surfers of all levels. Uncrowded.

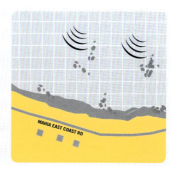

Boat Harbour

From Mahia, take Mahia East Coast Rd past the Spit to Boat Harbour.

Area features an extreme right-hander breaking over a shallow reef. Expect a sucky, vertical takeoff. The bottom will drop out from under you. Pull in to the fat hollow tube. Often barrel will double-up in meaty swells. Easy paddle out from rocks to outside line up. Optimum wave size 3-6ft (1-2.5m). Experts only.

Auroa Point

Head east from Boat Harbour. Look for a large white house on the right side of the road.

Point features a big sucky right-hander breaking off the reef and rocky out crops. Fickle spot, can produce massive ledging barrels and intense speed walls. Gnarly break. Optimum wave size 4-7ft (1-2m). Experts only.

Find various other breaks at Diners Beach on the eastern side of the Mahia Peninsula. Get there by taking Mahia East Coast Rd south. Expect a very long drive.

Coast offers a myriad of reefs and beaches. Very isolated, there are gems to be discovered here.

328 MA1

Mahia SE Coast

Take Mahia East Coast Rd south on the Mahia Peninsula. Long winding metal roads lead to various beaches and bays. Easy to lose hope and turn around. Very easy to get lost.

The southeastern coast of the Mahia Peninsula features 22km of coastline covered with an endless array of breach breaks, reefs and points. This area is very isolated and access is difficult. There are some gems hidden here just waiting to be surfed, finding them with waves is no problem as the coast nearly always has swell. Breaks are exposed to onshore winds. Isolated and uncrowded. Experienced surfers only.

INFO

The Quarters - Accommodation
- Complementary crayfish (when in season) corn bread & ground coffee
R.D. 8 Nuhaka, Hawkes Bay
Ph 06 837 5751 Fax 06 837 5721
www.quarters.co.nz
Email: m.rough@xtra.co.nz

Sunset Point Sports Bar & Bistro
Cnr Newcastle & Ratau Sts, Mahia Beach, Mahia
Ph 06-837 5071

Surf Reports - Nationwide - Online
www.surf2surf.com

Surf Reports - Phone
Wavetrack 0900 99 777 (Calls 99c/min)
Groms ask your parents first

LAST CHANCE. PHOTO: SURF2SURF.COM

MA1

Hawkes Bay

Welcome to the Hawkes Bay. This area comprises of Wairoa, going south through Napier and continuing to Waimarama located on the southern east coast.

This region features a diverse range of waves and is perhaps one of the most underrated surfing destinations in the country. This could be due to its relative isolation along with the fact that it is flanked by legendary surf destinations such as Mahia and the Wairarapa.

Located 154km southeast of Taupo on the North Island's East Coast, the Hawkes Bay is quite a trek from New Zealand's larger centres but it is most certainly worth a visit as the region features a thriving wine industry, beautiful rolling countryside and the charming coastal city of Napier.

While Napier doesn't boast the crown-jewel surf breaks of the east coast, a short drive will have you surfing some quality breaks which are known to produce perfect and powerful waves on occasion. The area's fickle river bars offer a fascinating option if you manage to get wind, swell and tide conditions perfect. Find these breaks working and you will experience very hollow, powerful waves.

Continuing south to Waimarama is an amazing and most worthwhile trip in itself as the journey will have you travelling through classic New Zealand rural countryside. When you reach the ocean you'll discover a rugged, swell-exposed coast which will provide you with a larger, better quality and more consistent wave than the areas around Napier City.

A depression descends from the north combining with the trade wind belt producing a classic squash. HB's northeast exposed reefs and river bars pump.

A depression holds and churns to the east. A large fetch fires solid swells to the Hawkes Bay's exposed breaks.

Massive low pressure system pours swell into Ocean Beach and Waimarama. Big swells wrap into breaks north of Napier City.

HB1	333
Wairoa	334
Waihua	334
Mohaka	335
Waikari	335
Aropaoanui	338
Waipatiki	338
Stingray Bay	339
Tangoio Beach	339
HB2	340
The Gap	341
Westshore	341
City Reef	341
Harding Rd	342
Awatoto	342
Haumoana	343
Te Awanga	343
HB3	346
Ocean Beach	347
Waimarama	348
Cray Bay	348
INFO	349

O'NEILL — AREA SEASONAL WETSUIT RECOMMENDATIONS

SUMMER
BOARDIES-
SPRINGY

AUTUMN
SPRING
SUIT

WINTER
4/3 STEAMER
+ BOOTIES

SPRING
SPRINGY-
STEAMER

HB1 AREA

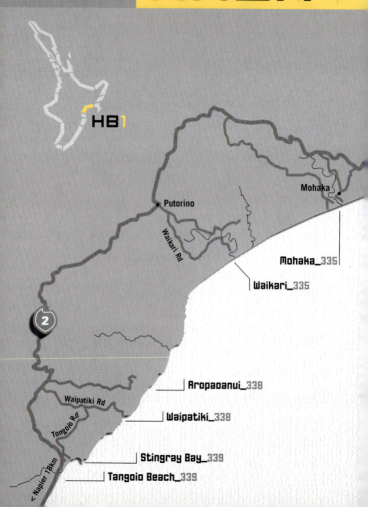

Mohaka

Putorino

Waikari Rd

Mohaka_335
Waikari_335

Aropaoanui_338
Waipatiki Rd
Waipatiki_338
Tongoio Rd
Stingray Bay_339
< Napier 18km
Tangoio Beach_339

333

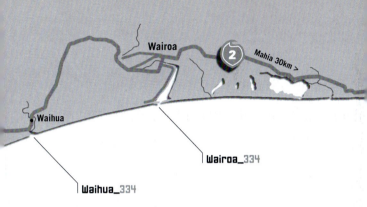

Waihua_334

Wairoa_334

334 HB1

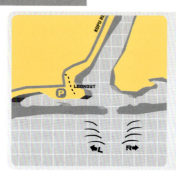

Wairoa River Mouth

From Mahia and Nuhaka take HWY 2 west to Wairoa. When you reach the round-a-bout, take a left down the main street. Follow the road and the river to the coast. As you approach the river mouth, check the surf at the lookout.

Break consists of a heavy river bar break producing a range of left and right peaks. Shingle banks are very shifty, river has massive water flow during floods which changes the dynamics. When it's on expect dredging, shallow barrels and murky water. Best on an incoming tide and offshores. Optimum 3-6ft (1-2.5m). Heavy local scene. Surf with respect and don't leave valuables in your car.

Waihua

Find Waihua 16km southwest of Wairoa off HWY 2.

Area features a variable beach and bar break. Banks are constantly on the move, but can produce quality waves on occasion. Optimum 3-5ft (1-1.5m) on an incoming tide. Uncrowded. Good for surfers of all levels.

HB1 335

Mohaka River Mouth

Head north from Napier on HWY 2. Take the road to East Beach. Drive past the small settlement and Marae. You'll pass the quarry - a good lookout/overview of the bars.

Mohaka offers a river bar break with constantly moving banks. Floods can change bar locations overnight. Find peaky left and right wedges either side of the river depending on bar location and swell angle. Expect a heavy, grinding wave breaking over shallow shingle. Muddy, murky water. Isolated spot. Uncrowded. Optimum wave size 3-5ft (1-2m). Picks up swell ranging from south through east. Serious currents. Competent surfers only.

Waikari

Drive north from Napier. Take a right at Putorino. Two options, take Waikari Rd to the southwest side of the river. From here it's a 2km hike to the mouth. Alternatively, take the first left off Waikari to the northeast side. Both roads are a bugger of a long winding metal road drive.

Area features a river bar break. River is high-volume, so floods change bar layout and banks constantly. Best a few days after a flood when flow settles. Also find reef options to the southwest. Very isolated and uncrowded. Cool camping and hike. Good for competent surfers.

HB1 STINGRAY BAY. PHOTO: ROB MACDONALD

338 HB1

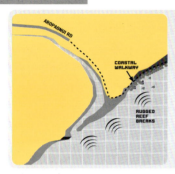

Aropaoanui

Head north from Napier on HWY 2. Turn right on Aropaoanui Rd. Long winding drive down to the river mouth and car park.

River bar break featuring a range of variable left and right peaks. Constantly shifty banks. The north end features a range of reef options. Find good lefts here during east swells. Optimum size 3-5ft (1-1.5m). Isolated and uncrowded. Good for surfers of all levels.

Waipatiki Beach

Take HWY 2 north from Napier. Take Waipatiki Rd to the coast. Long winding road down hill to beach. Don't be tempted to drive over the sand - you'll get stuck.

Bay features good left and right beach break waves. Secluded, it is a good place to get a wave to yourself. At the north and south ends find a range of reef breaks with good lefts at the north end. Fickle break as it shuts down on larger swells. Optimum 2-5ft (.5-1.5m). Uncrowded and isolated. Good for surfers of all levels.

HB1 339

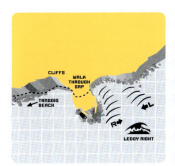

Stingray Bay

Head north from Napier on HWY 2. Take a right at the Tangoio turnoff. Take another right to Tangoio beach. From here, take the track east below the cliffs to Stingray Bay. Arduous hike of 20 minutes +.

Bay features a quality right-hand reef break at the west end and a good left at the eastern end.

The jewel is the right. Expect a jacking ledge takeoff followed by a quick bowl/wall. High-performance wave, great for lip bashes, cutties and barrels. Bowl especially likes northeast swells. Point will also line-up perfectly with southeast and east swells. Optimum size 3-6ft (1-2.5m). Gets crowded. Isolated. Intermediate to expert level surfers.

Tangoio Beach

Take HWY 2 north from Napier. Take a right at the Tangoio turnoff. Take another right to the beach. Parking is in front of the batches.

Area features a variable beach break producing a range of short punchy peaks. Left and rights break over shallow shingle. Use caution entering and exiting surf, the shorebreak can be head high and gnarly. Optimum wave size 4-6ft (1.5-2.5m). Break is sheltered during northerly winds. Good for competent surfers.

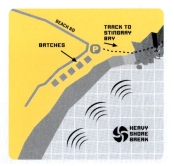

HB2 AREA

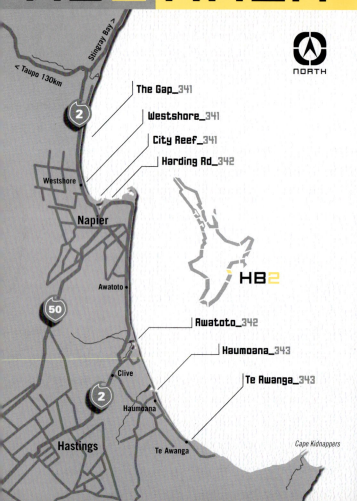

HB2 341

Westshore/Gap

Head north of Napier on HWY 2. Take a right to Westshore and the Surf Club car park.

Area from Westshore north to the gap in the houses. Find a long sweeping beach break with a steep profile. Expect long walled waves with a heavy shorebreak. Prone to stong undertow and rips. Uncrowded waves.

City Reef

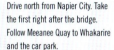

Drive north from Napier City. Take the first right after the bridge. Follow Meeanee Quay to Whakarire and the car park.

Located at the southern end of Westshore beach is a reef break producing a peak with good left and rights. The lefts tend to peel better while the rights are a little fatter. Mellow, fun wave with a faster inside section and pocket especially on the lower tides. Break picks up swell northeast through large southeast. Optimum wave size 3-5ft (1-2m). Tends to close-out when bigger. Gets crowded. Paddle out without getting your hair wet. Good for surfers of all levels.

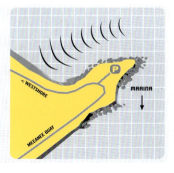

342 HB2

Harding Rd

From HWY and Napier City Centre, take Hyderabad Rd/Bridge St to Hardinge Rd. Hardinge Rd and the break are located west of the Port of Nelson.

 Break consists of an inconsistent right-hand point. Extensions to the Port over the years have effectively blocked swell from reaching this perfect point set up. Break can produce a classic long walled wave during a mega east/southeast swell. Rarely gets bigger than knee high. There are stories from the 60's of classic days of surf and amazing rides. Cars would be used to shuttle surfers back to the takeoff zone after very long rides. Good for surfers of all levels.

Awatoto

Head south from Napier on HWY 2. You'll see the fertiliser works and industrial area. Pull off to the left and drive (4WD) or walk to the river mouth from here.

 Quality river bar break which produces grunty double-up barrels. Needs a strict set of conditions to produce quality, can be perfect. Best with offshore winds, east/southeast swells and an incoming tide. Council control water flow from the river by digging and closing the river mouth. Banks constantly change with flooding. Optimum wave size 3-5ft (1-2.5m). Intermediate to experts only.

HB2 343

Haumoana/Tukituki

Take HWY 2 south from Napier to Clive. Take a left at the Haumoana/Te Awanga turnoff. Head to Haumoana and the mouth of the Tukituki River.

Grunty right-hand river bar break. Breaks in extremely shallow water over gravel. Screaming currents from the river create sucky double-ups and square barrels. Lots of water moving. The bigger it gets, the heavier it breaks. Best on incoming tide with offshores and a swell from the east or southeast. Optimum wave size 4-6ft (1-2.5m). Needs perfect conditions to work. Intermediate to experts only.

Te Awanga

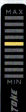

Head southeast from Haumoana towards Cape Kidnappers. Travel through the village and continue to the point and motor camp.

Area features a mellow, fun right-hand point break. A Malibu California setup, it is an excellent longboard wave on its day. Waves are soft and mellow with wrapping southeast swells. Break gets a little gruntier during northeast/east swells. Great wave for toes on the nose. Optimum wave size 3-6ft (1-2.5m). Closes-out across bay during maxed-out swells. Gets crowded. Good for surfers of all levels.

AWATOTO. PHOTO: ROB MACDONALD

HB3 AREA

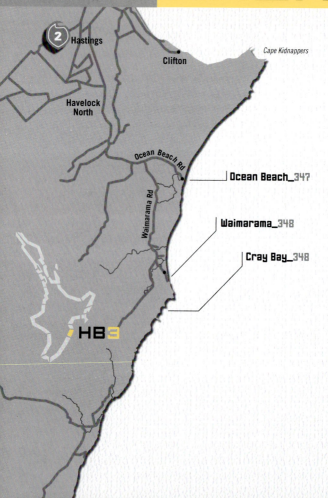

HB3 347

Spot X

Big left and right-hand reef break. Produces massive barrels on solid swells. Ask a friendly local.

Ocean Beach

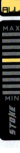

Get to Ocean Beach by travelling southeast from Havelock North. Take the long, winding road to the beach.

Area features a long beach stretching north and south. Find variable left and right peaks breaking on inner and outer bars. Grunty wave complete with sand/boil-ups. Generally breaks over sand, but also rock/sand combo banks. Heavy wave on a solid swell. Hot local scene. Difficult paddle out on sizey days. Isolated beach. Optimum size 3-6ft (1-2.5m). Good for surfers of all levels.

348 HB3

Waimarama Beach

From Ocean Beach, head back to Waimarama Rd - drive south to the township. Parking is located at the southern end of the beach.

Here you'll find a variable beach break breaking over sand and rock. The south point features a range of peaks which break out from the car park. Often good rights peel through to the beach. North at the boat ramp you'll find a couple of reef breaks producing rights and good lefts. Paddle out via the channel. Hot local crew. Optimum 3-6ft (1-2.5m). Break picks up all swell angles. Head to the southern end for clean waves during southwest winds. Good for surfers of all levels.

Cray Bay

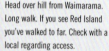

Head over hill from Waimarama. Long walk. If you see Red Island you've walked to far. Check with a local regarding access.

Area features a range of quality left and right reef breaks plus a steep profile beach break. Paua Point features a freight train left which can suck dry. The 100m wide reef also features a right-hander. Surf the left on a mid-high tide. At Cray Bay you'll find a big jacking takeoff followed by a hollow, shallow ledge and bowling section. Look for clean barrels on the inside. Best mid to high tides. Optimum 4-6ft (1-2.5m). Handles 6-8ft (2-3m). Crowded takeoff zone. Expert level surfers only, gets heavy when big.

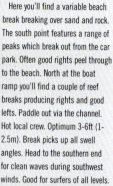

HAWKES BAY

Beach Culture Ltd
111 Heretaunga Street, Hastings
Ph 06 878 1219, Fax 06 878 1219

Boardzone Surf Co
Surfboards/Accessories/Clothing
176 Hastings Street, Napier
Ph 06 835 7363
341 Heretaunga St West, Hastings
Ph 06 876 0171

Notionlab
Advertising, Marketing, Book Design, New Media
Designers of the Wavetrack New Zealand Surfing
Guide - www.notionlab.co.nz

Surf 2 Earth
243 Gloucester Street, Taradale, Napier
Ph 06 844 7065

Surf Reports - Nationwide
www.surf2surf.com

Surf Reports - Phone
Surfline 0900 47 873 (Calls $1.20/min)
Groms ask your parents first

Vortex Surf
157 Emerson Street, Napier
Ph 06 835 6998

Wairarapa

Getting to the Wairarapa coast takes approximately three hours from New Zealand's capital Wellington. The coast is rugged and exposed featuring 200km of complex reefs, beaches and river bars all perfectly positioned to pluck any swell from east through to south. A wave magnet for deep southern ocean swells the area is known for producing large, powerful waves.

We've broken the region down into two areas. To the north find Castlepoint, and to the south find White Rock and Tora. In between is 50km of isolated reefs, beaches and points just waiting to be explored and surfed. The region is large and access is tricky. Much of the coast offers no road access.

White Rock is a classic New Zealand surf destination. Get there by driving south from Martinborough or alternatively take a 4WD adventure from Cape Palliser. Driving access has been closed recently - a controversial decision. To enter you will need to purchase a key to the gate. Walking access is open to the public. The area offers a range of quality reef and point breaks which can hold seriously large waves. Check out the deer stalkers hut. During the 70's the hut was the only accommodation in the area and was located 150m from the shore. Massive storms demolished the shoreline banks and came close to taking the hut with it. The hut was subsequently moved to higher ground.

Heading north you'll find Tora, Riversdale and Castlepoint. These areas also offer a range of quality breaks for the travelling surfer.

A depression descends from the north combining with the trade wind belt producing a classic squash.

A depression holds and spins to the east. A massive fetch pumps solid swells to the exposed Wairarapa coast.

A deep southern ocean system fires swell north. Huge swells wrap into Wairarapa's famous reefs and point breaks.

WR1	353
Schnappes	354
The Desert	354
Seconds	355
The Spit	358
White Rock Point	359
Dolphin Bay	359
Gnarlies	360
God Squad	360
Shipwrecks	361
Toilet Bowls	361
Tora Tora	364
Tora Stream	364
Tora Pit	365
Stony Bay	365
WR2	368
Slipperies	369
Castle Point Beach	369
The Gap	370
Xmas Bay	370
Riversdale Beach	371
Uruti Point	371

O'NEILL AREA SEASONAL WETSUIT RECOMMENDATIONS

SUMMER
BOARDIES-
SPRINGY

AUTUMN
SPRINGY-
STEAMER

WINTER
4/3 STEAMER
+ BOOTIES

SPRING
SPRINGY-
STEAMER

WR1 AREA

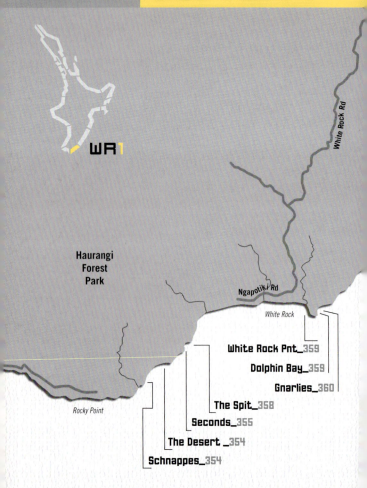

353

- Stony Bay_365
- Tora Pit_365
- Tora Stream_364
- Tora Tora_364
- Toilet Bowls_361
- Shipwrecks_361
- God Squad_360

Tora Rd
Te Awaiti Rd
Tora Farm Settlement Rd

NORTH

354 WR1

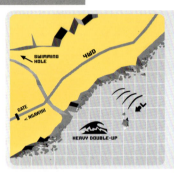

Schnappes

Schnappes is the first break in the area as you head around Cape Palliser from Ngawihi on the 4WD track.

Find it near the stream and look for the large rock offshore. You can often find cattle munching on bull kelp - serious tasting beef bro!

Break features challenging left-hand double-wammy pits. Be prepared for huge, ledgy takeoff. Schnappes is board breaker heavy. If you don't pull-in expect a beating. Optimum size 4-6ft (1-2m). Serious wave for expert level surfers.

The Desert

Follow the 4WD track back towards Ngawihi. When crossing the desert look to your left for a rocky outcrop.

Break is mostly surfed when the points are blown out. Can produce a heavy, ledging left-hander. Features a solid wave which has no problem handling the big swells. Isolated and spooky with tons of bull kelp hugging the rocks. Sharky. Optimum wave size 4-7ft (1.5-2.5m). Expert level surfers.

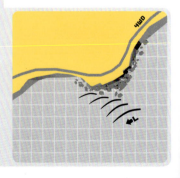

WR1 355

Seconds - Ngapotiki

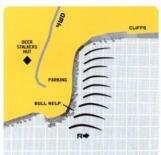

Get to Seconds by heading south from Martinborough (40km) to White Rock Rd and the coast. Take Ngapotiki Rd to the end, then the cliff top walkway/road southwest to the deer stalkers hut. Find the break peeling around the point directly in front of the hut.

Quality right-hand point break producing a long peeling top to bottom wave. Expect a jacking takeoff followed by a long wall complete with hollow sections and wide barrels peeling close to the rocks. The wave offers few sections to cutback as it rifles off perfectly down the line.

The break has no problem handling a solid swell and will pick up southeast through to a big southwest swell. Keep an eye out for sneaker sets on big days as there are few indicators to show their arrival. Entry to the break can be tricky due to heavy bull kelp, rolling rocks and sweep on bigger days. When it's solid, it's easier to launch from further inside the bay and make the longer paddle. Point is prone to devil northwest winds which hug and howl through the mountain putting an ugly surface chop on the break.

Fun wave when small, serious proposition when huge. Optimum wave size 3-8ft (1-3m). For competent/expert level surfers. Break gets crowded, but still feels isolated. One of NZ's gems.

Expect a jacking takeoff followed by a long wall complete with hollow sections and wide barrels peeling close to the rocks.

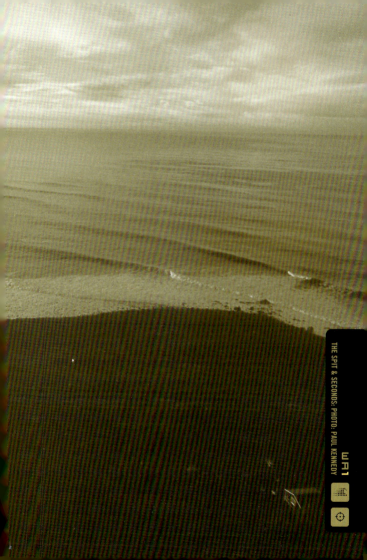

THE SPIT & SECONDS: PHOTO: PAUL KENNEDY

The Spit

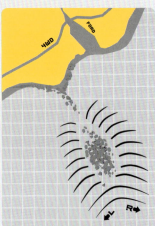

Find White Rock and the Spit 40km to the south of Martinborough. As you approach the coast take Ngapotiki Rd. You will pass a shearing shed. From here look for the gate/cattle stop. Gate is sometimes locked. Access from here is 4WD only. You'll have to negotiate rough terrain and cross fords which can be flooded. You won't have any trouble spotting The Spit if it's breaking. Park in the paddock overlooking the break.

The Maori name for The Spit is Tai Raukauwhakamataku, which means beware of the long breaking wave.

White Rock features a world-class reef/point setup. Two peaks break and peel for great distance either side of a long rock spit.

The southern side of the Spit offers a grunty left-hand peak which peels off a large rock. This break can handle macca swells. A huge takeoff is followed by a big solid wall. Optimum wave size 6-10ft (2-4m). Experts only.

The north side features an excellent right-hander which breaks off the end of the spit and bends as it peels around the rocky spit. Be ready for an intense takeoff followed by speed wall, cutback and epic barrel sections, all of which come at you as the wave bends and wraps. Best surfed at 3-6ft (1-2.5m).

The right is the most surfed break, so expect solid crowds. Good for intermediate to expert level surfers. Access both breaks by long, arm-numbing paddle either side of the spit. Caution: wave size can be deceptive from the shore.

WR1 359

White Rock Point

From Martinborough head south. Follow the long and winding metal road to the ocean. White Rock Point is the first break you'll see when you hit the coast - look to the left towards Te Kaukau point.

Point features a fickle left-hander. Break works best in medium sized swells and produces a ledgy wave with heaps of power. A sucky takeoff grinds into fast sections. Can be a fun wave and a good alternative option if the points are crowd-maxed. Optimum wave size 3-6ft (1-2m). Competent surfers.

Dolphin Bay

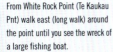

From White Rock Point (Te Kaukau Pnt) walk east (long walk) around the point until you see the wreck of a large fishing boat.

Break consists of a variety of beach/reef breaks producing various peaks. Spot is a swell magnet and a good option if the points are being hammered by strong northwest winds. Find mostly rights with the odd left, and various peaks breaking on rocky outcrops. Isolated and uncrowded. Experienced surfers.

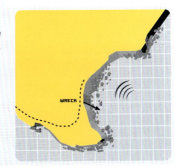

360 WR1

Gnarlies

From Dolphin Bay continue northeast until you spot a big wedge imploding over shallow reef.

 A favourite spot for body boarders and knee boarders, Gnarlies consists of a left-hand double-wedge beast of a wave. It is suitable for expert level surfers only.

 Be ready for a massive ledgy jack-up as the wave hits the reef and pitches horizontal. Take the drop and pull in for a hell or a heavenly barrel - the wave will decide. Isolated, uncrowded, dangerous spot.

God Squad

From Martinborough, head south on White Rock Rd. Take a left on Tora Rd and head to the coast. When you reach the ocean take Tora Farm Settlement Rd southwest to the break.

 The southern most Tora break, God Squad features a left and right reef peak. Here you'll find user friendly waves on mid-sized swells. Expect fun peaks and good workable walls. Optimum wave size 3-5ft (.5-2m). Good for surfers of all levels.

WR1 361

Shipwrecks

From Martinborough head to Tora. Take Tora Farm Settlement Rd southwest to Shippies. Break is located a little south of Toilet Bowls. Look for a peak behind the wreck.

Here you'll discover a clean right-hand peak which likes small to medium size swells. It features a easy takeoff followed by a fast peeling workable wall. Good for big roundhouse cutties. Easy paddle out when small to mid-sized. Gets gnarly when big. Northeast swells ledge-up more on the takeoff. Optimum wave size 3 to 5ft (.5 to 1.5m). Watch out for the rusting remains of wreck on the inside. Heaps of sheep poo.

Toilet Bowls

Head south along Tora Farm Rd. Park before the old boiler from the shipwreck. Look to the left, if breaking you will see two distinct peaks working.

Another classic Tora break consisting of twin peaks firing off a small point with various rocky outcrops. Expect shifty peaks depending on swell angle. Small swells mean fun, easy waves. The more size the break gets, the meaner the bowls and suckier the wave. Access is an easy paddle out under 4ft. Optimum wave size 3-5ft (1-2m). Competent surfers.

PHOTO: PAUL KENNEDY

364 WR1

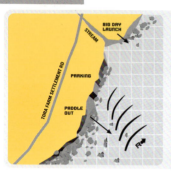

Tora Tora

Find Tora Tora off Tora Farm Settlement Rd 200m (or 500m when big) to the south of Tora Stream.

Break consists of an epic right-hand reef break. Ledgy suck-ups fire off down the line. Be prepared for a ledgy takeoff complete with boil-ups if the tide is mid to low. From here it's a speed run offering super hollow barrel sections and high performance walls. The bigger it gets, the further out it breaks. Line-up can be shifty, varies with swell angle. Very consistent spot. Optimum 3-8ft (1-4m). When it's solid paddle out south of Tora stream, otherwise a straight paddle out through the lulls. Expert surfers.

Tora Stream

Head to Tora from Martinborough via White Rock Rd. Take Tora Rd to the coast. Make a right on Tora Farm Settlement Rd, pass the old run-down shearing sheds. Tora Stream is the first break as you head southwest - find a car park beside the stream.

Classic break producing a quality A-frame peak. Expect a short hollow left and longer sucky rights. Break gets hollow as the tide drops producing good barrels and fast sections. Heaps of rock boil-ups. Easy paddle out unless it's maxing. If it's huge, expect a gnarly shore break. Optimum wave size 2 to 5ft (.5 to 2m). Good for surfers of all levels.

WR1 365

Tora Pit

Find Tora Pit approximately 500m northeast of Tora Stream.

Break features a left and right point/reef setup. Big wave magnet which can be a beast during huge swells. The lefts generally offer the longer rides while the rights offer hairy inside ledging sections which get hollow. Optimum wave size 4-8ft (2-4m). Expert level surfers only.

Stony Bay

From Tora Rd take a left on Te Awaiti Rd when you hit the coast.

Area northeast of Tora Stream features a range of rugged and rocky bays. Look for various peaks breaking over reef and sand. Area offers many options to get a wave to yourself. Good for surfers of all levels.

DANIEL KEREOPA. PHOTO: CORY SCOTT

WR2 AREA

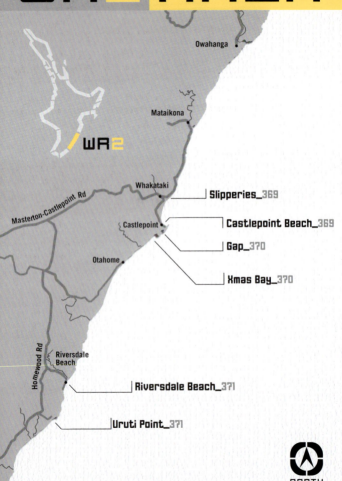

Slipperies_369
Castlepoint Beach_369
Gap_370
Xmas Bay_370
Riversdale Beach_371
Uruti Point_371

Slipperies

Find Slipperies off Castlepoint Rd. Spot breaks in front of the Whakataki Hotel.

Here you'll find a grunty left-hand reef break. Expect a powerful, jacking takeoff followed by a quality workable wall. Break holds a solid swell. At times it can get crowded. Optimum wave size 3-8ft (1-3m). The Whakataki Hotel welcomes surfers and surf club visits. For $20/night, it's a great place to stay and surf.

Castlepoint Beach

From Masterton take Masterton-Castlepoint Rd east to the coast and Castlepoint.

In front of the store and campground find a variable beach break producing a range of left and right peaks. Break works in a range of swells and can be a good option during maxed out swells from the south/southeast. High tide is generally too full causing the beach to close-out. Good for surfers of all levels.

370 WR2

The Gap

Take Masterton-Castlepoint Rd to Castlepoint. Head to the eastern end of the township. Walk past the lighthouse over the sand to The Gap.
 Narrow inlet featuring a beach break setup. The Gap is sheltered from strong winds and can often have the best surface conditions in the area. Needs a solid swell to get in the bay. Be ready for grunty left and right peaks and long workable walls with the odd tube section. Quality depends on sand banks. Best 3-5ft (1-1.5m). Good for surfers of all levels.

Xmas Bay

From the Gap, walk southwest over the hill. Takes about 15 minutes.
 Bay features a beach break offering various left and right peaks. Xmas Bay is a south swell magnet and can be surfed on north/northeast winds. Optimum wave size 3-5ft (1-1.5m). Good for surfers of all levels. Uncrowded and isolated break.

WR2 371

Riversdale Beach

From Masterton take Masterton Castlepoint Rd to Blairlogie. Take the next right to Riversdale Beach.

Long beach features variable beach break waves. Expect fun left and right peaks. Beach will pick up all swell angles - closes out over 6ft. Optimum wave size 2-6ft (0.5- 2m). Good for surfers of all levels.

Uruti Point

Get to Uruti Point by taking Homewood Rd to Waiorongo Rd and the coast.

Bay features a variable beach break producing good left and right multiple peaks over sandy bottom. Quality depends on sand build up. Break better in smaller swells, optimum 2-5ft (0.5 to 2m). Beach bends, so can be surfed in winds ranging from northwest through southwest. Uncrowded and Isolated. Good for surfers of all levels

Wellington

Wellington is the capital of New Zealand. It also has the distinction of being the windiest city in the country. For this guide we cover the area from Wellington east to Palliser Bay. The region offers the travelling surfer many interesting options. The city is prone to inconsistent conditions and strong winds. Topographic layout, with the Cook Strait on its back doorstep means it can receive a battering from winds of north or south direction.

Wellington offers some good reef and beach break options, but heading out of town will get you into waves of better consistency and quality. Palliser Bay can be an oasis from the savage weather which batters the southeast coast. The Rimutaka Ranges to the west and the Aorangi Ranges to the east can divide weather systems, offering shelter to the Palliser Coast.

On occasion Lyall Bay can have strong southerly onshores, while the Palliser area will be calm and glassy with sunshine. Palliser can be prone to strong north to northwest winds which lacerate the surface of many breaks with a lumpy cross offshore. The area is a wave magnet. It features a complex layout of reefs which are positioned to pick up the powerful southern ocean groundswells. The deepwater canyons of Cook Strait offer little resistance to large ocean swells, allowing them to hit the reefs with full force. Surfing here you look to the south and see the sun set over the Seaward Kaikoura Range. Be sure to check out the hard core fisherman at Ngawhi as they launch their boat using bulldozers, their knowledge and timing of sets is something to behold.

A large low pressure wave factory hovers to the east. A huge fetch pumps waves into Palliser Bay, wrapping swells bend into Wellingtons reefs and beaches.

A deep depression to the south churns up the Southern Ocean firing huge swells towards Wellington. Palliser Bay takes it on the chin.

A massive low pressure system sends swell north hugging the coast. Palliser Bay and Baring head net the swell - Welly pumps.

WL1	375
Rat Island	376
Houghton Bay	376
Lyall Bay	377
Airport	377
Propellers	380
Breaker Bay	380
Eastbourne	381
WL2	383
Wainui	384
Lake Ferry	384
Batches	385
Whata Bombie	385
Whata Station	386
Humenga Point	386
Humenga OS's	386
Pararaki Stream	387
Humenga Lodge	387
Otakaha Stream	388
Dee Dees	388
Raspberries	389
Little Ning Nong	389
Craps	389
Big Ning Nong	389
Windies/No 4	390
INFO	391

WL1
WL2

O'NEILL   AREA SEASONAL WETSUIT RECOMMENDATIONS

SUMMER
BOARDIES-
SPRINGY

AUTUMN
SPRINGY-
STEAMER

WINTER
4/3 STEAMER
+ BOOTIES

SPRING
SPRINGY-
STEAMER

WL1 AREA

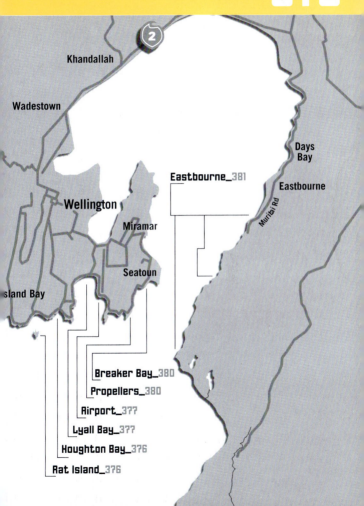

376 WL1

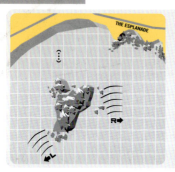

Rat Island

From Houghton Bay head west along the Esplanade. Look for Taputeranga Island off Elsdon Pnt. Find a left off the west side of the island. Features a big sucky speed run - watch the first section as it sometimes closes out. Handles 6 to 8ft (2 to 4m).

During medium sized south swells the east side can provide a quality right. Expect a big sucky takeoff and perhaps a barrel. First section prone to occasional shut downs. If you make it through, it'll wind through another section complete with a big rock boil-up mid way. Optimum size 3 to 6ft (1.5 to 2.5m). Easy but long paddle. Competent surfers only.

Houghton Bay

From Lyall Bay head west along Queens Drive through Princess Bay to the Esplanade. Find the car park on the left. Houghton Bay was the venue for the 1968 New Zealand Surf Nationals.

Bay features various left and right peaks. Quality depends on banks and swell size. During bigger swells a solid right-hander ledges off the rocks. During medium sized swells a sucky, hollow left-hander is the more consistent break. Optimum size 3-5ft (1-1.5m). Caution: heavy board-breaker shore break. Gets crowded. Intermediate to expert level surfers

Airport

From Lyall Bay follow the airport runway south on Moa Point Rd. Look for a big exploding peak breaking off the end of the runway.

Semi sheltered spot from strong northwest winds. Fun wave up to 5ft (1.5m). Expect a personality change when it's big - turns into a brute. Surfers need cast iron balls to takeoff. A strong offshore will hold you up as it jacks. It'll follow with a short, fat, heavy wall usually ending with a hideous close-out. Uncrowded break for expert level surfers only.

Further east is Moa Point. It features a fickle right hand reef break. Avoid surfing here due to sewerage outfall.

The bay features a variety of peaks with constantly changing banks. The wall next to the airport offers the best quality. Expect a super sucky takeoff and quick tube. A workable wall will peel through to the inside and close-out. Spot gets insanely crowded.

The Maranui end of the bay can offer good peaks. It picks up southeast swell as well as south, but is prone to howling northerlies which scream through the hills. Big swells break on the bombie reef located off Arthurs Noose. Optimum wave size 3 to 6ft (1 to 2m). Good for surfers of all levels.

ISLAND BAY. PHOTO: PAUL KENNEDY

380 WL1

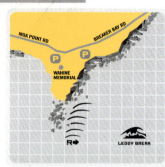

Propellers

From Lyall Bay head along Moa Point Rd east to the Wahine Memorial Park. Find the car park on the right. Look for the propeller from the wreck of the Wahine.

Break features a long, ledgy right-hander producing long, solid walls and fat tubes. When sizey it gets intense. Serious locals spot - respect and surf in harmony. Optimum wave size 3 to 6ft (1 to 2m). Expert level surfers.

Breaker Bay

Head north from Props along Breaker Bay Rd. The break is on the right just before the road heads inland towards Seatoun.

Grunty right reef break featuring a gnarly takeoff which can suck dry. Beware, break produces double deep tube rides and super fast sections. Holds solid swells. Use the outside rock as an indicator for sneaker sets. Best surfed glassy, optimum size 4-8ft (2-3m). Gets crowded. Experts only.

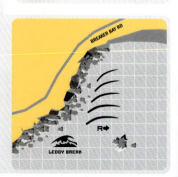

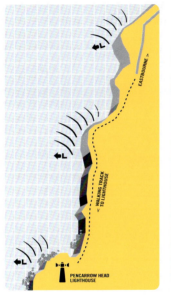

Eastbo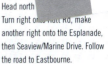

Head north
Turn right onto Hutt Rd, make another right onto the Esplanade, then Seaview/Marine Drive. Follow the road to Eastbourne.

Here you'll find numerous left-hand point breaks which break on big southerly swells. All the points are surfable with southerly onshores but best with glassy conditions. The waves are smallest towards Eastbourne (due to refraction) and largest south near the Pencarrow Head Lighthouse. Check out Lion Rock for the best line-up. Good for surfers of all levels. Uncrowded.

wavetrack
0900 99 777

Updated accurate surf reports since 1992

Calls 99c per minute - Groms ask your parents first

2 AREA

WL2

Baring Head

Wainui_384

Coast Rd

Orongorongo

Turakirae Head

NORTH

383

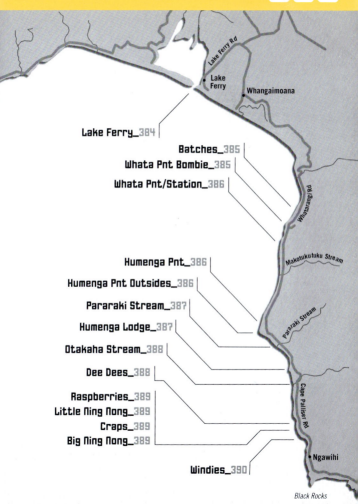

384 WL2

Wainui

Head to Wainuiomata. Take the Coast Rd to Orongorongo.

Area features three breaks. Find a grunty left reef break in front of the river mouth. It features a ledgy takeoff followed by fast sections through to an intense inside section. Break holds a big swell and is prone to strong northerly winds.

Further east find Dribbles, a fun right reef break and another left breaking over a rock ledge. Spots hold large waves. Optimum size 4-6ft (1-2m). Expert level surfers.

Lake Ferry

Drive south from Martinborough through Tuhitarata and Pirinoa. Turn right onto Lake Ferry Rd heading towards Lake Onoke. Find the car park overlooking the the entrance (pub on the left).

Fickle spot which occasionally produces heavy barrels. If it's on, be ready for super sucky A-frames (the wave can actually suck gravel into the barrel) and fast walls. Find various left and right peaks at the entrance - board breakers. Optimum wave size 2 to 6ft (.5 to 2.5m). Expert level surfers.

Whata Point/Bombie

From Batches head southeast along Whatarangi Rd. You'll drive around steep cliffs with the sea below.

The point features a peeling left with good fast, makeable sections. The break works well during macca swells. If Ning Nong is closing out, Whata can be a good option.

Outside you'll find a bombie peak. For competent surfers, this wave is a beast and has no problems handling huge swells. Caution: when it's big there will be tons of water moving. Best surfed when glassy or light northeast offshore. Serious paddle out. Handles 6 to 10ft (2 to 4m). Experts only.

Batch

From Martin... the coast and... Rd. As you dive south along the coast you will spot a bunch of batches, some which have succumbed to the sea due to serious erosion of the coast. Drive a little further and park on the side of the road.

Batches offers good shelter during huge swells and wind - it is surfable with strong south/southeast winds. Here you'll find a left and right peak which sucks up over the reef. Expect fun rights and longer lefts. An outside break features another peak which handles the macca swells. Good for surfers of all levels.

WL2

Whatarangi Station

Head southeast towards Ngawihi. Look for the Whatarangi Station on your left.

If the break is working you'll spot various left handers wrapping through rocky outcrops. Outside the homestead is a fun mal wave featuring long ripable walls. At times sections can link and peel for 200-300m. Another peak further along can produce good barrels. Optimum wave size 2 to 8ft (.5 to 3m). Uncrowded break - competent surfers only.

Humenga Point

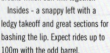

Head further south towards Ngawihi. Park on right side of the road as it curves around the point.

Area features four different breaks which can link together.

Insides - a snappy left with a ledgy takeoff and great sections for bashing the lip. Expect rides up to 100m with the odd barrel.

Outsides features an even longer ride. Be ready for an intense takeoff and super speed run of 300m with deep pits when it's cranking.

South point is a mellow peak which breaks on smaller swells and offshore in northwest winds.

Also, find Michelles by the boat ramp - a peaky swell magnet. All breaks for competent surfers only.

Pararaki

Drive south from Whatarangi Point until you cross a bridge. Find the car park on the right after the bridge.

Stream mouth features fun left and right peaks. Mellow wave, very ripable. Banks are constantly changing due to flow from the stream. Break picks up all swells south through southeast. Optimum wave size 2 to 4ft (.5 to 1m.) Good for surfers of all levels.

Humenga Lodge

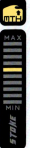

Head south towards Ngawihi - look for Humenga Lodge on your left. Break located south of the Lodge.

Grunty left-hand reef break which peels around the point. Expect a big ledgy takeoff and two workable sections. Break likes big powerful south swells, so stay sharp, this wave will give you a serious drubbing if you're not careful. Optimum wave size 4 to 8ft (2 to 4m). Intermediate to expert level surfers only.

Otakaha Stream

Head south on Cape Palliser Road. Travel past the Humenga Lodge to the mouth of the Otakaha Stream.

Stream mouth features a good left and right peak producing fun sucky waves and punchy walls. Banks are constantly moving due to stream flow and flooding. Further south find a right hander. Optimum size 3-5ft (1-1.5m). Good for surfers of all levels.

Dee Dees

Head south towards Ngawihi. Find Dee Dees opposite Kawakawa Station as the road bends south. Various car parks along the coast.

Dee Dees features a classic A-frame peak producing ripable walls. Generally the rights are longer than the lefts. Great top to bottom hotdog wave. Gets gnarly and mean when it's big. Best with light northeast offshores to groom to perfection. Optimum wave size 2-5ft (.5 to 1.5m). Good for surfers of all levels when small. Gets crowded.

Little Ning Nong - Big Ning Nong

Head south towards Ngawihi. Look for a white toilet on the right side of the road. You'll see a range of areas to park.

Point features a range of quality breaks. Tricky place to explain as every local has his (or her) own definition and opinion of break names and layout. Simply put, the point features a long left reef point break with the exception of Craps, which offers short right barrel.

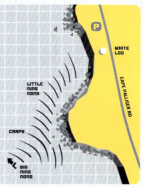

From the inside out. First up is Little Ning Nong or Raspberries. A fun wave, it features a range of medium intensity sections and is best at full tide. It can handle solid swells but is still surfable on grovelly 2ft days.

Next up is Craps. Expect a solid left and right peak with the left offering the best quality. A ledgy takeoff fires off down the line with 3 or 4 long sections of fully workable walls. Impress your mates as you wind down past the car park. Handles swells up to 8ft (3m) and works all tides.

Outside of Craps you'll spot Big Ning Nong or Freight Trains. Big Ning Nong will only fire on a big swell. For very experienced surfers, it is a beast of a wave offering a serious big wave option for the area. When big it features a massive cranking takeoff, long fat walls and barrel sections. It'll wind through Craps and continue all the way to Dee Dees. Starts working at 6ft and will hold well over 10ft waves.

Confused? Just to cap it off, south of Craps you'll find another named section - Super Tubes. It likes smaller clean swells in the 4 to 6ft range (1.5 to 2m). Here you can get into some hollow, deep pits. If you're committed look out for billys rock (a massive boil-up).

WL2

Windies/No:4

Head southeast from Craps. Look for the Ngawihi golf course. Here you'll find two right handers which are good options when the crowd factor gets intense at Craps.

Windies is a fun wave and features 2 or 3 sections which peel through for 100m. Good wave for surfers of all levels.

Next is No:4, another right which handles large swells. Find it directly opposite the golf course. It is surfed during strong northwest winds and seems to handle them while other spots are torn to shreds. Good for surfers of all levels.

Spot X

Find various other breaks in the area. Hells Corner, a beach break with multiple peaks. Surf with seals and other sea life at Wins - a long left hander which breaks 500m offshore. Other breaks with no names - go search.

WELLINGTON - PALMERSTON NORTH

Amazon Queensgate
Queensgate Mall, Lower Hutt
Ph 04 922 3607

Amazon Johnsonville
34 Johnsonville Rd, Johnsonville Mall
Ph 04 461 6104

Boardriders Surfboards
53 Willis Street, Wellington
Ph 04 499 3655

Colorado Palmerston
169 The Square, Palmerston North
Ph 06 357 6575

Colorado Wellington
Lido Centre, 75-87 Willis Street, Wellington
Ph 04 472 3224

On Surf - Custom Surfboards
Surf School Board Hire
Lyall Bay Parade, Lyall Bay, Wellington
Ph 04 387 7182

Notionlab
Advertising, Marketing, Book Design, New Media
Designers of the Wavetrack New Zealand Surfing
Guide - www.notionlab.co.nz

Surf n Snow - Surfboards
45 Cuba Street, P O Box 11 - 127, Wellington
Ph 04 473 3379
email: surfnsnow@xtra.co.nz

Surf Reports - Nationwide
www.surf2surf.com

Surf Reports - Phone
Wavetrack 0900 99 777 (Calls 99c/min)
Groms ask your parents first

The Real Surf Company
Goodtime Surf Products
Crn Kingsford Smith & Lyall Bay Parade
Lyall Bay, Wellington
Ph 04 387 8798

Titahi Bay Surf Coaching Services
Qualified Surf Coach, Titahi Bay
Ph 025 246 7984

C 2 C Surfshop
276 Cuba Street, Palmerston North
Ph 06 354 9963
email: c2c surfshop @ xtra.co.nz
www.c2c surfshop.co.nz

Ocean & Ice
72 Broadway Ave, Palmerston North
Ph 06 355 1122

wavetrack™   SURF2SURF.com

Kapiti

Fifty minutes drive from downtown Wellington is the Kapiti - Mana coast, named because of the proximity of two large islands offshore.

Covering nearly 50 kilometres of coastline, the area offers a range of surfing options with beaches, points and reefs that can create great waves. But for most of the time this coast is missing that magic ingredient called swell. Although it's part of the West Coast it is shielded from the Southern Ocean swells by the South Island to the west.

Occasionally a southwest swell will wrap round into the Kapiti Coast but it generally relies on a very narrow northwest swell window. During certain weather patterns Tasman storms and equinoxial gales pound the coast. If the wind drops all the reefs and points can provide a welcome escape valve for Wellington surfers.

Titahi Bay is the centre of surfing on the coast and is known as the onshore capital of New Zealand. But it's not all bad: even in a howling northwesterly it's still very surfable with a user-friendly rip and semi-clean wave faces. Many of Wellington's true surf chargers started surfing at the Bay.

If the surf is flat the coast offers a host of activities such as hiking, fishing, restaurants, bars and amazing sunsets.

Five kilometers off the coast lies the mysterious Kapiti Island. If a solid northwest groundswell is pulsing down the coast with calm wind conditions the island can offer some quality point breaks for the adventurous.

Deep southern ocean system creates a massive southwest fetch. Huge southwest swells bend and wrap around the South Island in to the Kapiti beaches.

Equinox - Roaring 40's deliver a hideous westerly onshore flow. 30-60kt onshore winds produce a 6-8ft Kapiti Coast washing machine which maxes T-Bay out.

A depression delivers a strong northwest flow. Solid swell penetrate Kapiti's narrow swell window bringing its beaches and reefs to life.

KP 393

KP1	394
Otaki Beach	395
Waikanae	395
Kapiti Island	396
Paekakariki	397
Pukerua Bay	397
Wairaka Reef	397
KP2	398
Titches	399
Pa Point	399
Hongoeka	399
Plimmerton	399
Titahi Bay	400
Steveos	400

O'NEILL — AREA SEASONAL WETSUIT RECOMMENDATIONS

SUMMER
BOARDIES-
SPRINGY

AUTUMN
SPRINGY-
STEAMER

WINTER
4/3 STEAMER
+ BOOTIES

SPRING
SPRINGY-
STEAMER

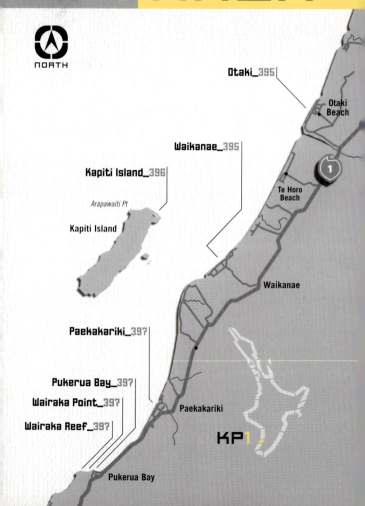

KP

Otaki

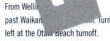

From Wellington, take HWY 1 north past Waikanae for 20km. Turn left at the Otaki Beach turnoff.

Here you'll find a variable beach break producing various left and right peaks breaking on inner and outer banks. Mellow, often crumbly wave with a swift cross current when big. Optimum wave size 3-5ft (1-1.5m). Good for surfers of all levels.

Waikanae

From Wellington, take HWY 1 north towards Paraparaumu. Take a left to Waikanae Beach.

Area features melow left and right beach break waves. Break will only handle small swells - great spot to learn to surf. Optimum wave size 1-3ft (.5-1m). Good for surfers of all levels.

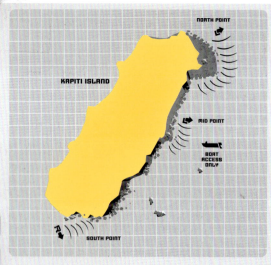

Kapiti Island

Boat access only. Permission required.

Island features three distinct breaks. North point features a long peeling point break wave which wraps producing long rides and fast, workable walls.

Find a little more spice at Mid Point - expect a sucky takeoff followed by a big round barrel section. Full-on walls wrap towards you as they bend around the point. Break will hold a solid swell 4-7ft (1.5-2.5m). Good option when North Point is maxing out.

The southern end of Kapiti Island features a right-hand reef break which breaks on a mega-southeast swell (believe it or not). Offshores for South Point are northwest through north.

Here you need to be ready for a grunty right reef with a big sucky takeoff followed by a long barrel section over shallow reef. Break gets heavy with pitching, fat lips. Handles a solid swell 4-7ft (1.5-2.5m). Isolated break for expert level surfers only.

KP1

Paekaka[riki]

Drive north [to] Paraparaumu. Take a left to Paekakariki Beach.

It's no G-land, but a great place to practice and learn how to surf. Beach features a variety of left and right peaks. Usually long walled close-outs. Fun waves for beginners. Optimum wave size 3-5ft (1-1.5m). Good for surfers of all levels.

Pukerua/Wairaka Reef

Head past Titahi Bay on HWY 1 northbound. Drive down the steep hill to the the Bay.

Area offers a range of reef break options. In front of the private homes find Brendens - a sucky right-hand reef break with a short fat shoulder. Gets hollow on occasion. Optimum 3-5ft (1-1.5m).

Find Wairaka Point west along the Frontage road. Quality left reef, breaks best in northwest swells. Expect a sucky takeoff and punchy sections. Optimum 3-7ft (1-2.5m).

Further west (2km walk) is Wairaka Reef. Grunty powerful waves on solid northwest swells. Hell drops - good barrels. Isolated. Expert level surfers only.

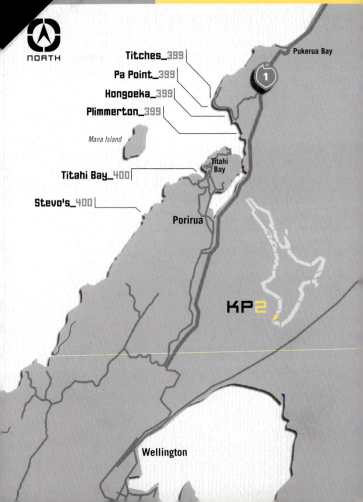

KP

Titches

Head ...
1. T...
foreshore road to the breaks.

Find *Hongoeka* in front of the Marae - permission required. Features various beach break peaks breaking around rocky outcrops.

Head west on foot past the quarry (1km) and you'll find *Pa Point*. Expect a sucky right-hand point offering grunty waves and good barrels. Optimum 3-5ft (1-1.5m). Best surfed mid to high tide.

Hike another 1km to *Titches*. Another right-hand reef/point, it features a fast, jacking takeoff and quick barrel section. Powerful wave. Optimum size 3-6ft (1-2m). Expert level surfers only.

Plimmerton

From HWY 1 turn off at Plimmerton. Cross the railway line, find car park in front of the railway station.

Area features a variable beach break producing a range of left and right peaks. Soft, mellow waves which suit learners. Optimum wave size 1-3ft (.5-1m). Good for surfers of all levels.

KP2

Titahi Bay/Slipperies

Head north on HWY 1 to Porirua. Take Titahi Bay Rd to Main Rd.

Bay features a beach break which breaks on a north/northwest swell. To the north find *Fishermans*. A beach/point break which produces sucky waves and big right-hand walls. Watch for serious rips and heaps of water moving. Best surfed mid-tide. Watch for rocks.

Inside Fishermans you'll find *Slipperies* - another beach break/point. A fun wave, it generally offers better rights. Break holds a solid swell. Optimum 3-9ft (1-3m).

To the south find Pete's Rock, a sucky left-hand reef best surfed mid to high incoming tide. Serious takeoff. Rocks. Experts Only.

Stevo's

Take the track south from Titahi Bay. Access through private land or long walk. Ask a friendly local. Get permission first.

Area features a powerful left-hand reef break. Breaks best with solid wrapping south lines. Be ready for a jacking takeoff followed by a hollow barrel section. Uncrowded and isolated break. Optimum 4-8ft (1.5-3m). Expert level surfers only.

A great place to visit, Nelson offers some of the finest weather in the South Island. It's a dry region famous for wine making, arts and culture. If all this puts you to sleep there's a ton of adventure based activities in the area.

On the surf front, the Nelson area is fickle. This is due to a very narrow swell window. Tucked up into Tasman Bay, between the Farewell Spit to the north and the Marlborough Sounds in the east, Nelson is blanketed from the mighty southwest swells of the west coast, which feed New Zealand's best surf regions. If you can pick the arrival of a northwest groundswell you'll be rewarded. Nelson definitely has the geographic setups to deliver high quality surf when swell is present.

Keep a lookout for low pressure systems or cyclones in the North Tasman Sea. These usually intensify and may sit for 48 to 72 hours systematically churning out long duration northwest swells directly into the Nelson Bays setting its points and bars alight.

Most of the time the reality for locals is to live off north to northwest short-fetch wind swells. These usually fade in a few hours so study the maps closely and be ready to score.

If desperation sets in the wild West Coast nearly always has swell and is a few hours drive over the mountains.

A depression tracks eastward from the north Tasman sending out pulses of north/northwest swell which penetrate the Nelson Bay's narrow swell window.

NB1	
Ruby Bay	406
Tahunanui Beach	406
The Cut	407
Lighthouse	407
Schnappers Point	407
The Glen	410
Cable Bay	410
Delaware Bay	411
Whangamoa	411

O'NEILL   AREA SEASONAL WETSUIT RECOMMENDATIONS

SUMMER
BOARDIES-
SPRINGY

AUTUMN
SPRINGY-
STEAMER

WINTER
5/3 STEAMER
+ BOOTIES

SPRING
SPRINGY-
STEAMER

NB1 AREA

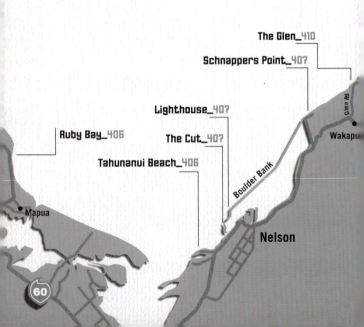

405

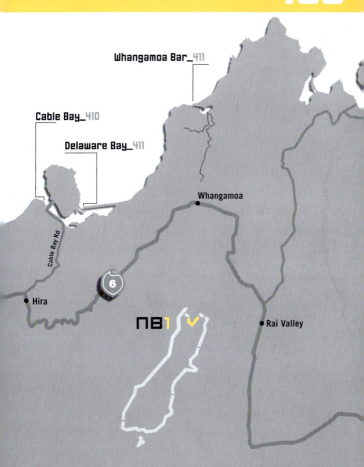

406 NB1

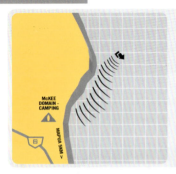

Ruby Bay

From Nelson take HWY 60 north 27km to Ruby Bay.

The north end of long bay features a fat/mushy left-hander which is rather slow breaking. Good mal wave with sections perfectly suited to the longer boards. Wave can offer extremely long rides with the right conditions. On large swells the break is prone to lots of water moving and sweep down the point. Good spot for surfers of all levels.

Tahunanui Beach

From Central Nelson take Tahunanui Drive HWY 6 to Beach Rd and Waikare.

Area features a mellow beach break producing soft waves. Needs lots of tide to work. The wave breaks a long way from shore then re-forms a number of times - great spot for beginners. Optimum wave size 2-4ft (0.6-1.2m).

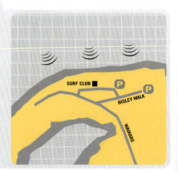

NB1 407

The Cut/Lighthouse

Access the break from Rocks Rd near the Port.
Long 1km paddle, boat access best.

Lighthouse needs a large (6ft+) lined-up cyclone swell to work. Expect big jacking takeoffs, super hollow sections and long workable walls. Can peel for over 1km with optimum conditions.

The Cut is best at low tide. It features a big scary peak, super fast drop - then it morphs into deep water. Strong rip on outgoing tide. Inside Cut works on high tide featuring a wedgey fast jacking takeoff and barrel. Comes out of nowhere, so be quick to your feet. Fickle and dangerous breaks. Competent surfers only.

Schnappers Point

Take HWY 6 northeast from Nelson for 7km. Take a left, follow the road to the coast. Car park is next to the oxidation pond. Walk along the boulder bank for approx 500m to the break.

Triangle reef which breaks off the bend in the boulder bank. Soft and fat at 3ft, turns sucky and hollow over 5ft (1.5m). Be ready for a screaming right-hand speed run down the line. Don't be tempted to go left or you will get a drubbing. Extreme jacking takeoff at low tide. Getting in on high tide can be tricky - ankle bitting boulders. Popular Nelson spot. Intermediate/expert surfers only.

410 NB1

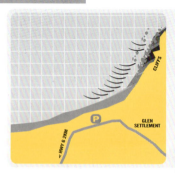

The Glen

From Nelson take HWY 6 northeast 10km. Make a left on Glen Rd. Park next to the boulder bank.

  This is the first break at the beginning of the infamous boulder bank at the Glen Headland. Don't get sucked into taking off on the outside, it is rocky and very shallow. 200m down the point is the second break. Pick your waves carefully, as fast sucky peaks will either close out or let you through for a long speed run. Expect thick punchy walls ending with a solid close-out. Difficult paddle. Intermediate to expert level surfers only.

Cable Bay

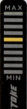

Take HWY 6 northeast from Nelson to Cable Bay Rd (13km). Take a left to Cable Bay. Car park is on the left - walk around the beach to the break.

  Bay features a grinding left which jacks up over shallow reef. Hesitation on takeoff can result in severe punishment for unwary surfers. Easy paddle out into deep water. Best to sit on shoulder and check it out until you get the takeoff sussed. Competent surfers only.

Delaware Bay

From Nelson, head to Cable Bay Rd. Long 2km walk across mud flats, then paddle across channel to the break.

Delaware features a fickle wave which is hard to get right. When the right swell hits it can be an epic left tube. In optimum conditions the peak can jack-up and double in size then pitch over the shallow sand bar. A 2 to 3ft swell can jump to 5 to 6ft. Good tube riding skills essential. Spot is prone to westerly side shore winds. Optimum size 2 to 4ft (.5 to 1m). Uncrowded. Intermediate to expert surfers.

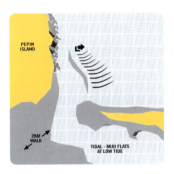

Whangamoa Bar

Take HWY 6 from Nelson towards Blenheim. Over the Whangamoa saddle head down through the forestry block to Hori Bay. At the high point look down to Whangamoa Bar. Car park located next to the road. Scramble down the hill before the cliff.

Shifty sandbars create various peaks along the beach. Best either side of the channel. Spot picks up more swell than Nelson due to angle. Uncrowded and difficult access. Best surfed 2 to 4ft (.5 to 1m). Good for surfers of all levels.

West Coast

The West Coast of the South Island - the final frontier of New Zealand surfing.

When creating this guide we had to determine how far we would go in documenting each area. When it came to the area south of Greymouth it was decided to leave well enough alone, as this is one of the last areas of New Zealand which has yet to be fully explored by surfers.

It is known that this rugged coastline features breaks of superb quality and consistency. We, the authors, can certainly vouch for this as we flew this stretch of coast at 500ft in a Piper Super Cub in preparation for this book. The surf was 6-8ft, glassy and an awesome sight to look down at river bars, hollow beach breaks, reefs and several cranking left-hand point breaks. Most of the breaks are isolated and miles from the highway so, basically its up to you to do the searching. Seek and ye shall find!

To the north, the West Coast offers a range of quality breaks. Massive rainfall means the river bars and inlets offer dynamic banks when not in flood and many of the breaks provide serious power and hollow barrels. For all this though, West Coast surfing is a spooky experience. Firstly, the swell is nearly always big, in fact it's often the case of waiting for it to drop and clean up before heading out. You will also be sharing the breaks with a wide range of marine life - many of which have big sharp teeth! Combine this with extremely cold and often murky water, and you have a true Kiwi hardcore surf destination.

CONSISTENCY 10

A massive system to the south delivers huge southwest swells to the west coast. As the depression moves east the swell drops and cleans up, West Coast breaks pump.

Equinox - Roaring 40's deliver a hideous westerly onshore flow. 30-60kt onshore winds produce an 8-10ft West Coast washing machine.

A depression tracks east from the Tasman Sea delivering lots of wind rain and messy northwest wind/ground swells to the coast.

WC 413

WC1	414
Blaketown	415
Wavetraps	415
Cobden	416
The Channel	416
Point Elizabeth	417
Spooky's	417
Chimney Pots	420
Nine Mile Bluff	420
14.16.17 Mile	421
WC2	424
Punakaiki	425
Punakaiki River	425
Safety Bay	426
Woodpecker	426
Fox River	427
Charleston	427
Nine Mile Beach	428
Tauranga Bay	428
Shingles	429
Westport Breakwater	429
WC3	430
Waimaire	431
Little Wanganui	431
Karamea	432
WC4	435
Anatori River	436
Paturau River	436
Whariki Beach	437
Pillar Point	437

O'NEILL — AREA SEASONAL WETSUIT RECOMMENDATIONS

SUMMER
SPRINGY
3/2 STEAMER

AUTUMN
STEAMER

WINTER
5/3 STEAMER
+ BOOTIES

SPRING
STEAMER

WC1 AREA

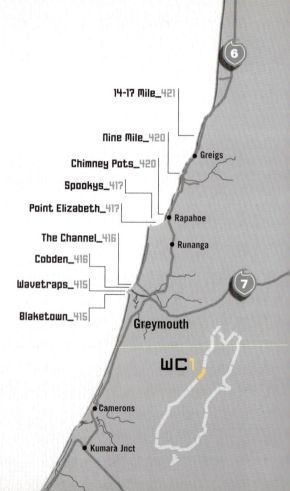

- 14-17 Mile_421
- Nine Mile_420
- Chimney Pots_420
- Spookys_417?
- Point Elizabeth_417
- The Channel_416
- Cobden_416
- Wavetraps_415
- Blaketown_415

WC1 415

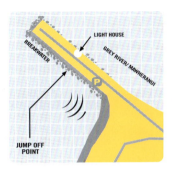

Blaketown

Head to the southside of the Grey River. Follow the road around the lagoon to the break.

Spot features a grunty peak/right-hander next to breakwater. Expect sucky fast bowls which throw out as far as the wave is high - very hollow and gnarly. Also find various left and right peaks further down beach depending on bank location - banks are shifty. Holds 6-8ft (2-3m). Optimum wave size 4-6ft (1-2m). Break is still pushy and grunty when it's 2ft. Expect heaps of drift. Paddle out through rip next to breakwater or jump off the rocks. Uncrowded. Intermediate to expert level surfers.

Wavetraps

Find Wavetraps on the north side of the Grey River. Break is located on a small beach inside the river mouth. From Cobden take the road out to the breakwater.

Break features a short sucky right-hand peak breaking over part boulder, part shingle. Spot is surfed when swell is huge and everywhere else is closing out. Spot has its hazards - beware of turds (from sewer pipe), large floating driftwood and even the odd dead cow floating down the river. Optimum wave size 2-4 ft (.5-1m). Good for surfers of all levels surfers especially hardened West Coast grommies.

416 WC1

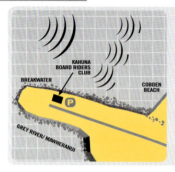

Cobden

Head to the north side of the breakwater at Greymouth.

Home of Kahuna Boardriders Club. Break features changeable shifty bars with a big mean hollow right peeling into breakwater. Expect ledgy drops and tight barrels - stay high in the pocket. Sometimes you'll find a grunty left as well. Super tough paddle out especially when it's big. Best entry is to jump off the rocks (watch out they're very slippery). Paddle out through bar when big. Break picks up all swell directions and handles 2ft (.5 m) through to 15ft (5m). Best for intermediate to expert level surfers.

The Channel

From HWY 6 take Bright St through Cobden, turn left at the Esplanade.

Here you'll find various beachies featuring quality short punchy peaks with long walls and multiple high-performance sections. Sand banks are shifty and change often. Handles solid 6ft. Optimum surfing on a small swell 2-4ft (.5-1m). Good break for surfers of all levels.

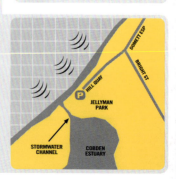

WC1 417

Point Elizabeth

Take HWY 6 north from Greymouth to Point Elizabeth. Turn left before Rapahoe river bridge into car park overlooking 'The Rock.'

Find various left and right beachies - banks are constantly shifting so just a matter of finding a peak and hitting it. Expect sucky A-frame peaks with swells from the northwest and longer lefts with wrapping southwest swells. Sheltered spot from southwest winds. Optimum wave size 3-5ft (1-1.5m). Suits surfers of all levels.

Spooky's

Same directions and parking for Point Elizabeth. Find Spookys breaking off 'The Rock' offshore.

Outside bombie off Port Elizabeth features a big solid chunky left-hand beast of a wave. Expect a sucky, gnarly take off followed by a short wall fading into deep water. Active seal population and Great White feeding territory.

Handles 8-12ft (3-4m). Good tow-in spot. For experts only.

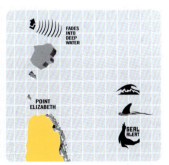

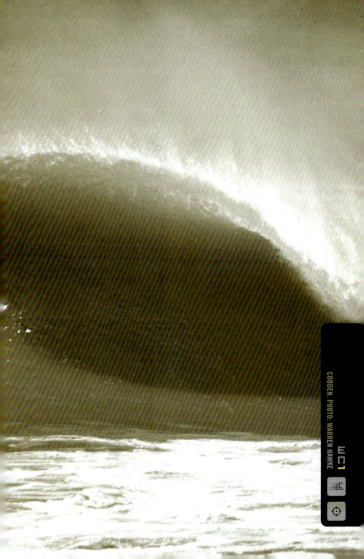

COBDEN. PHOTO: WARREN HAWKE

420 WC1

Rapahoe/Chimney Pots

From Greymouth, head north 10km on HWY 6.

Beach features various peaks and sandbars. Often long left-handers form in front of the river mouth. Sand always shifting. Optimum wave size 2-4ft (.5-1m). Major rip and current on larger swells. Good for surfers of all levels.

Nine Mile

Take HWY 6 12.5km north of Greymouth. Park on the side of the road, walk down through bush to break below.

Left hand point/reef/sand combo. Features a sucky takeoff barrel over rock and live mussel beds followed by long ripable walls until it closes-out on the inside. Optimum wave size 3-5ft (1-1.5m). On bigger swells it closes-out and is prone to serious rips with heaps of water moving. Uncrowded. Suits intermediate to expert level surfers.

14, 16, 17 Mile Bluff

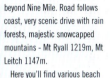

Head up HWY 6 from Greymouth beyond Nine Mile. Road follows coast, very scenic drive with rain forests, majestic snowcapped mountains - Mt Ryall 1219m, Mt Leitch 1147m.

Here you'll find various beach breaks with a myriad of rock fingers and reefs poking out. It's just a matter of having a good look and finding the best spot for the swell and tide. The rewards can be very high. Optimum size for area 2-4ft (.5-1m). Uncrowded and isolated. Best for intermediate/expert surfers.

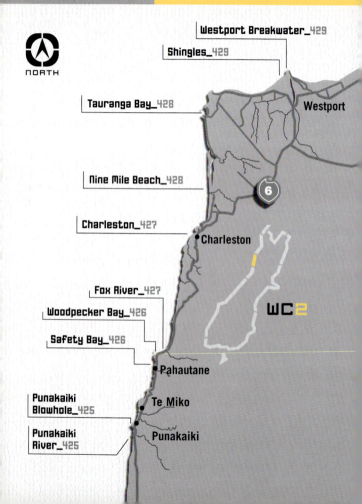

Punakaiki Blowhole

From Greymouth head north on HWY 6 (41km).

Wind sheltered beach break producing mellow/fun workable walls. Swell magnet, always bigger than the rest of coast. Good place to surf when the coast is small. Beautiful backdrop - 100m limestone cliffs covered in rain forest descend to the waterline. Spot works best 2-6ft (.5-2m). Good for surfers of all levels.

Punakaiki River

Take HWY 6 south 2km from Punakaiki. Park at the river bar just before Razor Back Point.

Launch from the north side of the river. Bar can feature a right semi-peaky hollow barrel with sucky close-outs on inside. Further north is a rarely surfed variable beach break which can get good (occasionally). Bay only handles up to 4ft (1m). Can have strong rips, so surfers should be competent.

Safety Bay

From Punakaiki head 8km north on HWY 6. Safety Bay is located 1km south of Woodpecker Bay.

Swell magnet - beach break which draws in any scrap of swell. Good option if the coast is flat. Here you'll find punchy left and right beachies which close out over 4ft (1m). Isolated. steep walk down cliff. Good for surfers of all levels.

Woodpecker Bay

Take HWY 6 north from Greymouth for 46km to Woodpecker Bay.

Bay features various fat left and right peaks. Break needs 6-10ft (3-4m) swell to work and features a massive wrap. Usually surfed after two weeks of screaming southwest winds and pounding swell. Cabin fever rehab spot. Good for surfers of all levels.

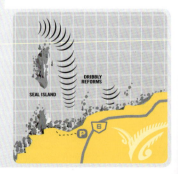

WC2 427

Fox River

From Greymouth take HWY 6 north past Punakaiki to Woodpecker Bay and the Fox River. Cross the bridge and see parking on the left.

Fox River features a river bar break producing mostly left handers. Expect a long breaking (100m) walled-up, semi-hollow wave. Mellow workable walls make for a fun wave. Holds up to 6ft (2m). Break is constantly changing due to shifty shingle banks. Be ready for freezing cold alpine water pouring out the river mouth. Uncrowded. Good for surfers of all levels.

Charleston

From Westport take HWY 6 south 22km to Charleston.

Left-hand point beach break combo. Southwest swell wraps around rocky outcrop producing a left with various sucky sections. Easy paddle out. Optimum wave size 3-5ft (1-1.5m). Break closes-out over 5ft. Uncrowded, good for surfers of all levels.

428 WC2

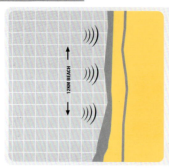

Nine Mile Beach

From Westport take the Cape Road south down the coast past Tauranga Bay.

Here you'll find a range of left and right peaky beachies producing grunty A-frame barrels. Expect sucky takeoffs and a tough paddle out in solid swells. Break offers shelter from north/northwest winds at northern end of beach. Optimum wave size 3-5ft (1-1.5m). Uncrowded. Good for surfers of all levels.

Tauranga Bay

Take HWY 67A Cape Foulwind Rd to Tauranga Bay Rd from Westport.

Bay features a solid left hander off the rocks at the southern end. Further up the beach you'll find shifty West Coast power peaks. During large swells there will be heaps of water moving with a large drift. Handles solid swell 3-6ft (1-2m). Good for all levels when small, competent surfers when big.

WC2 429

Shingles

Find Singles west of the Buller River at Westport.

Various left and right peaks break over shifty banks which are constantly changing due to water movement. Murky water. Spooky place to surf. Optimum wave size 2-4ft (.5-1m). Good for surfers of all levels.

Westport Breakwater

Head to the breakwater located at the Buller River Mouth, Westport.

Break features peaky left and right-handers on a northwest swell (best angle). Be ready for sucky takeoffs and pitching lips which throw out wide. Break is prone to strong currents and heavy water movement. Chilly surfing as cold fresh water spills out from Buller River. Optimum 3-5ft (1-1.5m). Uncrowded. Sharky murky water. Competent surfers.

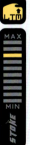

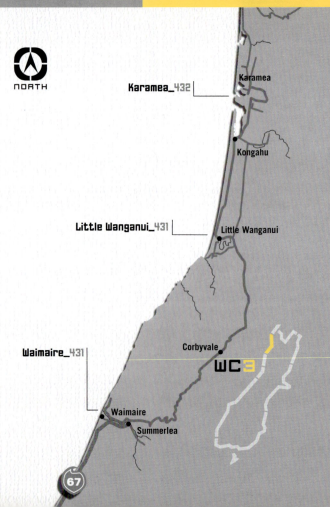

WC3 431

Waimaire

Get to Waimare by taking HWY 67 north 40km from Westport.

River bar/beach break features a range of shifty peaks up and down the beach. Quality depends on shingle location. Find lefts and rights on either side of the river mouth - tricky currents on high river flow days. Good A-frames on northwest swells. Optimum wave size 3-5ft (1-1.5 m). Uncrowded. Murky cold water. Competent surfers.

Little Wanganui

Find Little Wanganui 15km south of Karamea.

River mouth bar break producing long walled left and right peaks. Break gets sucky. Expect sudden bowls. Gets hollow depending on swell angle and shingle location. Uncrowded/isolated. Murky water. Optimum size 3-5ft (1-1.5m). Best for competent surfers.

432 WC3

Karamea River Mouth

From Westport take HWY 67 north for 75km past Little Wanganui to Karamea.

Left and right river bar break which only handles small swells. Lots of flow from the river means the banks are constantly changing. Watch for serious rips. Uncrowded break, lots of spooky, murky water. Optimum 2-4ft (.5-1m). Competent surfers only.

PHOTO: WARREN HAWKE

WC4 AREA

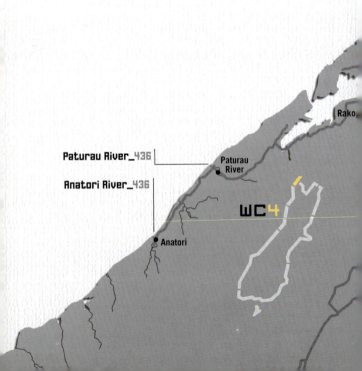

Paturau River_436

Anatori River_436

435

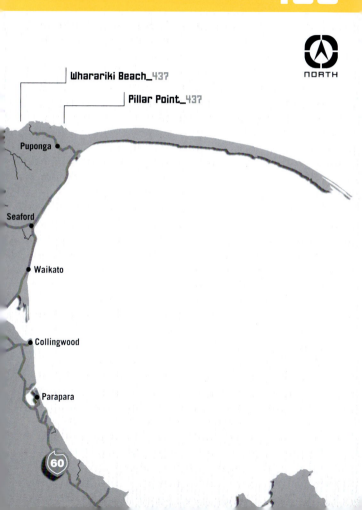

436 WC4

Anatori River Mouth

From Collingwood head north until you hit the Pakawau Bush Rd. Turn left, take the road 32km south down the coast to Anatori.

Left-hand river bar break producing long and punchy waves. Multiple sections peel through to the sandy beach. Sand and shingle are constantly moving due to river flow. Further north you will find a variety of beach breaks. If you have a 4WD head south - very isolated area is home to more point breaks and river bars. Best for competent and experienced surfers.

Paturau River

From Collingwood, head north until you hit the Pakawau Bush Rd. Turn left. Take the road 22km to Paturau River. Park next to the woolshed at the river mouth.

Left-hand river bar/beach combo. Find a mellow left peeling over the bar through to the inside. Best on southwest swells. Also, variable beach breaks further to the north. Banks are constantly changing from stream flow. Optimum wave size is 3-5ft (1-1.5m). Good for surfers of all levels.

WC4 437

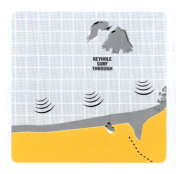

Wharariki Beach

From Collingwood head north out to the Spit. Drive west past Puponga - car park is located at the top of the hill. Follow the sheep track over the sand hills to Wharariki Beach.

Beautiful bay featuring a range of variable beach breaks. Long beach stretches west to Pilch Point. Offshore are the Archway Islands - try surfing through the keyhole on big swells. Optimum size 3-5ft (1-1.5m). Good for surfers of all levels. Isolated, uncrowded break.

Pillar Point

From Collingwood head north on HWY 60. Check the surf from the hill overlooking Farewell Spit.

Here you'll find a range of left-hand beach breaks which work best on solid southwest swells. Can get good. Breaks are offshore with south/southwest winds. Can be an interesting West Coast option. Optimum size 3-4ft (1-1.5m). Good for surfers of all levels. Uncrowded, isolated.

Kaikoura

Located on the northeast coast of the South Island the Kaikoura area is famous for its diving and whale watching. Running parallel to the coast is the Seaward Kaikoura Range. Rising to 2600 metres it offers a spectacular backdrop while surfing and it's not unusual to be deep inside the tube and look out to snow capped mountains framed by the barrel. Below the surface things get interesting as well. Offshore are three ocean trenches, the Conway Trough, Kaikoura Canyon and the Hikuranga Trough. Some Kaikoura surf breaks are affected by massive tidal upwelling and a break can jump in size from two to five feet in ten minutes with the change of tide. The deep trench upwelling brings the cold nutrient rich water close to shore so you could be sharing these waters with seals, dolphins, orca, whales and the odd great white shark.

Surfing the Kaikoura region offers numerous options condensed into a small geographic area. The surfing is world class at certain breaks and most are located close to the main highway. The area features it's own micro climate. The mountains funnel winds and onshores can switch to offshores in minutes, as can perfect glassy surf instantly change to un-ridable junk.

Like other parts of the South Island, winter requires quality equipment to make surfing enjoyable. Water temperatures can dip below eight degrees so a quality steamer and accessories are required.

The town of Kaikoura offers a range of surf shops, accommodation and restaurants making it a great place to visit and surf.

A depression to the east combines with a high pressure system. A classic squash fires swell towards the coast - Kaikoura's breaks pump.

A low pressure system holds and spins to the southeast. Solid swell hits the east coast - Kaikoura points fire.

A deep southern ocean system sends huge swells north. As they hug the coast they bend and wrap around the Kaikoura Peninsula.

K1 439

K11	440
Robin Hood Bay	441
The Cut	441
K12	442
Kekerengu	443
Clarence Point	443
Clarence	446
Sandy Bay/Okiwi	446
Blue Duck	447
Iron Gate	448
Mangamaunu	449
Ocean Fun Reefs	452
Graveyards	452
Meatworks	454
Whale Watch	455
Gooch's Beach	455
Jimmy Armers	456
Kahutara	456
Kahutara Reef	457
Oaro Beach	457
INFO	461

K11
K12

O'NEILL AREA SEASONAL WETSUIT RECOMMENDATIONS

SUMMER
SPRINGY - 3/2
STEAMER

AUTUMN
3/2 - 4/3
STEAMER

WINTER
5/3 STEAMER
BOOTS, GLOVES + HOOD

SPRING
4/3 STEAMER
BOOTIES

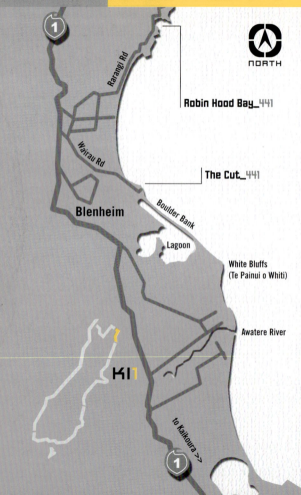

KI1   441

Robin Hood Bay

Head northeast from Blenheim on HWY 1. Turn right at Tuamarina, follow road through Rarangi.

Area features a beach break which usually features fat long walls. Spot is prone to backwash. Expect mostly close-outs. While this is no J-Bay, it is a great indicator of conditions for the legendary point breaks of Kaikoura. See KI2.

The Cut

Head north on HWY 1 from Blenheim to Spring Creek. Take a right to Wairau Bar Rd. Break is situated northwest of a large lagoon.

The break features a right-hand river bar/point. Like most river mouths, it is dependent on shingle movement and location. Optimum conditions are a southeast/east swell at around 3-5ft (1-1.5m). Good for surfers of all levels.

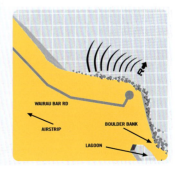

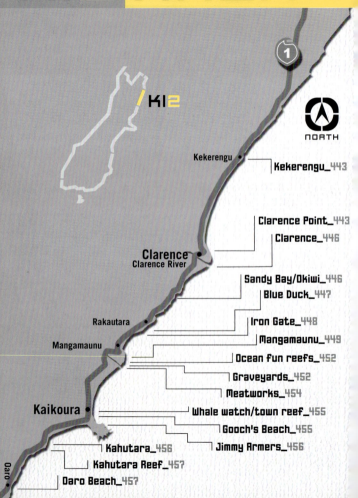

K12 443

Kekerengu

From Blenheim head south down HWY 1 towards Kaikoura. Kekerengu comes up after Tirohanga - you'll see the local store.

Break consists of a right-hander breaking over rocks and moving shingle. It features a fat takeoff followed by short right peeling sections. Good sheltered spot on a large south swell. Optimum wave size 3-5ft (1-1.5m). Good for surfers of all levels.

Clarence Point

Head south from Blenheim on HWY 1 towards Kaikoura. You'll see the break before the road heads inland past the township of Clarence. Access the break over railway line and farm.

Classic right-hand point break set up. A series of 50m sections wrap down the point for up to 100-200m depending on swell size, direction and tide. Break generally offers fat waves with occasional hollow sections. Optimum size 3-5ft (1-1.5m). Uncrowded and isolated. Suitable for surfers of all levels.

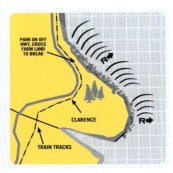

446 K12

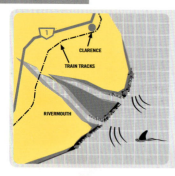

Clarence

Located south of Clarence Township. Cross the railway tracks. Difficult access - walk across the farm land to the break.

  The break is sheltered from northeast winds and features a ledgy, sucky takeoff followed by a hollow barrel. Expect short, fat and fast waves. You'll be amazed to see pebbles churn up inside the barrel. Tricky takeoff and line-up. Best for competent surfers. Uncrowded and isolated. Watch for Noahs and seals (they bite!)

Sandy Bay / Okiwi

Head south on HWY 1 from Clarence. Look for car park on the left after the bridge. Right sweeping corner overlooks the bay.

  Break features average beachies breaking over a combo of sunken rocks and sand. Generally ok depending on banks. Spot is sheltered from the northeast wind (cross offshore). Good learners wave. Optimum wave size is 2-4ft (.5-1m).

KI2 447

Spot X

Filthy right point somewhere on the Kaikoura coast - hook a local up with some crays and a tray - it may be worth your while. Good luck.

Blue Duck

Find Blue Duck north of Mangamaunu and south of Half Moon Bay on HWY 1. Keep an eye out for the Blue Duck Stream. Access the break by crossing the railway line.

Blue Duck is another spot sheltered from northeast winds. It features a combo of rock and sand beachies. Expect mostly fat close-outs. Worth a check when Meatys and Mangas are blown-out. Optimum wave size 3-5ft (1-1.5m). Uncrowded. Good for surfers of all levels.

448 K12

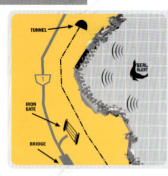

Iron Gate

Head north on HWY 1 from Mangamaunu. You'll drive through many sharp bends in the road. Look for a rusty old iron gate on right side of the road. Access the break by crossing the railway line.

Average beach/rock combo wave, long crumbly walls which generally close-out. Fun and scenic. Easy paddle out. Optimum size 3-5ft (1-1.5m). Picks up a range of swell from north through to south. Uncrowded. Good for surfers of all levels. Caution: watch out for seals (especially in spring) they can get frisky!

Spot X

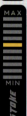

Ledgy reef break. Short punchy waves. Holds big swells. Ask a friendly local.

Mangamaunu

Take HWY 1 north from Kaikoura 13km. Cross the Hapuku bridge. At end of straight you'll find the car park located on the left side of the road. Watch for traffic when crossing the highway.

Mangamaunu is an epic right-hand point break which peels for 100-300m depending on swell angle. Large south swells create a strong rip which sucks around the point making it difficult to stay in the line-up. Mangas works best with clean lines of southeast and east swell allowing the sections to link into one long amazing wave.

Mangas features three distinct sections: Outsides - expect a big hollow ledgy takeoff followed by quick barrel sections and a long workable wall. A big cuttie section will link you through to Middles. Here you'll pull into another barrel section and a long speed wall with cutback sections. From here Insides takes over and can get very hollow and fast. Mangas is the ultimate wave for short or long boards and anything in between. After rides you'll be in for a long walk around the point to the line-up.

Works 2-6ft (.5-2m). Best 4-6ft (1.2m-

Manga's is the ultimate wave for short, long boards and anything in between. After rides you'll be in for a long walk around the point back to the line-up.

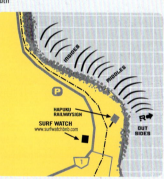

2m). To launch, walk next to the railway line past the Hapuku sign - use various rips. Gets crowded with a hot local crew. Good for surfers of all levels. Watch for seals, Noahs and extremely slippery rocks due to growth of "Korengo" - a local seaweed which is edible and healthy.

MANGAMAUNU. PHOTO: SURF2SURF.COM
K12

Ocean Fun Reefs

Find Ocean Fun Reefs south of Mangamaunu. Head along the railway line and rocks south from Mangas. Paddle out in front of the Surfwatch Lodge and Marae on hills.

Break consists of various left and right peaks with mostly rights breaking on outer reefs. A fun hollow wave with a big sucky takeoff and long walls. Down the line it will back off then suck-up again through the shorey. Optimum size 3-4ft (1-1.5m). Uncrowded. Good for surfers of all levels. Accommodation - Surfwatch Lodge - www.surfwatchbnb.com

Graveyards

From Kaikoura take HWY 1 north. When you reach the end of the Hapuku Straight (where HWY 1 meets the ocean) cross the railway line next to the graveyard on Kiwa Rd (metal road).

The break features a powerful right-hand reef which is sometimes fat and pushy. East and southeast swells produce longer peeling waves. Break features various hollow and steep sections. Expect a ledgy, steep takeoff with rock boils-ups. Optimum size 3-6ft (1-2m). Uncrowded. Best for intermediate to expert level surfers.

454 K12

Meatworks

Head past the Graveyard on Kiwa Rd. Continue past the line of pine trees, carpark is on the left.

Series of grunty left and rights breaking over rolling boulders. The rights peel longer, while the lefts are shorter and more hollow. Expect a fat fast pocket with ledgy sections. Meaties is a south swell magnet - watch for macca clean-ups on big days. Tricky launch - slippery moving rocks and heavy shorey. Optimum size 3-6ft (1-2m), handles 6-8ft (2-3m). Competent surfers. Meatworks gets its name from the days before booties, when surfers cut their feet up on the moving rocks getting in and out of the water.

Spot X

Filthy reef break. Heavy, powerful, hollow wave holds 8-10ft (3-4m). Experienced surfers only. Bribe a local, you may be rewarded.

K12 455

Whale Watch Reef

Head under railway bridge at Kaikoura township to Whale Watch and the Railway Station car park.

Hollow ledgy right-hand reef break. Mean takeoff with a fat pocket and short wall. Fades off into deep water. Optimum wave size 3-5ft (1-1.5m). Uncrowded. Competent surfers.

Goochs Beach

Find Goochs along the Esplanade from Kaikoura township. Travel past the swimming pool, car park is on the left after pool.

Bay features a left and right crumbly close-out breaking over beach and rock boil-ups. Fun wave for groms and learners. Optimum 2-4ft (.5-1m). Good for surfers of all levels.

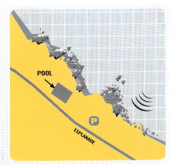

456 K12

Jimmy Armers

Head southeast along the Esplanade past the wharf and the Fifeshire (pink) historical house. Find the carpark on left.

Sheltered spot. Good for big maxed-out swell days. Swell wraps lefts and rights into small bay producing fat peaks, short walls and ledgy rock boil-ups. Optimum size 3-4ft (.5-1m). Competent surfers.

Kahutara

Drive south from Kaikoura on HWY 1 past the Peketa camping ground. Turn left along a metal clay road and through willow trees. Car park is located at the top of a small hill.

Legendary right reef point featuring big jacking takeoffs. Fast hollow sections come at you as the wave jacks and gets bigger. Stand up barrels. Room for occasional cutties as it winds down inside. Caution: heavy shorey and meat grinder rocks. Steep bank. Paddle out at the river entrance. Optimum wave size 4-6ft (1-2 m), handles 6-10ft (2-4m). Crowded - hot locals. Intermediate to expert level surfers.

K12 457

Kahutara Reef

Head south over the bridge from Puketa. See car park on the left side.

Break consists of a dry sucking reef takeoff followed by short fast sections and a big rock boil-up. Wave cranks with ripable 50 to 70 metre walls finishing with a big heavy shorie. Shallow - watch for submerged rocks. Optimum size 3 - 6ft (1-2m). Expert level surfers.

Oaro Beach

Travel south from Kahutara on HWY1. Car park is on left before you get to the railway bridge. From here the highway heads inland to Hundalee. Various left and right peaks depending on swell angle. Picks up more north swell than Manga. At the southern end of beach a right hand reef produces good workable walls. Expect lots of bull kelp floating around. Optimum wave size 3-5 ft (1-1.5 m). Uncrowded and isolated. Good for surfers of all levels.

Head further south along the tracks and find more reefs.

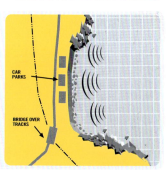

emmit tucker

RPM.co.nz

INFO 461

Board Silly Adventures
Surf School Snow tours
134 South Bay Pde, Kaikoura
Ph 0800 787 352

Kaikoura Surf
4 Beach Rd, Kaikoura
Ph 03 319 7173

Notionlab
Advertising, Marketing, Book Design, New Media
Designers of the Wavetrack New Zealand Surfing
Guide - www.notionlab.co.nz

R & R Sport
14 West End, Kaikoura
Ph 03 319 5028, www.rrsport.co.nz

Seaward Pottery & Accomodation
Kepa Road - Meatworks, Kaikoura
Ph 03 319 5795
email: seawardnz@xtra.co.nz

Surge Surfboards
Meatworks, Kaikoura
Ph 03 319 7011
www.surgesurfboards.com

Surf Reports - Nationwide - Online
www.surf2surf.com

Surf Reports - Phone
Surfline - Detailed Telephone Surf Reports -
Call 0900 47873, Calls $1.20/min, groms ask
your parents first

Surfwatch Lodge
RD 1, Mangamanu, Kaikoura
Ph 03 319 6658
www. surfwatchbb.com

Ocean Fun Publishing Ltd
P O Box 26, Kaikoura
Ph 03 319 6658
email: davidrob@ofu.co.nz

wavetrack™   SURF2SURF.com

Christchurch

Located midway up the east coast of the South Island, Christchurch is a picturesque city which sits on a river plain with the Southern Alps in the distance. For this guide we cover the area from Gore Bay in the north, to Banks Peninsula, and down to Timaru. Along this stretch of coast you'll find a fascinating range of beach breaks, river bars, and points, which pick up swells from the north through to south west.

Banks Peninsula, an hour or two from Christchurch, provides the best surf. Its convoluted coast contains numerous long bays at the bottom of huge valleys. The southern bays, notably Magnet Bay, receive the serious Southern Ocean swells, but the eastern and northern bays get their share of great surf too. Uncrowded breaks and amazing scenery make exploration of Banks Peninsula rewarding for those who take the time to search.

Surfing the Christchurch area during summer is fun but its beaches are exposed to strong northeast onshores, as well as the notorious north westerly gales. Surfing here during winter can be as cold as you'll find anywhere in the world. Melting snow from the alps feeds the rivers which pump cold, murky water into the ocean. Chilly southerly fronts pound the south, their winds cut to the bone.

Christchurch features an international airport and is the perfect place to launch on your South Island surf experience. Here you'll find everything you need including surf shops, board manufacturers and surf schools in the area.

A depression descends from the north combining with a blocking high. A classic squash fires swell towards the coast - Christchurch beaches pump

A low pressure system holds and spins to the southeast. Solid swells hit the Banks Peninsula and wrap into the city beaches.

A deep southern ocean system sends huge swells north. As they hug the coast they bend and wrap - Magnet goes off.

CH 463

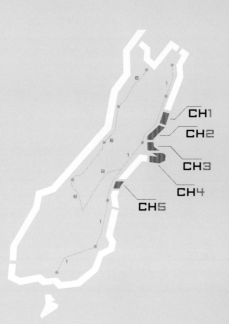

CH1	464
CC's Reef	465
Gore Bay	465
CH2	467
Port Robinson	468
Hurunui Mouth	468
Fields	469
Motunau	472
Mid Shore	472
Amberley	473
Leithfield	473
CH3	474
Waikuku	475
Pines	475
Waimairi	476
North Beach	476
New Brighton	477
South Shore	477
Sumner Bar	478
Sumner	478
Taylors Mistake	479
CH4	483
Raupo Bay	484
Le Bons Bay	484
Hickory Bay	485
Robin Hood Bay	485
Te Oka Bay	486
Tumble Down	486
Magnet Bay	487
CH5	490
Smithfield	491
Patiti	491
Jacks Point	492
Lighthouse Reef	492
INFO	493

O'NEILL AREA SEASONAL WETSUIT RECOMMENDATIONS

SUMMER
SPRINGY - 3/2
STEAMER

AUTUMN
3/2 - 4/3
STEAMER

WINTER
5/3 STEAMER
BOOTS, GLOVES + HOOD

SPRING
4/3 STEAMER
BOOTIES

CH1 AREA

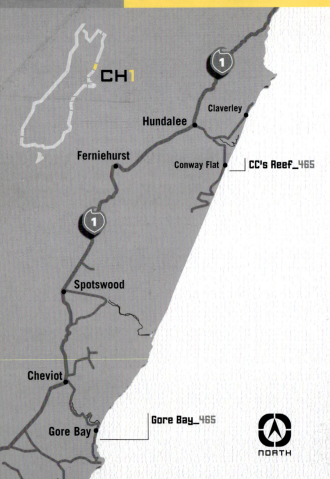

...take a right and wind down metal road along cliff. Difficult access down cliff face.

CC's is sheltered from strong offshore winds and picks up swells from east through to south. It features a sucky takeoff followed by a heavy ledgy section and short intense barrel. A fickle spot, it is isolated and uncrowded, so getting a wave to yourself shouldn't be a problem. Optimum wave size 3 - 5ft (1 - 1.5 m). Good for surfers of intermediate/expert ability.

Gore Bay

From Cheviot head southeast to the coast via a winding and, in parts, loose metal road.

Gore Bay is a swell magnet picking up swells northeast through southeast. Here you'll find various left and right peaky beach breaks amongst various rocky outcrops. Break gets crowded on weekends. The southern end of the beach offers good shelter from south/southwest winds. Gets very cold in winter with low sun. Good at 3 - 5ft (1 - 1.5m). Good spot for surfers of all levels.

AREA 2

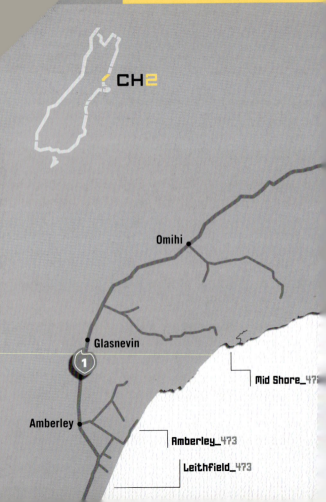

CH2

Omihi

Glasnevin

①

Mid Shore_47?

Amberley

Amberley_473

Leithfield_473

467

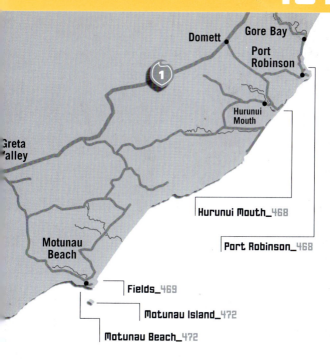

Hurunui Mouth_468
Port Robinson_468
Fields_469
Motunau Island_472
Motunau Beach_472

468 CH2

Port Robinson

From Gore Bay, follow the road signs to Manuka Bay. Park at the end of the road. From here it is by foot to the break.

Fickle spot which can produce quality waves. Needs a sizeable swell at the right angle - best with long straight east groundswell lines or a big southeast swell. Rocky, kelpy and sharky. Optimum conditions 4-6 ft (1-1.5 m). Intermediate/expert surfers.

Hurunui River Mouth

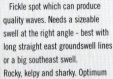

Head south from Cheviot on HWY1. Take a left on Hurunui Mouth Rd - Drive 8km to the river mouth.

Spot consists of a changeable river bar break with variable shifting sand and shingle. Banks change constantly with shingle movement from heavy river floods. Spot picks up a wide band of swell from northeast through to southeast angles. Experienced surfers only.

CH2 469

Spot X

Left point featuring long, ripable walls and sucky sections. Ask a friendly local.

Fields

From HWY1 take Motunau Beach Rd to Stonyhurst Rd, cross over the river to car park. Long walk down the fence line to the beach.

Fields is a good quality beachie featuring variable left and right peaks. Quality depends on sand location and swell angle. Find various breaks up and down the beach with an occasional good right reef break located at the southern end. Uncrowded and isolated. Optimum size 3-6ft (1-2 m). Good for surfers of all levels.

CH2

MOTUNAU ISLAND. PHOTO: SURF2SURF.COM

H2

Motunau Beach/Island

Take HWY 1 north from Amberley to Motunau Beach Rd (44km). Drive 13km to the coast.

Here you'll find a quality beach break with peaks and long workable walls breaking through from the outer bars. Fun mal wave. The north end of beach offers good shelter from strong winds. The northeast sea breeze often swings to a valley offshore in the evenings. Uncrowded.

Offshore is Motunau Island featuring good reef breaks. Solid south/southeast swells wrap around both sides of island. Picks swells northeast through to south. Optimum size 3-5 ft (1-1.5m). Good for surfers of all levels. The Island - intermediate/expert.

Mid Shore

From Christchurch take HWY 1 to the Waipara junction. Take a right and drive to end of road. Park at the stockyards - approx 20 minute walk across paddock and down the hill to the break.

Mid Shore features two breaks. A fun beach break producing sucky lefts and rights - excellent mal wave. At the northeastern end of the beach you'll find a primo left point break in solid swells. Expect long workable walls and big fat sections, great for roundhouse cutties. Uncrowded and isolated. Scenic spot. Quality at 2-4ft (.5-1m) 4-5ft (1.5m) on the point. Intermediate to expert surfers.

Features an average beach break with constantly changing banks due to sand/shingle movement. Breaks better in peaky swells. Picks up swells from the east through southeast. Uncrowded. Optimum wave size 2-4 ft (.5-1m). Good for surfers of all levels.

Leithfield Beach

Head north from Christchurch on HWY 1 turn right at Leithfield - two car parks at the beach.

South swell magnet features various beach breaks, quality dependent on sand movement. Tends to close-out - likes peaky swells. Best shape at 2-4ft (.5-1m). Good for surfers of all levels. Great beginners wave.

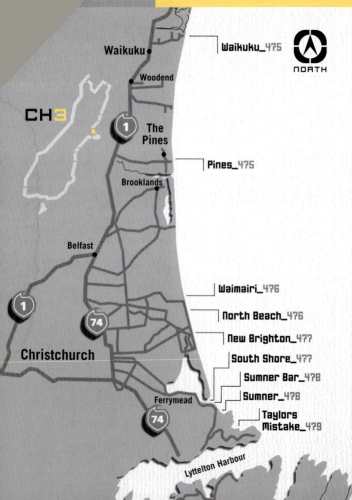

CH3 475

Waikuku

Head north from Christchurch on HWY 1 to Waikuku. Make a right before crossing the Ashley River bridge on Waikuku Beach Rd. Car park located near the river mouth.

Waikuku offers a good quality bar break at the mouth of the river in clean south swells. The beach features variable left and right peaks - often a consistent bank in front of the surf club. Gets crowded on weekends. Picks up swells from the south and southeast. Optimum 3-5ft (1-1.5m). Good for surfers of all levels.

Pines

From Christchurch take HWY 1 north. When you reach Kaiapoi, take Beach Rd to Pines Beach.

Here you'll find various beach breaks and a river bar break which can get very hollow. Watch for savage rips from Waimakariri River. Works on south and southeast swells. Optimum wave size 3-5ft (1-1.5m). Intermediate surfers.

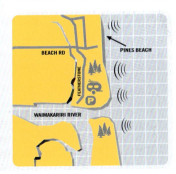

476 CH3

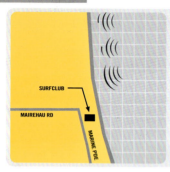

Waimairi Beach

Head north from Brighton on Marine Parade. Waimairi Beach is located at end of the road.

   Features wind-exposed beach breaks which pick up onshore northeast winds early. Break can pump on clean south swells. Find various peaks up and down the beach. Optimum size 3-5ft (1-1.5m). Good for surfers of all levels.

North Beach

Find North Beach on Marine Parade 1.4 km north of New Brighton Pier.

   Area features average beachies, quality depends on sand location and movement. Wind affected break - prevailing northeast devil wind cuts it to pieces. With the right conditions can be a fun wave. Picks up swells from the northeast through to the southeast. Northeast swell causes major drift. Good at 2-4ft (.5-1m). Good for surfers of all levels - good learners spot.

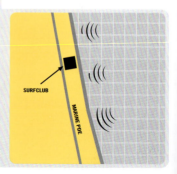

CH3 477

New Brighton

Find New Brighton 12km east of the central city.

Consists of various beach breaks and peaky lefts and rights either side of the pier. Quality can be attributed to construction of the new pier and the rip formed beneath it. Break picks up any swell northeast through to south, works best with east and south swells. Expect lots of drift on north/northeast swells. Enter break by paddling out at beach, locals often jump off the pier. Caution: serious jump. Watch for fishing lines and hooks. Popular Christchurch spot, gets crowded. Exposed to the northeast devil wind. Optimum size 3-5ft (1-1.5m).

South Shore

Head southeast from Brighton down Marine Parade. Turn left on Rockinghorse Rd, follow to the end.

Find a good wave at the estuary outlet. Sucky right-hander breaks off the bar in dirty water. Also a variety of beach breaks in the area featuring various left and right peaks - similar quality to Brighton. Needs south or southeast swells. Heaps of drift. Works best 2-4ft (.5-1m). Good for surfers of all levels.

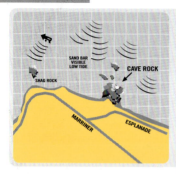

Sumner Bar

Drive to Sumner Park near Cave Rock. Check the surf by climbing the rock.

Good quality bar break when the conditions are right. Produces short intense rides with hollow barrel sections. Waves connect with right swell angle producing long peeling walls - mostly left-handers. Picks up swells east through south. Large south swells wrap 150° around the Banks Peninsula lining up on the bar. Break is fickle with the change of tide. Long paddle out to line-up, prone to serious rips. Optimum wave size 3-5ft (1-1.5m). Intermediate to expert surfers.

Sumner Breakwater

Drive to Scarborough, take a left down Esplanade, follow the road to the breakwater.

Mellow soft beachie, good wave for mals and learners. When it gets sizey the outer peaks can crank with big ledgy takeoffs and long rides.

Very severe rips at times. Break is sheltered from prevailing winds. The Cave Rock end of the beach picks up more south swell but is more exposed to devil onshore northeast winds. Spot gets crowded. Mellow friendly locals. Look out for honey bee. Good for surfers of all levels. Optimum wave size 3-6ft (1-2m).

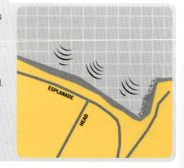

CH3 479

Taylors Mistake

From Sumner head up Scarborough Hill Rd over the top to Taylors Mistake Rd. Wind down the hill to the car park.

Taylors features a grunty beach break producing powerful wedgy peaks and pitching takeoffs. Needs north or northeast swells - spot is bypassed by all those killer southerly swells. Here you'll find strong rips and a difficult paddle out when it's big. Solid swells tend to wedge together, serious pummelings go with the territory. When it's big use launch pads along Godley walkway. Break gets super crowded. Intermediate to expert surfers. Optimum wave size 3-6ft (1-2m).

Checkout the Worlds Best Legend Series Longboard Skaters, Pope Bisect Travel Boards and great New Zealand made surfing accessories all at Wholesale prices direct to the public on our website or phone 021-384280

The New Zealand Longboard Co

WWW.NZLONGBOARD.COM
or come see us at Taylors Mistake, Christchurch

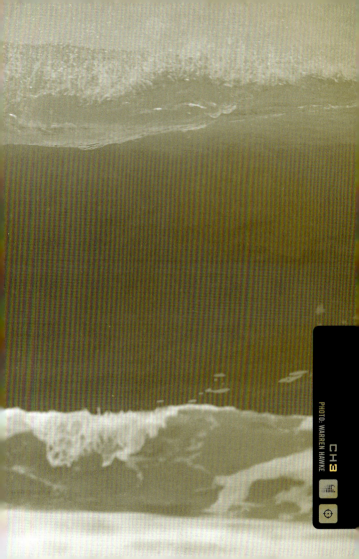

CH3
PHOTO: WARREN HAWKE

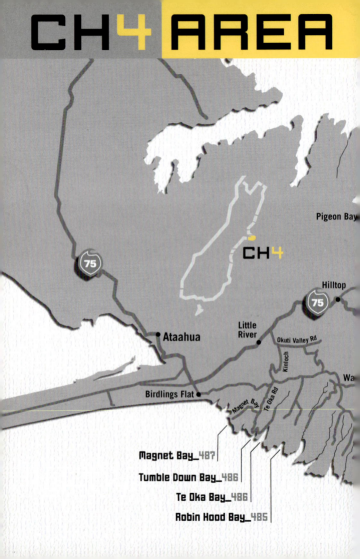

483

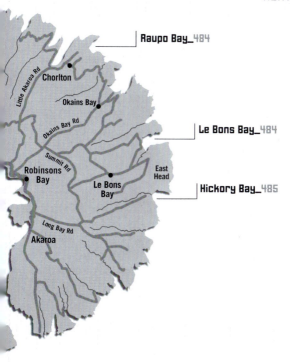

Raupo Bay

From the Summit Rd turn down little Akaroa Rd - go past the boat ramp and park at end of the road. Follow the Raupo stream (a long walk down to the bay).

Raupo features various left and right beach breaks. At the northern end of the bay you'll find a left-hander which works on all tides and gets hollow at low tide. Needs a northeast swell or big north swell. Beautiful scenic bay. Good for surfers of all levels.

Le Bons Bay

Take the Summit Rd turn down Le Bons Bay Rd, turn left across the stream, park at picnic area.

Mellow variable beach breaks with a perfect right-hander off the eastern end of bay - needs solid swell (3ft+) from the north, northeast or east. Great learners wave - very safe beach. Optimum wave size 3-5ft (1-1.5m). Good for surfers of all levels.

CH4 485

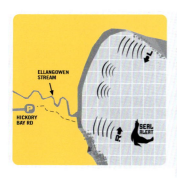

Hickory Bay

From Summit Rd turn down Hickory Bay Rd through Ellangowan scenic reserve to the carpark. When you reach the end of the road walk down the hill to the break.

Bay is a swell magnet and offers a powerful beachbreak with tons of grunt. The northern end of the bay features a excellent left-hander which deflects off the cliffs. Find a right in front of the rivermouth at the south end. Picks up south and southeast swells. Be ready for a very long drive from Christchurch. Isolated, exposed bay. Optimum 3-6ft (1-2m). Intermediate to expert level surfers.

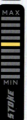

Robin Hood Bay

From Te Oka scenic reserve take Gap Rd to the end of Robin Hood Bay Rd. From there it's a long walk to the bay.

Deep water reef breaking in the bay on south swells. Best access is by boat. Best at mid tide. Isolated and uncrowded. Advanced to expert surfers only.

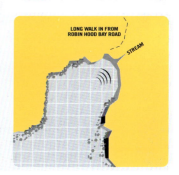

486 CH4

Te Oka Bay

From Little River head south on Kinloch Rd. At the summit Te Oka turn right on Bossu Rd, then Te Oka Bay Rd.

Bay features a sheltered beach break producing a mellow, fun wave which is good for mals. Beach is sand at low tide and boulders at high tide - watch your fins. Good at 2-4ft (.5-1.2m). Good break for surfers of all levels.

Tumble Down Bay

From Bossu Rd, head south down Te Oka Bay Rd - steep winding road with carpark at the end.

Here you'll find a sheltered beach break - good small wave spot for grommies. Best 2-3ft (.5-1m). Perfect for learners.

CH4 487

Magnet Bay

From Little River head south on Kinloch Rd. Take a right down Bossu Rd. Turn off onto Te Oka Bay Rd and follow Magnet Bay Rd to end.

Here you will find a long left-hand point break peeling over a rock and boulder bottom. Entry is via the flat table rock on the right side of the stony beach. On small to medium sized days walk out to the point and paddle from the rocks.

Expect a long peeling wave featuring a range of good sections. With grunty swells the break offers more of a pocket and can produce the odd good barrel. Be ready for large crowds as Magnet is one of the more popular breaks in the Christchurch area.

Magnet is best surfed on a low to mid tide with mid-sized to large swells. When the swell fades, surf the incoming tide for the best waves. The point will hold a solid 6ft plus - optimum size is 3-5ft (1-1.5m). Break works best with true south swells which hug the coast as they travel north. Competent surfers only.

Expect a long peeling wave featuring a range of good sections. With grunty swells the break offers more of a pocket and can produce the odd good barrel.

MAGNET BAY. PHOTO: PAUL KENNEDY
CH4

CH5 | 491

Smithfield

Take HWY 1 north from Timaru. Take the right to the Smithfield Freezing Works and the beach.

Grunty right-hander breaks on the reef in front of the Freezing Works. Expect a ledgy takeoff and an intense section over shallow reef. Heavy break - expert level surfers.

Patiti

Drive south from the Main St of Timaru, take Domain Rd to South St and Patiti Point.

Patiti features a left-hand reef break. A sucky takeoff is followed by multiple high performance sections. Break is a swell magnet - it'll pick up a range of swell from northeast through south. Its consistency means it's a popular break for locals. Good for intermediate level surfers and up.

492 CH5

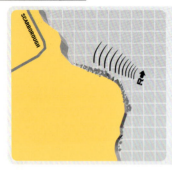

Jacks

Get to Jacks by taking HWY 1 south from Timaru to Scarborough Rd.

Jacks is a right reef break offering a range of good sections. Optimum wave size 2-5ft (1-1.5m). Competent surfers only.

Lighthouse Reef

Find Lighthouse Reef south of Jacks. Here you'll find a right-hand reef break. Be ready for a sucky takeoff and a range of grunty sections as it peels through. Look for the barrel. Optimum wave size 4-6ft (1-2m). Reef can hold a chunky swell. Competent surfers only.

INFO 493

Kaiapoi

SURFBOARDS
SUNAMIE SURF Custom Built NZ Surfboards, 44 Charles Street, Kaiapoi Christchurch, Ph 03 327 3350

Christchurch

SURFBOARDS
BARRON SURFBOARDS - NZ Made
Unit 1/18 Bower Ave, Ph 03 981 2268
www.barronsurfboards.co.nz

SURF SHOP
OUTER ISLAND
Gracies New Brighton Ltd, 81 New Brighton Mall
Ph 64 3 388 9263, www.outerisland.co.nz

SURF SCHOOL
SISCOS SURF SCHOOL
12 New Brighton Mall, New Brighton
Ph 03 382 6969, www.surfsouth.co.nz

SURF SHOP
EASTCOAST BOARDRIDING CO
1091 Ferry Rd Woolston, Ph 64 3 384 3788
www.eastcoast.co.nz

SURF MISSIONS
PACIFIC SURFARI- DOUG YOUNG
Surf Missions/Surf School. Ph 0800 4 SURFING
(478 734) email: dougfunstar@hotmail.com

SURF SHOP
URBAN SURF
25 D Marriner Street, Sumner
Ph 03 326 6023, Fax 03 326 6528

SURF COACH
LEARN TO SURF - AARON LOCK
Surf School / Surf Tours, Scarborough Beach
meeting place cnr Stoke St and Esplanade
Ph 0800 80 SURF (80 7873) www.surfcoach.co.nz

SURF SHOP
EXIT SURF SHOP - 1020 Ferry Road,
Woolston. Ph 03 384 2813, www.exitsurf.com
SURFTECH NZ - Expoxy Boards -
email surftech@exit.com, www.surftech.com

CHRISTCHURCH

Barron Surfboards
Agent South Coast Surf Blanks
Custom Built NZ Surfboards
Unit 1/ 18 Bower Ave, Christchurch
Ph 03 981 2268, email: barron 1@ xtra.co.nz
www.barronsurfboards.co.nz

Amazon. Riccarton
Shop 63 Riccarton Mall, Ph 03 348 5689
Fax 03 3487369

Amazon Christchurch
Shop 44 The Palms Mall, Shirley
Ph 03 385 5166, Fax 03 385 5826

Central Surf
239 High Street, Christchurch, Ph 03 377 9714

Eastcoast Boardriding Co
1091 Ferry Rd Woolston, Christchurch
Ph 03 384 3788, www.eastcoast.co.nz

Euphoria Surf Snow Skate
Cnr Colombo & Lichfield St, Christchurch
Ph 03 366 5100

Exit Surf Shop
1020 Ferry Road Woolston, Christchurch
Ph 03 384 2813, www.exitsurf.com

Learn To Surf
Aaron Lock / Professional Surf Coach
Surf School / Surf Tours, Scarborough Beach
Ph 0800 80 surf (80 7873)
www.surfcoach.co.nz

Onboardnz.com
632 - 634 Colombo St, Christchurch
Ph 03 366 6516, email: info@onboardnz.com

Outer Island Surf Shop
Gracies New Brighton Ltd, 81 Brighton Mall
New Brighton, Ph 03 388 9263
email: gracies @ xtra.co.nz
www.outerisland.co.nz

Outer Island Surf Shop
9 Wakefield Ave, Sumner Christchurch
Ph 03 326 7444

Pacific Surfari
Surf Missions / Surf School, Doug Young
Ph 0800 4 Surfing (478 734)
email dougfunstar@hotmail.com

Snow & Surf Ltd
85 Tuam Street, Christchurch
Ph 03 366 7351

Siscos Surf School
12 New Brighton Mall, New Brighton
Ph 03 382 6969, email: surfsouth@hotmail.com
www.surfsouth.co.nz

Sunamie Surf - Kaiapoi
Custom Built NZ Surfboards
44 Charles Street, Kaiapoi, Christchurch
Ph 03 327 3350

Surf Tech NZ
Epoxy Surfboards, email: surftech@exit.com
www.surftech.com

Urban Surf
25 D Marriner Street, Sumner Christchurch
Ph 03 326 6023, Fax 03 326 6528

Wipeout Clothing Co Ltd
28 - 40 High Street, Rangiora
Ph 03 313 3480

Dunedin

Dunedin represents one of the finest areas for waves in New Zealand. As you head south, it also becomes one of the least populated regions. Welcome to the deep south. This section spans from the north coast to the area west of Invercargill.

From Oamaru to the south coast you'll find an amazing range of beaches, reefs, points and islands. If you have an appetite for adventure you'll find a hundred more quality breaks which are not mentioned in this guide.

The south coast is the home of New Zealand big wave surfing. Power is present wherever you go and much of the coast feels the full effect of grunty southerly swells. Deep water reefs create some of the largest waves in the South Pacific.

Like any surfing paradise there's a downside. In this case it's winter. If you plan to surf here from May through to October you better be prepared with thick rubber. Deep southern lows are prevalent and often produce rain, sleet and snow.

Some of the breaks, like the reefs and beaches between Dunedin and the Taieri River, offer classic small surf, while the Catlins Coast, south of the Clutha River, is no place for beginners. Marine life can add another dimension to your surf mission. You may be sharing waves with seals, the rare Hectors Dolphin, as well as various shark species.

Dunedin features a strong local surfing scene and offers a range of surf shops, board manufacturers and accommodation.

A depression descends from the north combining with a blocking high pressure system. A classic squash fires swell towards the deep south.

A low pressure system holds and spins to the southeast. Massive fetch pumps solid swells to the exposed Southland Coast.

A deep southern ocean system sends huge swell north. The Catlins big wave spots harness the energy - dust off the Jetski.

DN 497

DN1	498
Oamaru Harbour	499
Oamaru South	499
Kakanui	500
Campbells Bay	500
All Day Bay	501
Waianakarua	501
DN2	502
Moeraki	503
Light House	503
Katiki	503
DN3	504
Matanaka	505
Karitane Point	505
Karitane Beach	506
Warrington	506
Potato Point	507
Murdering Bay	507
Aramoana Spit	510
Pipikaretu	510
DN4	513
Victory Bay	514
Allans Beach	514
Sandfly Bay	515
Smails Beach	515
Tomahawk Bch	516
Lawyers Head	516
St Kilda	517
St Clair	517
DN5	518
Black Head	519
Ocean View	519
Brighton	520
Taieri Mouth	520
DN6	523
Kaka-Nuggets	526
Cannibal Bay	526
Long Point	527
Papatowai	527
Tautuku	530

Beatons	538	Porpoise/Curio Bay	530	
Porridge	538	**DN7**	533	
Frenches Reef	539	Oreti Beach	534	
Blue Cliffs	539	Riverton Rocks	534	
INFO	540	Colac Bay	535	
		Nicks Point	535	

O'NEILL — AREA SEASONAL WETSUIT RECOMMENDATIONS

SUMMER
SPRINGY - 3/2
STEAMER

AUTUMN
3/2 - 4/3
STEAMER

WINTER
5/3 STEAMER
BOOTS, GLOVES + HOOD

SPRING
4/3 STEAMER
BOOTIES

DN1 AREA

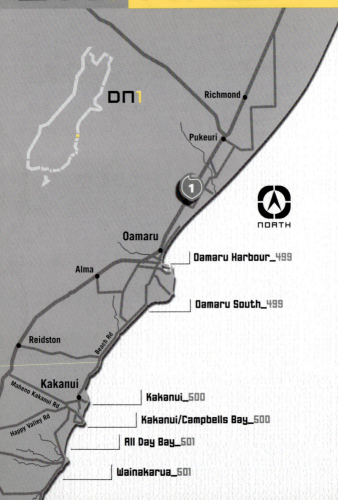

DN1 499

Oamaru Harbour Entrance

From Thames St head south to Arun St then to Marine Parade and the North Mole.

Break is located at the entrance to the Oamaru harbour. Find it at the north end of the MacAndrew Breakwater.

Spot consists of a man-made right which breaks over a mixture of rock and sand. Needs a large swell to work and picks up northeast and east swells. Optimum wave size 3-5ft (1-1.5m). Good for surfers of all levels. Keep an eye out for boats and beware of submerged rubble.

Oamaru South

From Oamaru take Kakanui Beach Rd to the coast.

Here you'll find a range of beach and reef breaks as you drive down Beach Rd. Find a good right-hand reef break near the crossroads. Area picks up swells from the northeast through to south. Optimum wave size 4-6ft (1-2m). Good for surfers of all levels.

500 DN1

Kakanui North

Head south from Oamaru on HWY 1. Take Maheno/Kakanui Rd to Cobblestone on the north side of the river or alternatively take Harbour Tce on the south side.

Break features a right reef break in the mouth of the Kakanui River and a beach break. Picks up a range of swells from northeast through to the south. Optimum wave size is 4-6ft (1-2m). Good for intermediate level surfers. Beware of old jetty pilings.

Campbells Bay

From Kakanui River Mouth continue on Harbour Tce around the point to All Day Bay. Parking and camping on the south side of point.

Here you'll find various beach breaks and a left point at the north end of the beach. Optimum wave size 3-6ft (1-2m). Good for surfers of all levels.

DN1 501

All Day Bay

Take HWY 1 south from Oamaru. At Maheno take the turnoff to Orore Point.

Stretch of coast features a range of variable beach breaks. Quality depends on location of sand. At the southern end of the beach you'll find a right reef break peeling around Orore Point.
Beach picks up swells from the northeast through south. Southern point is sheltered from winds. Optimum wave size 4-6ft (1-2m). Good for surfers of all levels.

Waianakarua

Drive south from Oamaru on HWY 1. Take the turn to Orore Point. Road continues past Orore point.

Variety of breaks (mostly reefs) breaking over a reef shelf which extends out to sea. Find grunty lefts and rights peeling off rock fingers protruding from the beach. At the south end of the beach you'll find a left river bar break. Expect speedy lefts and strong currents. Optimum wave size 3-6ft (1-2m). Best for expert level surfers.

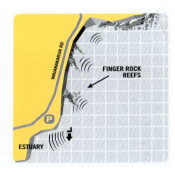

DN2 AREA

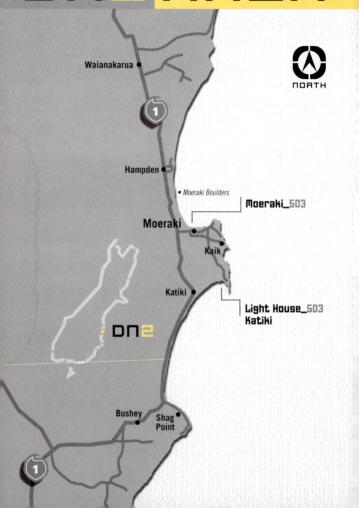

DN2 503

Moeraki

Find Moeraki 37km south of Oamaru off HWY 1.

Moeraki is famous for its large spherical boulders scattered along the beach north of town. They are formed by a process similar to that of oyster pearls from ancient seafloor sediments. The scenic reserve is worth a visit if you are surfing the area.

On the surfing side, you'll find a range of variable beach breaks - generally a soft wave. The southern end of the beach features a right-hand reef break which breaks best on an east swell. Bay is sheltered from wind. Optimum 4-6ft (1-2m). Good for surfers of all levels.

Light House

From Moeraki take Hillgrove - Moeraki Rd to Tenby St. Take a right on Light House Rd to the point.

Variety of beach breaks featuring range of left and right peaks. Area takes the southerly swells head-on. Spot is best surfed during smaller swells. Wind protected from strong offshore north/northwest winds.

Check with farmer to access - area is a protected Yellow-Eyed Penguin breeding ground (leave your dog at home). Also, healthy seal population. Optimum 3-5ft (1-1.5m). Good for surfers of all levels.

Head further south and you will find a range of beach and reef breaks at Katiki.

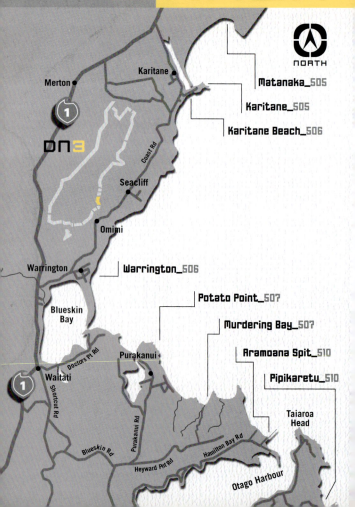

Matanaka

Take HWY 1 35km north of Dunedin. Make a right at Beach when you reach Waikouaiti.

Variable beach breaks producing left and right peaks along the beach. An occasional left-hander breaks along the reef and cliffs at the north end of the beach. Great place to learn to surf.

Optimum size 2-4ft (.5-1m). Any bigger and it will close-out. Good for surfers of all levels.

Karitane

Located 32km north of Dunedin. Take Coast Rd 3km to Sulisker St.

Karitane features two quality breaks on the north side of the Huriawa Peninsula.

The river mouth features a long right bar break. Expect a sucky takeoff followed by several barrel and cutty sections. Paddle out through the river.

Further out find The Point - features a heavy right which breaks close to the rocks. Be ready for a sucky takeoff surge through the kelp followed by heavy barrel sections which hug the rocks. Serious wave. Optimum bar: 2-5ft (1-2m). Point: 5ft-huge (1.5m - completely insane).

Karitane Back Beach

From Dunedin take HWY 1 north 32km. Turn right on Coast Rd to Karitane, drive 3km to beach.

Back beach features a range of beach breaks producing left and right peaks. Quality depends on sand location/movement. Optimum size 3-4ft (1-1.5m). Good wave if you're new to the sport.

Warrington

Head north from Dunedin on HWY 1. When you reach Evansdale (20km) take a right on Coast Rd to Warrington.

Warrington features a range of mellow beach breaks and a left point located at the north end of the beach. Good learners spot. Optimum wave size 2-4ft (.5-1m).

DN3 507

Potato Point

Head north from Port Chalmers to Purakanui (8km) via Blueskin Rd and Purakanui Rd.

The main break is a right-hand point located on the eastern side of Purakanui Bay. Spot features 3-4 sections as it peels around the rocks and steep cliffs. Sheltered spot from strong southerly winds. Paddle out from mouth of the river. Optimum size 3-6ft (1-2m). Good for surfers of all levels.

Murdering Bay

From Port Chalmers take Blueskin Rd to Heyward Point Rd. Look for the signpost to Murderers. Caution: steep, slippery access road.

Bay features a high quality right point break producing very long peeling waves. Expect a sucky takeoff and long walls with multiple sections. Look for the barrel on the inside. Breaks over combination of reef, boulders and sand. Quality can be changeable due to sand location. Pumps on a northeast groundie at 1-8ft (1-3m). Awesome longboard wave on the smaller days. Intermediate/expert level spot.

PHOTO: MARK STEVENSON

510 DN3

Aramoana Spit

From Port Chalmers take HWY 88 northeast 10km to Aramoana.

Aramoana is located on the edge of the Otago Harbour and is home to one of New Zealand's finest beach breaks. Here you'll find hard-breaking peaks producing very hollow barrels when conditions are right. The Spit is a heavy wave when it's big. The Mole located at the south end of the beach can provide an easy way out the back when it's pumping.

The Spit is always a little bigger than Murderers and optimum size is 4-8ft (1-2.4m). Best for intermediate or expert level surfers. Caution: sharky break.

Pipikaretu

From Dunedin take the road out to the Peninsula - follow the harbour until you get to Pipikaretu Rd (25km). Take a right. Access is difficult from end of the road - check with the farmer first. Area is often closed during lambing.

The bay features a range of grunty A-frame beach breaks. When it's cranking and offshore you'll be in for sucky takeoffs and nice hollow barrels.

In south swells there can be a right at the south end of the beach. Optimum wave size 2-4ft (1-1.5m). Tricky break, best for intermediate or expert level surfers.

ARAMOANA SPIT. PHOTO: WARREN HAWKE

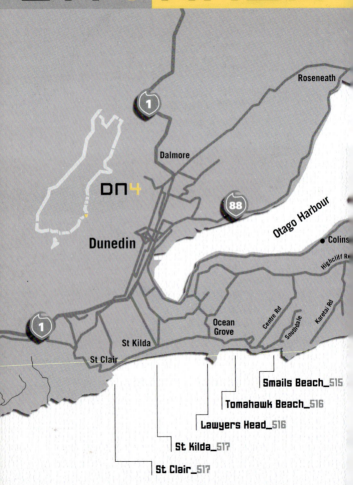

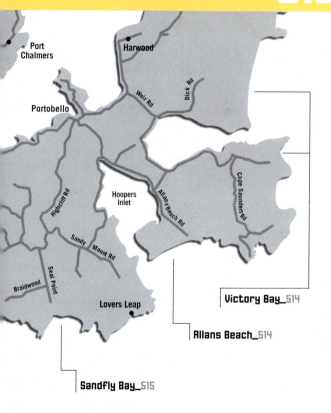

514 DN4

Victory-Wickliffe Bay

From Pipikaretu Point south to Cape Saunders find a range of high quality beach breaks. Many of the breaks are swell magnets and offer waves larger than other Dunedin breaks. Area picks up a range of swell from northeast to south.

Many spots are tricky to access due to reluctant farmers and conservationists limiting entry. Be polite and courteous and you may score. Isolated area with abundant sea creatures of all shapes and teeth sizes. Leave your dog at home.

Allans Beach

From Portobello take Allans Beach Rd southeast to the coast. The breaks are a short walk to the beach from the car park.

Heavy variable beach breaks. Various left and right A-frame peaks on the the beach producing solid waves which can break in very shallow water. Spot is often bigger than the city beaches.

Optimum 4-6ft (1-2m). Good for intermediate level surfers.

DN4 515

Sandfly Bay

From Dunedin head out on the Otago Peninsula. Take Highcliff Rd to Seal Point Rd. Drive to the end of the road. From here it's a solid 1km hike down very steep sandhills to the break. Tricky hike with a mal.

Sandfly features a beach break with various left and right peaks along the beach. Quality depends on sand location. Best surfed in a smaller swell - optimum size 2-4ft (.5-1m) at low tide. Good for surfers of all levels - difficult access. Leave dogs at home - Yellow Eyed Pengiun reserve.

Smails Beach

From St Clair or St Kilda take Victoria Rd to Tomahawk Rd. Follow signs to Smails Beach.

Smails features a range of beach breaks which work best on a small swell. The bay is prone to serious rips, especially the area between the beach and Bird Island. Best 2-4ft (.5-1m). Good for surfers of all abilities.

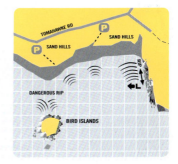

516 DN4

Tomahawk Beach

From St Kilda take Victoria Rd to Tomahawk Rd. Follow the signs to the beach.

Variable beach break producing peaks along the beach. Find the best waves at the eastern corner in a small swell - 2-5ft (1-1.5m). Don't surf the western end of the beach - heavily polluted. Good for surfers of all levels.

Lawyers Head

From St Kilda take John Wilson Ocean Drive to Lawyers Head.

Located east of St Kilda Beach, Lawyers Head offers variable beach break waves with constantly changing sand banks. Breaks best in smaller swells, optimum 2-5ft (.5-1.5m). Avoid surfing here during an east swell due to sewage outfall. Good for surfers of all levels.

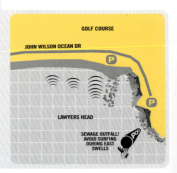

St Clair

From St Kilda head southwest down Victoria Rd.

St Clair is the centre for surfing in Dunedin. It attracts a large local following who head there to surf and hang out.

Here you'll find a beach break and a right point. The beachie offers consistent waves of good quality. When the swell picks up, it can offer punchy waves complete with hollow barrels.

The point breaks over a kelpy reef and sand. As it peels inside it sucks up offering multiple sections. The beach picks up a range of swells. The point is can be surfed with a clean south swell between 2 and 10ft. Good for surfers of all levels.

sand banks. Beach can produce hard-breaking heavy waves offering good barrels and speed walls. Optimum wave size 3-6ft (1-2m). Good for surfers of all levels.

DN5 | 519

Black Head

From Dunedin head south on HWY 1 to Brighton Rd. Take Brighton Rd to Blackhead Rd.

Variable beach breaks featuring grunty left and right peaks and quality barrels. Area prone to strong rips. Optimum wave size 3-5ft (1-1.5m). Expect better quality with east swells. Break is sheltered in strong north and east winds. Caution: beach has had pollution problems in the past. Good for surfers of all levels.

Ocean View

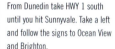

From Dunedin take HWY 1 south until you hit Sunnyvale. Take a left and follow the signs to Ocean View and Brighton.

Ocean View offers a range of beach breaks producing grunty hard breaking waves. The beach picks up a range of swells from east through to south. Optimum size is in the 3-6ft range (1-2m). Good for surfers of all levels.

520 DN5

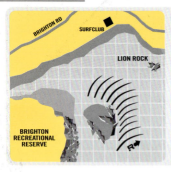

Brighton

From Ocean View continue south on Brighton Rd. Find parking at the surf club.

Brighton features a mellow right-hand point break which peels around a large rock and bends into the estuary. Point breaks over a combination of rock, boulders and kelp. Look for good barrels on takeoff. Break will hold big waves, but paddling out becomes difficult. Works best in a clean south swell at 2-10ft (1-2m). Good for surfers of all levels.

Taieri Mouth

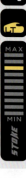

From Brighton follow the coast southwest for 16km on Taieri Mouth Rd. Enjoy a beautiful coastal drive - you'll pass an amazing range of reefs and beaches.

Taieri Mouth features breaks either side of the river mouth. The north side offers a right bar break which breaks hard and fast. The south side features a left reef which breaks on the back of the island. Size can be deceptive. Expect hard breaking waves producing hollow barrels. Watch for dangerous currents. Optimum south/southeast swells 4-6ft (1-2m). Good for intermediate to expert level surfers. Caution: sharky break!

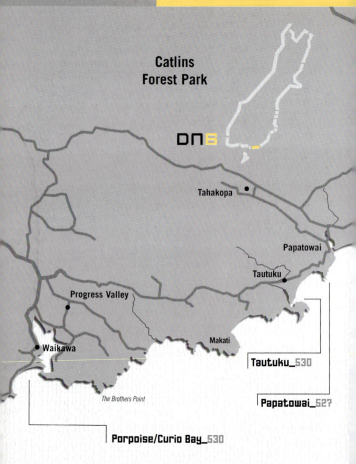

523

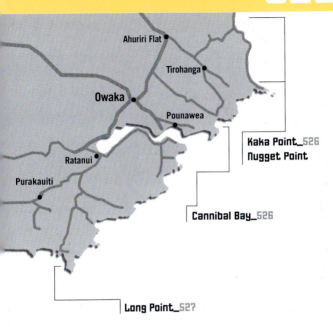

Kaka Point_526
Nugget Point

Cannibal Bay_526

Long Point_527

PHOTO: MARK STEVENSON, POSITIVE PICS

526 DN6

Kaka-Nugget Point

From HWY 1 Balclutha take the Owaka HWY through Otanomomo 17km to Kaka Point.

From Kaka Point to Nugget Point (7km stretch of coast) the scenic coastal road will give you access to a myriad of beach and reef breaks. All break on swells from the northeast, east and large southeast angles. Optimum size 3-6ft (1-2m). Good for surfers of all levels.

Cannibal Bay

Area from Cannibal Bay 11km to the south of Kaka Pnt. From Kaka Point get back on the Owaka HWY, follow the signs to the bay.

Swell exposed beach break producing grunty A-frame peaks. Takes the southerly swells head-on, so expect pure southern power and hollow barrels when conditions are clean. Optimum wave size is 4-6ft (1-2m). Tough paddle when it's big. Good for surfers of all levels.

DN6 527

Long Point

From the Papatowai HWY head south past Ratanui. Take Purakanui Bay Rd until you see the road sign to Long Point. Marginal access due to the farmer limiting access over his farm (he has been burnt in the past - if you get in, show respect for his property).

   Quality heavy grinding left reef point break producing long ripable walls. Expect a ledgy takeoff followed by top to bottom speed walls and power-pocket cuttie sections. Takes southerly swells head-on. Gets very heavy in larger swells. Optimum surfing 4-8ft (1.2-2.4m). Will hold bigger. Best for intermediate/expert level surfers.

Papatowai

Head to Papatowai if you dare!
   Area is the centre for New Zealand big wave surfing. Here you will find a massive right-hand reef break along with a suicidal left. Break starts to work at 10ft and will hold solid 25ft (7.5m) waves. The break has potential to hold even larger waves. Expect a massive ledging takeoff followed by a 300m avalanche barrel section. Caution: Papatowai is a dangerous wave. Watch for rocks and kelp. Observe the locals before paddling out.

   Break needs a 5m+ ocean swell to break. Usually these conditions are accompanied by snow. Hardcore, dangerous wave. Experts only.

PHOTO: MARK STEVENSON, POSITIVE PICS

530 DN6

TAUTUKU PENINSULA

Tautuku

Find Tautuku off the Southern Scenic HWY 87km east of Invercargill.

Tautuku is the first of many breaks along the Catlins stretch of coast towards Invercargill. The coast is wild and the surf is often big.

Tautuku features a beach break producing a range of grunty peaks. Quality depends on sand location. Optimum wave size 3-6ft (1-2m). Break can be surfed with winds from the northwest through to the southwest. Good for surfers of all levels.

Porpoise Bay

Take the Southern Scenic HWY east 67km to Niagara Waikawa Rd and Curio Bay.

Porpoise Bay features a grunty beach break exposed to the might of southern swells. The northeastern end of the beach features big exposed peaks, while the south end can produce powerful, hollow left barrels. Optimum size 3-8ft (1-2.4m). Good for surfers of all levels. Friendly Hectors Dolphins regularly hang around here.

TO INVERCARGILL
NORTH HEAD
BIG BOMBIE

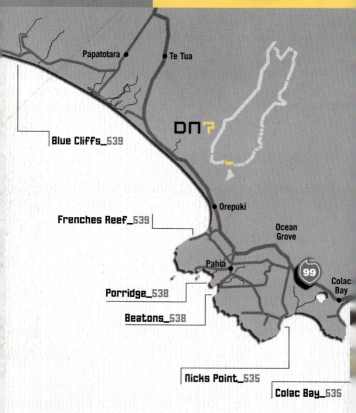

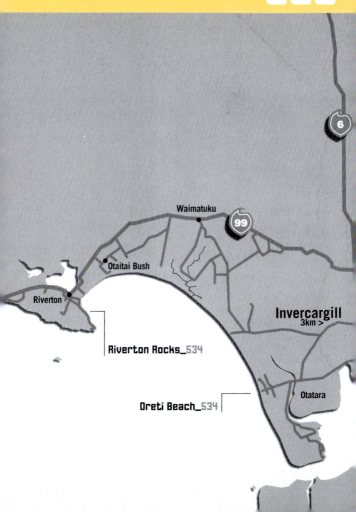

534 DN7

Oreti Beach

From Invercargill take Stead St to Dunns Rd and Oreti Beach.

Features a range of beach breaks with constantly shifting banks. Usually soft and often closes out. Good at 3-5ft (1.1.5m). Good for surfers of all levels.

Riverton Rocks

From Invercargill take HWY 99 west to Riverton. When you reach New Windsor take Bay Rd and Church St to the Taramea Rocks HWY.

Bay features a series of long right-hand points. Fickle break which rarely reaches its true potential. Spot needs a large swell to break. Point can link up when conditions are right to produce a very long wave. Best 4-6ft (1-2m). Good for surfers of all levels.

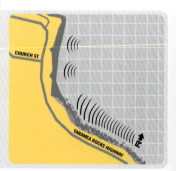

Colac Bay

From Riverton take HWY 99 to Colac Bay.

Bay features a variable beach break producing fun waves. Quality depends on sand location. Optimum size 3-5ft (1-1.5m). Good for surfers of all levels.

Nicks Point

From Riverton take HWY 99 to Colac Bay Rd. Continue on Colac Foreshore Rd to the point.

Southwestern end of Colac Bay features a right-hand reef/point combo. Best with a large west or south swell. Optimum size 4-6ft (1-2m). Best for intermediate/expert level surfers.

PHOTO: MARK STEVENSON, POSITIVE PICS

538 DN

Beatons

From Colac Bay take HWY 99 west. Take the turnoff to Pahia. Check with the farmer for permission to access to this spot.

Break consists of a rocky left reef/point break. Breaks best in a mid sized southerly swell at mid-tide. Always looks bigger from the car park. Optimum 4-6ft (1.2-2m). Expert level surfers.

Porridge

From HWY 99 and Pahia take Pahia Rd to the coast. Checking with the farmer for access is mandatory. Once you have permission the break is a 5 minute walk over the hill.

Quality point break producing mechanical grinding lefts over a reef and boulder bottom. Expect ledgy takeoffs and long speed walls with a variety of filthy sections. Gets hollow offering quality barrels. The point takes the southerly swells head-on, so it gets heavy. Optimum wave size 4-8ft+ (1.2-2.4m+). Best for intermediate/expert level surfers especially when it's big.

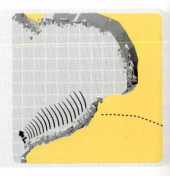

DN7 539

Frenches Reef

From Colac Bay take HWY 99 towards Te Waewae Bay and Orepuki. Take the road left past Monkey Island out to the point.

Left reef break producing a heavy wave in large swells. Needs to have a sizeable southerly swell to break. Good at 4-6ft (1.2-2m). Best for intermediate level surfers.

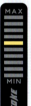

Blue Cliffs

From Orepuki take HWY 99 inland past Te Tua. Take a left on Papatotara Rd to the mouth of the Waiau River.

Right-hand river bar break. Fickle spot which can produce good waves occasionally. Best surfed at 3-5ft (1-1.5m). Good for surfers of all levels. Uncrowded.

There are many breaks around the south coast from Riverton West, Taewae Bay and further afield, including offshore islands. Just remember you are in the Southern Ocean and you need to respect the area and watch conditions closely.

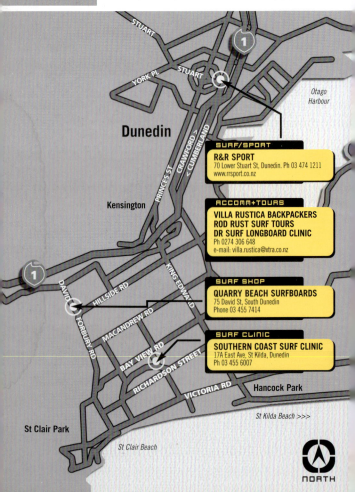

DUNEDIN

Boardbase
140 George St, Dunedin, Ph 03 477 7426

Hydro Surf
410 George St, North Dunedin, Ph 03 477 0429

Notionlab
Advertising, Marketing, Book Design, New Media
Designers of the Wavetrack New Zealand Surfing
Guide - www.notionlab.co.nz

Positive Pics Photography
376 George Street, Dunedin, Ph/Fax 03 477 5777
www.positivepics.co.nz

Quarry Beach Surfboards/Surf Shop
75 David St, Caversham, South Dunedin
Ph 64 3 455 7414

R & R Sport
70 Stuart St, Dunedin, Ph 03 474 1211

Southern Coast Surf Clinic
17 A East Ave, St Kilda, Dunedin, Ph 03 455 6007

Surf Reports - Nationwide - Online
www.surf2surf.com

Surf Reports - Phone
Surfline - Detailed Telephone Surf Reports -
Call 0900 47873, Calls $1.20/min, groms ask
your parents first

Villa Rustica Backpackers
ROD RUST Surftours & DR SURF longboard Clinic
Ph 0274 306648, e-mail villa.rustica @ xtra.co.nz

TIMARU

Soul Surf & Skate - Timaru
235 Stafford St, Timaru, Ph 03 684 4844

MEMBERSHIP CLUB

Join the Surfing New Zealand Membership Club and receive a stylish membership card. Present it at selected surf retail outlets and surfboard manufacturers throughout New Zealand and receive membership discounts and benefits.
Get a quarterly newsletter jam packed with all the latest surfing info and a full colour Surfing NZ events poster. Plus heaps of sponsors products, giveaways and more.

For further details and an application form
contact Surfing New Zealand
Phone 07 825 0018 or e-mail: surfingnz@xtra.co.nz
or join online at:

www.**surfingnz**.co.nz

545

Index

Index

3 Points	284
14,16,17 Mile	421
90 Mile Beach	55
Ahipara Beach	55
Ahu Ahu	152
Airport (WL)	377
Airports (BP)	253
Albatross Point	131
All Day Bay	501
Allans Beach	514
Amberley	473
Anatori River	436
Anaura Bay	281
Anawhata	91
Aramoana Spit	510
Aranga Beach	68
Arataki	241
Arawhata Road	168
Aropaoanui	338
Auroa Point	326
Awakino	137
Awana Bay	110
Awatoto	342
Back Beach	149
Batches	385
Baylys Beach	69
Beatons	538
Bell Block	142
Belt Road	148
Bethells	89
Big Ning Nong	389
Black Head	519
Black Jacks	190
Black Swamp	41
Blacks Cliffs	314
Blacks Reef	314
Blaketown	415
Bland Bay	29
Blue Cliffs	539
Blue Duck	447
Bluehouse	62
Boat Harbour (MA)	326
Bog Works	148
Boulder Bay	146
Bowentown	234
Breaker Bay	380
Brighton (DN)	520
Cable Bay	410
Campbells Bay	500
Cannibal Bay	526
Castle Point Beach	369
CC's Reef	465
Charleston	427
Chimney Pots	420
City Reef	341
Clarence	446
Clarence Point	443
Cobden	416
Colac Bay	535
Cooks Cove	289
Craps	389
Cray Bay	348
Crushers	164
Daniels Reef	44
Dee Dees	388
Delaware Bay	411
Desperation Point	169
Dolphin Bay	359
Eastbourne	381
Elliot Bay	29
Fields	469
Fin Fucker	164
Fishermans Reef	77
Fitzroy	146
Forestry	42
Fox River	427
Frenches Reef	539
Glinks Gully	69
Gnarlies	360
Goat Island	43
God Squad	360
Gooch's Beach	455
Gore Bay	465
Graveyards	157
Graveyards	452
Great Exhibition	19
Greenmeadows	173
Hahei	192
Happy Jacks	320
Harding Rd	342
Hariki Beach	266
Haumoana	343
Hawai	263
Helena Bay	30
Henderson Bay	20
Hickory Bay	485
Hicks Bay	270
Hokianga	63
Hongoeka	399
Horseshoe Bay	271
Hotwater Beach	193
Houghton Bay	376
Houhora Heads	20
Humenga Lodge	387
Humenga OS's	386
Humenga Point	386
Hurunui Mouth	468
Indicators	124
Iron Gate	448
Jacks Point	492
Jimmy Armers	456
Kahutara	456

Kahutara Reef	457	Matata	253
Kaiaua Bay	284	Matauri Bay	27
Kai-iwi	178	Meatworks	454
Katiki	503	Medlands	111
Kaitoke	111	Mid Shore	472
Kaituna	244	Midway/Pipe	303
Kaka-Nuggets	526	Milford Reef	80
Kakanui	500	Mimiwhangata	33
Kapiti Island	396	Moeraki	503
Karamea	432	Mohaka	335
Karekare	93	Mokau	137
Karioitahi	97	Motiti Island	245
Karitane Beach	506	Motu	266
Karitane Point	505	Motukahakaha	23
Kawerua Reefs	68	Motunau	472
Kekerengu	443	Moureeses	34
Kina Road	168	Mukie 1	59
Kiritehere	131	Mukie 2	59
Kuaotunu Reef	189	Murdering Bay	507
Kumene Road	156	Muriwai Beach	87
Kumera Patch	154	Mussell Rock	115
Laings Beach	39	New Brighton	477
Lake Ferry	384	New Chums	187
Last Chance	319	Newdicks	248
Lawyers Head	516	Ngunguru Bar	36
Le Bons Bay	484	Nicks Point	535
Leithfield	473	Nine Mile Beach	428
Light House	503	Nine Mile Bluff	420
Lighthouse	407	North Beach (CH)	476
Lighthouse Reef	492	North Mole	179
Little Ning Nong	389	North Reef	81
Little Waihi	250	Nth Makorori	293
Little Wanganui	431	Nth Matakana	234
Loisells	290	O'Neills	89
Long Bay Reef	77	O'Neills Reef	80
Long Point	527	Oakura Bay	30
Longbeach Drive	178	Oakura Beach	152
Lyall Bay	377	Oamaru Harbour	499
Magnet Bay	487	Oamaru South	499
Mahanga Point	320	Oaro Beach	457
Mahia Reef	319	Ocean Beach	37
Main Beach (BP)	240	Ocean Beach (HB)	347
Maketu	248	Ocean Fun Reefs	452
Makorori Centres	294	Ocean View (DN)	519
Makorori Point	294	Ohope	254
Makorori Reef	293	Okupe Beach	33
Mangahume	172	Old Mans	322
Mangamaunu	449	Omaha Bar	45
Mangawhai	41	Onemana	201
Manu Bay	120	Opito Bay	190
Maori Bay	88	Opotiki	262
Maraenui	263	Opoutama Beach	318
Marsden Point	38	Opoutere	199
Matakana	237	Opunake	169
Matanaka	505	Oraka Beach	322
Matarangi	188	Oreti Beach	534

Orewa Bar	76
Orewa Beach	75
Orokawa Bay	233
Otakaha Stream	388
Otaki Beach	395
Pa Point	399
Paekakariki	397
Pakiri Beach	43
Palmers	110
Papamoa	244
Papatowai	527
Paradise Bay	23
Pararaki Stream	387
Pataua Bar	37
Patea	176
Patiti	491
Paturau River	436
Pauanui	199
Peaks	58
Piha	92
Pillar Point	437
Pines (CH)	475
Pines (GS)	296
Pines (NW)	59
Pipikaretu	510
Plimmerton	399
Point Annihilation	315
Point Elizabeth	417
Porpoise/Curio Bay	530
Porridge	538
Port Robinson	468
Port Waikato	98
Potato Point	507
Pouawa Beach	293
Pouto	71
Propellers	380
Pukehina	250
Pukerua Bay	397
Punakaiki	425
Punakaiki River	425
Puniho's	156
Puwheke Beach	21
Rangiora Street	179
Rarawa Beach	19
Raspberries	389
Rat Island	376
Raupo Bay	21
Raupo Bay	484
Red Beach	76
Rimmers	87
Rings	189
Ripiro Beach	71
Riversdale Beach	371
Riverton Rocks	534
Robin Hood Bay	441
Robin Hood Bay	485
Rocky Lefts	158
Rocky Rights	158
Rolling Stones	315
Ruapuke	125
Ruby Bay	406
Russell	28
Safety Bay	426
Sailors Grave	197
Sandfly Bay	515
Sandy Bay (NE)	36
Sandy Bay/Okiwi	446
Schnappers Point	407
Schnappes (WR)	354
Scott Point	51
Seconds	355
Shark Alley	240
Shark Alley (GB)	111
Shingles	429
Shipwrecks	361
Sky Williams	172
Slipperies	369
Smails Beach	515
Smithfield	491
South Beach (TN)	180
South Reef	81
South Shore	477
Southeast Coast	328
Spirits Bay	18
Sponge Bay	298
Spooky's	417
St Clair	517
St Kilda	517
Stent Road	160
Steveos	400
Stingray Bay	339
Stock Route	296
Stony Bay	365
Sumner	478
Sumner Bar	478
Sunset Beach	97
Supertubes	59
Tahunanui Beach	406
Taieri Mouth	520
Taipa Beach	22
Tairua	197
Takou Bay	27
Tangoio Beach	339
Tanutanu	63
Tapotupotu Bay	18
Taupo Bay	23
Tauranga Bay (WC)	428
Tautuku	530
Tawharanui	45
Tay Street	241

Taylors Mistake	479	Wainui (TN)	177
Te Akau	115	Wainui (WL)	384
Te Arai	42	Wainui Beach (WK)	116
Te Araroa	274	Waipaoa River	306
Te Awanga	343	Waipatiki	338
Te Oka Bay	486	Waipiro Bay	277
Te Paki	52	Waipou Reefs	67
The Bluff (NW)	52	Waipu Cove	39
The Box	62	Waipu River	38
The Channel	416	Wairaka Reef	397
The Cliff	298	Wairoa	334
The Cut (KI)	441	Waitara	142
The Cut (NB)	407	Waiwera Reef	75
The Desert	354	Waiwhakaiho	143
The Gap (HB)	341	Warrington	506
The Gap (WR)	370	Waverley	176
The Glen	410	Wavetraps	415
The Groyne	143	Weld Road	153
The Island (GS)	299	Westport Breakwater	429
The Point (TN)	177	Westshore	341
The Spit (MA)	323	Whakatane	254
The Spit (WR)	358	Whale Bay	121
Titahi Bay	400	Whale Watch	455
Titches	399	Whales	296
Toilet Bowls	361	Whananaki Nth	34
Tokata	271	Whanga Beach	208
Tokerau Beach	22	Whanga Estuary	208
Tokomaru Bay	281	Whangamata Bar	204
Tolaga Bay	289	Whangamoa	411
Tom Bowling	19	Whanganui Mouth	180
Tomahawk Bch	516	Whangapoua	188
Tora Pit	365	Whangapoua	108
Tora Stream	364	Whangara	290
Tora Tora	364	Wharariki Beach	437
Torere	262	Whata Bombie	385
Tracks	318	Whata Station	386
Tuehuru Reefs	323	Whatipu	93
Tumble Down	486	Whiritoa	210
Twilight Beach	51	White Rock Point	359
Uruti Point	371	Whites	91
Victory Bay	514	Whitianga	192
Waianakarua	501	Windies/No 4	390
Waiapu	277	Woodpecker	426
Waihau Bay (EC)	270	Wreck Bay	58
Waihi	233	Xmas Bay	370
Waihua	334		
Waikanae	303		
Waikanae	395		
Waikari	335		
Waikawau	187		
Waikuku	475		
Waimaire	431		
Waimairi	476		
Waimamaku	67		
Waimarama	348		